A Concise Dictionary of English Idioms

William Freeman

3rd Edition
Revised and Edited by
Brian Phythian MA, BLitt

The English Universities Press Ltd

ISBN 0 340 16268 6 (Boards edition)
ISBN 0 340 16267 8 (Paperback edition)

First published 1951
Reprinted 1951
Second edition 1952
Reprinted 1963, 1965, 1967, 1970
Third edition 1973

The English Universities Press Ltd
St Paul's House, Warwick Lane, London EC4P 4AH

Printed in Great Britain by
Butler & Tanner Ltd
Frome and London

Preface

In revising William Freeman's Dictionary, I have done nothing to change the two objects he had in view. The first was to furnish both the native or the foreign reader with a simple and practical guide to the most frequently used idiomatic expressions in English—those countless expressions which everyone uses, which usually evade the normal rules of grammar, and which often have implications quite unconnected with the normal meanings of the words themselves. The second was to give the origin and history of some of these. I have, however, made substantial alterations to the text. Many archaic idioms have been deleted, and over 1200 new ones have been added. In many cases, the alterations are simply a result of differences of judgment between myself and the original compiler in deciding where the line ought to be drawn, in a concise dictionary, between expressions which are common enough to deserve inclusion and those which are not. In some cases, however, the amendments have been necessitated by changes in the language during the twenty years or more since the original publication of this Dictionary: such changes are specially prominent in the areas where idiom shades into colloquialism and slang, and where idiom has to do with social customs and conventions.
The user of this Dictionary should be aware that it has frequently been difficult to decide under what word an idiom should be entered. Should 'See how the land lies' be entered under 'See', 'Land' or 'Lie'? Cross-references have frequently been used, but complete cross-referring would have increased the size of this volume several times; accordingly, if an expression does not appear in the place the reader expects, he is asked to look it up under another key word in the expression. Similar difficulties have occurred in deciding on the correct alphabetical order of idioms within any one entry; idioms usually consist of several words, and have more than one key word, with the result that exact alphabetizing is impossible. Again the reader is requested to bear with the editor, and to be prepared to look in more than one place under an entry.
There are a number of deliberate omissions from the Dictionary: foreign words or phrases, commercial and technical idioms, dialect words, and, for the most part, single words—the idiomatic variations of which can be discovered in any ordinary dictionary.

Some slang expressions are included, but for a more comprehensive coverage of slang, the reader should consult our companion volume *A Concise Dictionary of Slang*.

In most cases, the explanations of idiomatic expressions are accompanied by illustrations, wherever it is felt helpful to show the idiom 'in action'. In other cases, it is hoped that the definition alone will suffice.

B. A. P.

Abbreviations

LIT Literal meaning

MET Metaphorical meaning

Old f. Old fashioned

Or. Origin

S Slang

U.S.A. American

A

A B C The first rudiments; the beginning. [Old f.]

Abeyance **Be in (*or* fall into) abeyance** Be in a state of waiting, or suspense (until some decision is made).
The whole matter is in abeyance until after Christmas.

Abide **Abide by (*or* with)** Remain faithful to (an agreement or decision).

Above **Above all** That which is of the greatest importance.
Above all, be careful.
Above-board Honest and unconcealed.
His conduct has been entirely above-board.

Abuse **Terms of abuse, *or* abusive terms** Bad, uncomplimentary, or violent language.

Accommodate **Accommodate oneself** Adjust oneself to the circumstances; accept the conditions.
They will have to accommodate themselves to hard work.
Accommodate with Supply with; allow the use of
We can accommodate you with a sitting-room and two bedrooms.

Accord **Of one's own accord** Voluntarily; without being compelled.
With one accord Unanimously; all together.
According to 1. As agreed or arranged. Similar to **in accordance with.**
The goods will be sent in accordance with your instructions.
2. As reported by. On the authority of.
According to the newspaper, it will rain later today.

Account **Account for** Explain (the cause of).
Did they account for the delay?
An account to settle [LIT] A debt to pay. [MET] A grudge or a grievance to avenge.
Call to account Summon, in order that statement of justification be made.
The cashier will be called to account in view of the loss of profit.
A good account of A satisfactory story about.
I was glad to receive a good account of the boy's work.
Give a good account of oneself Behave in a way which brings credit to oneself.
The whole team gave a very good account of themselves.
Keep an account of Keep a record of.
Of no account Of no value or importance.
On account As partial payment.
He owed £50, and sent me £10 on account.
On account of Owing to; because of.
She left her husband on account of his cruelty.

On no account In no circumstances.
On no account walk home by yourself.
On that account For that reason.
Open an account Deposit a sum of money (e.g. in a bank) for the first time.
Square accounts Take some action which will cancel out a wrong or disadvantage, and make one equal.
Take account of Estimate. Include in one's calculations.
Take into account Make allowance for. Consider.
Taking into account all the circumstances, he felt it wise to say nothing further.
Turn to (good) account Make useful.
She turned her illness to good account by knitting socks all day.

Accountable **Be accountable for** Be responsible for.

Ace **Within an ace of** Within a very little distance of; very near indeed to.
The boy was within an ace of being drowned.

Achilles **Achilles' heel** The weak or vulnerable spot in a man's character or circumstances. [Or. According to the legend, Achilles, with the exception of one heel, was protected against every weapon his enemies might use.]

Acquaint **Acquaint one with** Make one aware of.

Acquire **An acquired taste** A liking for something unusual; a taste developed gradually.
I don't know whether you'll like this drink; it's rather an acquired taste.

Acquit **Acquit oneself** Conduct or exhibit oneself; behave; perform a part or function.

Act **Act a part** Conceal one's real emotions, etc., as an actor does.
Act upon Take definite action as a result of (what one knows).
The police immediately acted upon the information they received.
Act up to Behave in accordance with.
I hope you'll act up to the advice I've given you.
In the act In the process (of doing something) (i.e. while doing it).
He was caught in the act of stealing the car.

Adam **Not known from Adam** Completely unknown and unfamiliar.
Mrs Smith is a friend of mine, but I don't know her husband from Adam.

Addition **In addition to** Furthermore; as well as.

Advantage **Have the advantage of** Be in a superior position because of.
He had the advantage of a first-class education.
Take advantage of 1. Gain through another person's ignorance or innocence.

The dealer took advantage of the woman's ignorance.

2. Act at a propitious or fortunate moment.

I took advantage of the fine weather to play tennis.

Affirmative **In the affirmative** Yes. Opposite : **in the negative.**

After **After all** In spite of everything that has been said or done.

Be after 1. Intend. Want.

What are you after?

2. Pursue.

He knew the police would be after him.

Again **Again and again ; time and again** Repeatedly.

Half as much again One and a half times as much.

Now and again Occasionally.

Age **At an advanced age** Very old.

She died at an advanced age.

Come of age Attain the age of legal responsibility.

For ages (and ages) For a very long time.

From age to age From one long historical period to another.

Ripe (*or* green) old age Very old (but often with the implication of being healthy as well).

Under age Less than the age specified by law.

Agog **All agog** In a state of excitement.

Aid **In aid of** To help ; with the object of assisting.

A concert will be given in aid of the Nurses' Fund.

Air **Air a grievance** Bring forward for discussion some hardship, grievance or other matter which should be made public.

These grievances were aired in Parliament last week.

In the air 1. In a state of uncertainty ; unsettled.

We go to Lancaster on Monday, but after that all our plans are in the air.

2. Spreading about.

Rumours of rebellion are in the air.

See **Castle.**

Into thin air Into nothingness. (To 'vanish into thin air' is to disappear entirely.)

Airs **Give oneself airs** Try to show one's (sometimes imaginary) superiority, usually to impress. Similar to **put on airs, put on side, show off.**

Alarm **Give the alarm** Give warning, usually when some danger or disaster is discovered.

False alarm Untrue report of disaster.

We heard that the brewery had been burnt down, but it was only a false alarm.

Alert **On the alert** In a state of awareness ; ready for anything that may happen.

Alive **Alive and kicking** [S] Vigorous and active.
I'm glad to see that Ben is still alive and kicking.

All **All along** All the time; from the beginning.
I suspected all along that he was unhappy.

All at once; all of a sudden Suddenly; unexpectedly.
All at once there was a tremendous crash.

All for the best All for the ultimate good. (Commonly used to console someone for bad news.)
If her husband has left her, it's probably all for the best.

All the best [S] A common form of farewell, an abbreviation for 'May all the best things happen to you'.

All but Very nearly.
The proposals are all but meaningless.

All ends up [S] In every way.
Manchester United won all ends up.

On all fours [LIT] On one's hands and knees, in the position of a four-legged animal. [MET] Level with; similar to. [Old f.]
This demand for money is on all fours with the one we received last week.

All in 1. Exhausted.
They're all in after this swim.
2. With everything included.
The holiday will cost £40 all in.

All in a day's work Part of one's responsibilities.

All in all In summary.

All my eye and Betty Martin [S] Complete nonsense. [Or. A term of contempt and disbelief said to be a corruption of 'Ah, mihi, beate Martini' = 'Ah, (grant) me, Blessed Martin!']

All one Of no importance; immaterial. Just the same.
It's all one to me whether you stay here or go home.

All out Using full power.
The builders are going all out to finish the job before the winter.

All over 1. Entirely covering.
There was ice all over the pavement.
2. Finished.
The funeral was all over by the time I arrived.
3. [S] Entirely in character; characteristic.
Bill arrived late and very untidy—but that's Bill all over.

All over the place 1. Scattered untidily.
Collect your papers; they are all over the place.
2. In many directions.
His work takes him all over the place.

All-round Complete. Many-sided. Hence **all-rounder**: a person with many skills, talents, etc.

All the same 1. Alike, in a general sense.

It's all the same to me; it will make no difference so far as I am concerned.

2. Nevertheless.

All the same, I'm not going.

All set Fully prepared.

All set? Then let's go.

All and sundry Everyone, individually and collectively.

All there [S] Mentally alert and fit. (*Note.*—This idiom is generally used negatively.)

The woman doesn't seem to be all there.

All-time Record.

Unemployment is at an all-time low.

At all In any way.

Did he promise anything at all?

In all In total number.

There are seventeen buses in all.

For all that Nevertheless; in spite of that.

When all's said and done The conclusion, stated briefly. When all the facts are considered.

When all's said and done, Peter is less to blame than John.

Allot **Allotted span** The time allowed.

Allow **Allow for** Take into consideration. Excuse. Leave a margin of time or space for.

Allow half-an-hour for the journey.

Allowance **Make allowance** Similar to **allow for.**

We must make some allowance(s) for her inexperience.

Along **All along** See *All.*

Along with In company with. In conjunction with.

We need to buy chairs along with the table.

Go along with [S] Agree, co-operate, with.

Alternative **Having no alternative** Having no choice or option; being unable to do otherwise.

Ambition **The height of ambition** Strongest, most powerful desire.

To be an airline-pilot was the height of his ambition.

Amends **Make amends** Compensate (e.g. for some injustice or wrong).

This will make amends for her disappointment.

Anchor **Come to anchor** [LIT] When a ship lowers her anchor, and ceases to move. [MET] Stop.

Ride at anchor Be anchored. (Sometimes, move gently with the tide while anchored.)

Weigh anchor Pull up the anchor prior to sailing away.

Answer **Answer back** Retort; reply impudently.

Answer (be answerable) for Accept responsibility.

The captain has to answer for the discipline of his company.

Answer to Have. Use.
A man answering to that description lives next door.
Know all the answers Be alert and well-informed.

Appear **Appear for** Represent legally or officially.
Keep up appearances Maintain an outward show.
We haven't much money, but we manage to keep up appearances.
Make (put in) an appearance Show oneself.
To all appearances To the eye; outwardly.
He was to all appearances a gentleman.

Appetite **Whet the appetite** Increase one's desire (to eat) or expectation.
The long walk had whetted the appetites of the guests.

Apple **Apple of one's eye** See under *Eye.*
Apple-pie order Perfectly tidy and neat.

Apron **Tied to one's (mother's) apron-strings** [MET] In the position of a small child who is compelled to rely on its mother for everything; humiliatingly dependent.

Argue **Argue something away** Argue that something does not exist. Attempt to get rid of something by argument.

Arm **At arm's length** [LIT] The length of one's extended arm.
He held the picture at arm's length.
[MET] In a state of formality and unfriendliness.
He prefers to keep his neighbours at arm's length.
A baby in arms [LIT] A child too young to walk. [MET] An inexperienced or immature person.
With open arms With warmth and pleasure.
The hotel welcomed the guests with open arms.

Arms **Up in arms** Concerned. Angry.
The residents are up in arms about the proposal to widen the road.

As **As it were** In other words; speaking metaphorically.
He was, as it were, intoxicated by the soft air and sunshine of spring.
Similar to **so to speak** and **in a manner of speaking**.

Ascendancy **Get** *or* **obtain the ascendancy (over)** Become more dominant (than).
As time passed, the wife gradually gained ascendancy over her weak-willed husband.

Ascendant **In the ascendant** Rising in power or popularity. Increasing in influence or ability. Hence:
One's star is in the ascendant One is growing in influence, etc.

Ashes **Reduce to ashes** Completely destroy by fire.
In less than an hour the cathedral was reduced to ashes.

Ask **Ask for it** [S] Behave in a way which invites trouble. Also **ask for trouble.**

Assurance **Make assurance doubly sure** Make absolutely certain. [Or. *Macbeth.*]

Astray   **Go astray** Stray. [LIT] Wander from the right path. [MET] Depart from what is correct. Become lost.
He has gone astray in his statement.

Attach   **Strings attached** Conditions. Restrictions.
We can have the use of the premises with no strings attached.

Attention   **Call (draw) attention to** Ask for consideration to be given to.
The waiter's attention was called to the fly in the soup.
Pay attention to Attend to; listen to.
Please pay attention to these instructions.
Rivet one's attention Concentrate; fix one's mind upon.

Attitude   **Attitude of mind** Settled way of thinking.
Strike an attitude Stand or sit in a dramatic, self-conscious position.

Avail   **Of (*or* to) little (*or* no) avail** Almost (or quite) without any result.

Avenue   **Leave no avenue unexplored,** *or* **explore every avenue** Employ every possible source or information; make every possible enquiry.

Aversion   **Pet aversion** Special object of dislike.

Axe   **Axe to grind** A private and personal object to achieve (or favour to obtain). A grievance.

B

Back   **Back and forth** From one place to another, then back again.
Backbone [MET] Chief support. Main strength.
Back down Abandon a claim.
Back out of Withdraw from an agreement.
George promised to contribute £20, but backed out of it when the time came.
Back stairs Indirect and unofficial. [Or. The inferior staircase used by servants in a large house. Hence **backstairs gossip**: gossip by subordinates.] Also **by the back stairs**: indirectly, unofficially.
Back up Give support to.
Beat back Compel to retreat.
The enemy attacked, but were beaten back.
Behind one's back When one is absent. Deceitfully.
Break one's back Overburden one. Hence **backbreaking**: very burdensome.
Break the back of Complete the most difficult or the chief part of.
We shall break the back of the work by tonight.
Go back *(a)* **on a person**; *(b)* **on one's word** *(a)* Betray; desert; *(b)* contradict or withdraw (a statement, etc.).
Hang back Linger; fail to advance.

Have one's back to the wall Be in difficulties.

On one's back Ill in bed.

Pay back Repay money or benefits.

Put one's back up [S] Annoy; make hostile. [Or. From the manner in which a cat arches its back when angered.]

See **rub up the wrong way.**

Take a back seat Occupy an inconspicuous position.

Turn one's back on Abandon.

When one's back is turned When one is absent, or occupied over some other matter.

Background **Keep (*or* remain) in the background** Remain inconspicuous and unnoticed.

I'm going to keep in the background during the discussion.

Backwards **Backwards and forwards** Similar to **to and fro.**

Bacon **Bring home the bacon** [S] Succeed in an undertaking.

Save one's bacon [S] Enable one to escape or succeed.

He would have failed the examination, but his history paper saved his bacon.

Bad **Bad Blood** Ill feeling.

There has been bad blood between the two countries for centuries.

A bad egg; a bad hat; a bad lot [S] A person with a bad character.

Bad debts Debts which are 'written off' as complete losses. See **write off.**

Bad for Damaging to.

Smoking is bad for your health.

Bad form Not accepted as socially correct; ill-mannered.

Go bad Become stale or rotten.

With bad grace Reluctantly.

He apologized, but with very bad grace.

Bag **Bag and baggage** Luggage; with all one's portable possessions.

He was turned out of the hotel, bag and baggage.

It's in the bag It is concluded successfully. [Or. The bag, behind the Speaker's Chair in the House of Commons, into which petitions are placed.]

The whole bag of tricks Everything.

Bail **Bail out** [LIT] Pay money as security so that a prisoner may be released pending trial. [MET] Come to the rescue in any way. See *Bale.*

Balance **Strike a balance** Balance or weigh certain objects or facts against one another, in order to discover their comparative value or importance.

On balance Taking everything into consideration. Having regard to all aspects of a matter.

Bald **Bald as a coot** Absolutely hairless. [Or. A coot is a water-bird, one

B

species of which has a flat covering on its forehead, which gives it an appearance of baldness.]

Bale **Bale (*or* bail) out** 1. Remove water or other fluid from a vessel by means of a ladle, pail, etc.

2. Escape from an aeroplane by parachute.

Ball **Have the ball at one's feet** Have every quality and opportunity of being successful. [Or. Football.]

Have the ball in one's court Be responsible for the next move. [Or. Tennis.]

The ball is now in their solicitors' court.

Keep the ball rolling Continue (the conversation, proceedings, etc.) successfully.

My host had very little to talk about, and it was difficult to keep the ball rolling.

Balloon **The balloon went up** Something began. Uproar broke out.

Bank **Bank holidays** General holidays on which all banks as well as shops are closed; consequently an official holiday.

Bargain **Bargain for** Anticipate; prepare for.

We didn't bargain for so many people coming to tea.

Drive a hard bargain Conclude a bargain the terms of which are harsh.

Jones agreed to finance the business, but he drove a hard bargain.

Into the bargain In addition; moreover.

He bought the house, and the furniture into the bargain.

Make the best of a bad bargain Accept difficulty, misfortune, etc., cheerfully.

Strike a bargain Reach a final compromise.

We argued for a long time over what I should pay, but finally struck a bargain.

Bark **Bark up the wrong tree** [S] Make a mistake or a false assumption.

If you think George was responsible for the rumour, you're barking up the wrong tree.

His bark is worse than his bite What he threatens to do is worse than what he actually does. His manner of speaking is deceptively severe.

Bat **Off one's own bat** On one's own initiative. Unaided. [Or. Cricket.]

Battle **Battle royal** A general fight.

Engage in battle Attack; fight.

Give battle Fight with; attack.

Pitched battle One in which both sides are fully engaged.

Bay **At bay** In a situation so desperate that one is compelled to turn and face one's enemies.

Bay the moon [LIT] Howl, as certain animals do, at the full moon. (To 'bay' is to utter a deep bark or cry.) [MET] Take futile action.

9

Be **Be it so** (*or* **so be it**) An old-f. version of 'Let it be so'. A general acceptance of a statement, etc.

Be no more Cease to exist; die.

Be off with you! A peremptory order to depart.

Beam **On one's beam-ends** In a desperate and almost hopeless condition. [Or. Nautical. The term is applied to a ship when it is tilted so far over that it is resting on the ends of its cross-beams, or supports, and is consequently in great danger of sinking.]

Tom's already spent all his pocket-money, and is on his beam-ends.

Bean **Full of beans** In high spirits. Having plenty of energy.

Without a bean Without any money left.

Bear **Bear a charmed life** Be almost incredibly fortunate in escaping disasters and accidents.

Bear down upon [LIT] To approach a vessel from the weather side. [MET] To approach with determination or with an obvious purpose. [Or. Nautical.]

Bear enquiry, investigation, *etc.* Produce a satisfactory answer to enquiries. (Frequently used in the negative.)

The business he has been connected with won't bear enquiry.

Bear false witness Swear to things which one knows to be untrue; tell lies about.

Bear malice (*or* **a grudge**) Retain bitter or angry feelings, usually as the result of a dispute or quarrel.

I hope you won't bear malice after what has happened.

Bear a meaning Convey a meaning.

That sentence doesn't bear the meaning you seem to think it does.

Bear in mind Retain in one's memory. Take note.

Bear in mind that the train leaves at midnight.

Bear the name of Possess the name of. Have the same name as.

Their son bore the name of his grandfather, and was christened Joseph.

Bear out 1. [LIT] Carry away.

They bore out the body.

2. Confirm; support.

His statement bears out what the police told me.

Bear up Sustain one's strength and spirits.

Her father's death was a terrible shock, but she is bearing up well.

Bear with Endure as sympathetically as possible.

The invalid is very irritable, but we try to bear with him.

Bear witness Act as a witness. Give evidence.

Bring to bear Apply.

The outcry in the local newspapers brought a good deal of pressure to bear on the Council.

Lose one's bearings Lose one's way or sense of direction.

No bearing on No connection with; irrelevant.
Bear a date, signature, *etc.* Have written upon it.
His latest letter bears the date April 1st.

Bear-garden A place—generally a room—in a condition of extreme tumult and confusion.
The children left the room looking like a bear-garden.

Beard **Beard the lion in his den** Confront boldly one's opponent (or superior) on his own ground (e.g. in his own home or office) to discuss a matter in dispute.

Beat **Beat about the bush** Avoid or delay a straightforward discussion; approach a subject in a roundabout way. [Or. Hunters beating bushes and similar hiding-places cautiously, to discover if game is hiding there.]
Beat down 1. Crush opposition.
The rebellion was beaten down.
2. Compel a person to reduce his price.
He wanted five pounds, but I beat him down.
Beat hollow [S] Be entirely superior to.
Beat it [S] Depart at once.
Beat off Repel.
The garrison beat off all the enemy attacks.
Beat up [S] Strike repeatedly and severely.
Dead beat Utterly exhausted.
After walking all day in the rain, we were dead beat.

Beck **At one's beck and call** In a position of being under one's domination.

Bed **Bed and board** Accommodation and meals.
Bed of roses A state of ease and luxury. (Frequently used with a negative.)
Life is far from being a bed of roses.
Between you, me and the bedpost In confidence.
Die in one's bed Die of natural causes, or peacefully.
Get out of bed on the wrong side Behave in a disagreeable fashion.

Bee **Bee in one's bonnet** [S] Obsession; some particular idea or conviction, usually slightly crazy.
Make (or follow) a bee line Proceed in a straight line (as a bee does on its way home).

Beg **Beg the question** Assume that something which is a matter for dispute is in fact true. (Often loosely used to mean 'avoid the issue being discussed'.)
Beg to differ Disagree. (Originally formal; now quite colloquial.)

Beggar **Beggars can't be choosers** People in need must take what is offered them. [Or. Proverbial.]

Beggar description Be so extraordinary that one cannot find words in which to describe it.

Begging **Begging the question** See *Beg*

Behalf **On behalf of** As a substitute for, or representative or spokesman of.

Behaviour **Be on one's good (*or* best) behaviour** Conduct oneself as correctly and properly as possible.

Behind **Behind the scenes** In private. Secretly and unofficially. [Or. Theatrical.]
Plans for the next election are going on behind the scenes.
Behind the times Late; unfashionable.
You are behind the times with your information.
Similar to **out of date.**

Belief **Beyond belief** Unbelievable; astounding.
To the best of my belief In my genuine opinion.

Below **Below one's breath** Almost inaudible (but intended to be heard). In a mutter, so as to be heard privately, not publicly.
Hit below the belt Attack unfairly. [Or. Boxing. A boxer may not strike his opponent below the belt worn round the waist.]

Beneath **Beneath contempt** So despicable as not to deserve even the effort of expressing one's dislike of it.
Beneath one's breath See *Below.*

Benefit **Give one the benefit of the doubt** Assume that one is right, or innocent, when it is not certain.
Confer a benefit Act beneficially; be advantageous.
This new discovery will confer a benefit on all invalids.

Bent **Bent upon** Determined to take a certain action.
John was bent upon walking the entire distance that same night.

Berth **Give a wide berth to** Avoid; keep as far from as possible. [Or. Nautical. A berth is any place in which a ship can anchor.]

Beside **Beside the mark *or* point** Irrelevant; unconnected with the matter being discussed.
Beside oneself In such a state of emotion that one is incapable of knowing what one is doing.

Best **At best** Even in the best possible circumstances.
A fox is, at best, an unsatisfactory pet.
Best man The bridegroom's chief friend and assistant at a wedding.
For the best; all for the best The best that can happen; for the ultimate good.
She has gone back to her husband, which is probably for the best.
Have the best of Win (an argument, contest, etc.).
Make the best of Be contented with.
Put best foot forward Walk as quickly as possible.
With the best As well as anyone.

Betake **Betake oneself** Go; proceed. [Old f.]

Better **Better half** Wife (a gently ironic complimentary phrase).

Better oneself Improve one's worldly position.

Get the better of Triumph over; prove stronger than.

His anger got the better of him, though he was sorry later.

Know better (than) Not to be so foolish (as).

He should have known better than to take the risk.

Think better of Reconsider, and decide to alter one's plan (usually from prudence or fear).

He was going to protest, but thought better of it.

Between **Between ourselves; between you and me; between these four walls; between you, me and the bed- (*or* gate-) post** Speaking privately and confidentially.

Between ourselves, I don't think he will live much longer.

Read between the lines Find [LIT, in a printed document; MET, in any situation] information which is not stated but implied.

Beyond **The back of beyond** The most remote part of the world.

Beyond (one's) expectation Beyond anything (one) expected.

The beauties of Florence were far beyond his expectation.

Beyond measure Exceedingly. Very much indeed.

Beyond the pale Unacceptable. [Old f.: beyond the limits of decent society, good manners and moral limitations.] [Or. In Ireland, the property of the English kings used to be separated from that owned by the inhabitants, which was thus beyond 'the pale' = heraldic term = sovereignty. 'Pale' also = fence, boundary—a more likely origin of the phrase.]

Bib **Best bib and tucker** Best clothes.

Bid **Bid fair to** Appear likely to.

The daughter bids fair to be even more beautiful than her mother.

Bid welcome, farewell To express a welcome, or a farewell greeting.

My hostess came to the door to bid me farewell.

Bill **Bill and coo** [S] Speak lovingly and intimately. [Old f.] [Or. An allusion to the sound—billing and cooing—made by doves and pigeons.]

Clean bill of health Assurance that one is in sound health.

The doctor gave him a clean bill of health.

Billingsgate Bad language; abuse. [Or. Billingsgate, the London market in which fish is bought and sold, is supposed—traditionally and unjustly—to be the place where the worst language is used.]

Bird **An early bird** An early arrival. [Or. The proverb, 'The early bird catches the worm.']

The entertainment did not begin till eight, but we were early birds, and got to the hall at seven-thirty.

Birds of a feather Similar people (e.g. having similar views, etc.). [Or. The proverb, 'Birds of a feather flock together.']

A bird in the hand Immediate possession is worth much more than a mere promise. [Or. The proverb, 'A bird in the hand is worth two in the bush.']

Bird of ill omen [LIT] A bird—e.g. the raven, the owl or the crow—whose appearance is supposed to indicate the coming of bad luck. [MET] Any person who has a reputation for bringing bad news. [Old f.]

Bird of passage [LIT] A bird like the swallow, starling, etc., which migrates from one country to another according to the season. [MET] A person who is constantly travelling from place to place and has no permanent home; one who remains only temporarily.

Get the bird Be badly received. (Usually applied to theatrical performances which displease the public.)

Kill two birds with one stone Produce two results with a single action.

When in town I'll kill two birds with one stone and visit Mrs Smith and my sister.

A little bird told me I refuse to say who told me.

Birthday **In (*or* wearing) one's birthday clothes, *or* suit** Wearing no clothes at all; naked (as one is born).

The small boy dashed out of the bath in his birthday clothes.

Biscuit **Take the biscuit (*or* cake)** Be incredible.

I've heard of some odd things, but this takes the biscuit.

Bit **Not a bit (of it)** Not at all.

Take (*or* have) the bit between one's teeth Become (or be) uncontrollably eager (to do something, etc.).

Bite **Bite (*or* lick) the dust** Be killed in battle. Be finished.

At the next election, I expect the Tories will bite the dust.

Bite one's head off Speak angrily and sharply to a person.

Bite off more than one can chew Undertake more than one can cope with.

Two bites at a cherry Two separate attempts to achieve a result.

Bitten **Once bitten, twice shy** Once having been hurt (damaged, disappointed, swindled, etc.), one is understandably careful.

Black **Black art** Art or craft derived from the Devil; vile or supernatural practices.

Black and blue Discoloured with bruises.

In one's black books In disfavour; with a bad reputation.

George has been in his uncle's black books ever since he forgot the old man's birthday.

Black looks Angry (sometimes evilly threatening) appearance.

He got black looks from his mother-in-law when he arrived late.

Black out 1. Obliterate; obscure. 2. Become unconscious.

(As) black as thunder (*or* a thundercloud) Very angry.
He gave him a glare as black as thunder, and asked him what he wanted.

In black and white In writing or print.

Blanket **Wet blanket** A person who by his manner or conversation extinguishes the cheerfulness and enthusiasm of others (as, literally, a wet blanket extinguishes fire).

Blind **Blind impulse** An illogical, sudden or thoughtless impulse.
Acting on blind impulse, she turned the car to the left.

None so blind No one is so difficult to persuade as a man who is determined not to listen to arguments or persuasion. [Or. Proverb, 'There's none so blind as those who won't see.']

Blind side The aspect of a man's character in which he is tender-hearted or weak. Also, in sport, the unguarded part of the field.

Blind to Incapable of appreciating.

To blind with science To confuse by using expertise, knowledge.

Turn a blind eye to Pretend not to notice or know about.

Block **A chip off the old block** One exhibiting the characteristics of his parents or ancestors.

Blood **Bad blood** Ill-feeling; antagonism.
There's been bad blood between them for ages.

One's blood being up Being excited and angry.
His blood was up, and a quarrel was inevitable.

Blood is thicker than water Relations are more closely connected than mere friends or acquaintances, and should receive better treatment.

Blood sports Sports that involve the shedding of blood, usually of animals. (e.g. fox-hunting, bull-fighting, etc.)

Blood-sucker [LIT] An animal, such as a leech, a vampire-bat, or a mosquito, which lives on the blood of living persons. [MET] One who lives by blackmail, lending money at high interest, or otherwise taking a cruel advantage of other people's fortune.

Blood-and-thunder Highly sensational; melodramatic. Hence, a story, book, film, etc., having such characteristics.
See **penny dreadful.**

Blue-blooded Aristocratic. [Or. The now discredited idea that the blood of aristocrats was bluer than that of other people.]

Get blood out of a stone Find evidence of human feeling in someone who lacks it. (More generally) Attempt the impossible.

Hot blood Quick temper. Anger.

In cold blood Deliberately; coolly.

In the blood Part of one's nature; born with one. Hence **runs in the blood** Is a family trait.

Make one's blood boil Make one furiously angry.

One's blood runs cold One experiences fear, acute apprehension or disappointment.

His ruthlessness makes my blood run cold.

A prince or princess of the blood A member of the Royal Family.

Blot **Blot on one's scutcheon** A disgrace; an injury to one's good reputation. [Or. Heraldry. The scutcheon (or escutcheon) is the shield on which a coat-of-arms is depicted.]

Blot one's copy book Spoil one's previously good reputation.

Blot out Efface; obliterate; forget.

It will be many years before memories of the accident will be blotted out.

Blow **Blow hot and cold** Be inconsistent and unreliable. [Or. Æsop's fable of the countryman who blew on his fingers to warm them, and then on his porridge to cool it.]

Blow (*or* hang) it! (*or* the expense, etc., etc.) Disregard it.

Blow (let) off steam Get rid of surplus energy.

Blow one's own trumpet Boast.

Blow out 1. (Verb) Extinguish.

Blow out the candles.

2. (Noun) [S]. A large and luxurious meal

We had a tremendous blow out at the hotel.

Blow over Subside. [LIT] Applied to a storm of wind, etc.

The storm will soon blow over.

[MET] Applied to quarrels, disagreements, etc.

We have frequent quarrels, but they soon blow over.

Blow up 1. Explode.

The mine blew up soon after the soldiers passed.

2. [S] Blame severely.

I'm going to blow up the builder for his bad work.

3. Inflate.

The tyre needs blowing up.

Hence: [MET] Exaggerate.

Its importance has been blown up out of all proportion.

Blue **Blue murder** An angry scene. (Also used in a number of phrases as emphasis, e.g. **shout blue murder** (= loudly), **like blue murder** (= very quickly).

There'll be blue murder when she hears of this.

Blue riband (*or* ribbon) Highest attainable honour or prize. [Or. The blue ribbon worn with the Order of the Garter.]

Dark blue and light blues The Oxford and Cambridge teams or crews respectively. [Or. The respective colours worn, especially in connection with the annual boat-race.]

Bluff **Call a man's bluff** Challenge a statement or action which one believes has nothing to support it. [Or. The card game of poker.]

If you think he's asking too much for the house, call his bluff by pretending you're not interested in buying.

Blush **At (the) first blush** At first sight.
At the first blush the Government proposals seem generous.

Board **Above board** Honest. Straightforward. In order.
Go by the board Be lost, forgotten or eliminated.
Sweep the board Take all the available rewards or prizes.

Boat **In the same boat** [S] Similarly situated.
It's no use grumbling—we're all in the same boat.

Bob **Bob up** 1. [LIT] Rise suddenly.
There was a splash in the pond, and a fish bobbed up.
2. [S] [MET] Arrive suddenly.

Body **In a body** Collectively; all together.
The deputies arrived in a body.
Keep body and soul together Remain alive. (Usually jocular.)
I'm managing to keep body and soul together.

Boil **Boil over** 1. [LIT] Boil so that the fluid rises above the edge of the saucepan or kettle. 2. [MET] Become so angry that self-control is lost.

Bold **Make bold to; make so bold as to** Presume to. Dare to. [Old f.] (Used ironically, usually.)
May I make so bold as to ask you for a match?

Bolster **Bolster up** Add to (e.g. one's confidence, a statement, etc.) in order to strengthen.
The Government bolstered up its position by imprisoning all its outspoken opponents.

Bolt **Bolt upright** Absolutely straight and perpendicular. [Or. 'Bolt' = short arrow of crossbow, therefore straight.]
A bolt from the blue A complete surprise. A sudden and entirely unexpected disaster. [Or. 'Bolt' = thunderbolt; 'blue' = a cloudless sky from which no storm is to be expected.]

Bone **Bone of contention** The subject of argument or dispute.
Bone-dry Quite dry.
A bone to pick A matter for reproof or blame.
I have a bone to pick with you in connection with your unpunctuality.
Feel in one's bones Be quite sure.
The train will be full; I can feel it in my bones.
Make no bones about Not attempt to disguise.
I'm disappointed, I'll make no bones about it.

Book **Bookmaker** Man, colloquially known as a 'bookie', who makes a living by accepting bets from the public (punters). The bets recorded form collectively a 'book'
Bring to book Bring to justice; punish.
Go by the book Adhere strictly to rules.

In one's good (or bad or black) books Liked and appreciated (or the reverse).
That young man is in everyone's good books.
Speak by the book Quote exactly and literally from some authority. (This phrase is more frequently used in the negative.)
Without speaking by the book, I am sure there is a law against cycling on that path.
Suit one's book Agree with one's plans.
That arrangement will suit my book very well indeed.
Take a leaf out of a person's book Follow his example.
I think I'll take a leaf out of his book and go to bed early.

Boot **To boot** In addition to; also. [Old f.]
The boot's on the other foot (or leg) The advantage (power, responsibility, truth, etc.) now lies on the opposite side to where it formerly did.
Get the boot [S] Be dismissed. Also **be booted out.**

Border **Bordering on** Near to; almost.
His manner was abrupt, bordering on insolence.

Born **Born before one's time** Possessing ideas and theories that belong to a later period in history.
In all one's born days In all one's life. (Used for emphasis.)
I've never been so surprised in all my born days.

Borne **Borne in upon one** Impressed upon one's mind.
It was borne in upon her that they would never meet again.

Borrow **Borrowed plumes** Anything worn or assumed to which one is not entitled. [Or. Æsop's fable of the jay who made herself ridiculous by adding peacock's feathers (or plumes) to her own.]

Both **Have something both ways** Choose two contradicting or alternative lines of action, etc., for one's own benefit, when only one is available.
If you don't give up smoking, you won't be able to afford a holiday: you can't have it both ways.

Bottle **Bottle-neck** A passage which becomes suddenly narrow, like the neck of a bottle, through which objects are compelled to move slowly; hence [MET] anything which causes a delay.
The Christmas rush has caused a bottle-neck in the postal services.
Bottle up Suppress.
He bottled up his anger and said nothing.

Bottom **At the bottom of** Really responsible for.
Bet one's bottom dollar Stake everything one possesses.
From the bottom of one's heart Genuinely. Most sincerely.
Get to the bottom of Find the truth, cause, meaning of.
Bottomless pit Hell.
Touch bottom [LIT] Reach the bottom of the sea.

B

The boat's keel touched bottom.
[MET] Reach the lowest depths (e.g. of misery, etc.). [Old f.]
See **rock-bottom.**

Bound **Beyond the bounds of** Outside the limits of.
This delay has gone beyond the bounds of reason.
I'll be bound I am certain.
He'll be late again tomorrow, I'll be bound.
Out of bounds Beyond the official boundary or limit.
All the hotels in the town have been placed out of bounds to the troops.
Within bounds 1. Within the official boundary or limit. 2. Within
reasonable limitations and restraint.
She could never keep her temper within bounds.
Within reasonable bounds Within restraint.
Within the bounds of possibility Just possible.
*It is, of course, within the bounds of possibility that the shipwrecked crew
may have reached some desert island.*

Bow **Bow to the inevitable** Accept what is unavoidable.
Draw the long bow Exaggerate.
Two strings (or another string) to one's bow More resources than
one. An alternative, a second plan in case the first should fail.

Bowl **Bowl along** Go fast and smoothly.
Bowled over 1. [LIT] Overturned; knocked down.
The nun was bowled over in the rush to the train.
2. [MET] [S] Overcome (usually with surprise, joy).
When I heard the news I was completely bowled over.

Box **Box on the ears** Blow on the side of the head.

Brain **Brain wave** Sudden good idea, plan; inspiration.
Brains trust A group of experts, meeting publicly to discuss and
answer questions, problems, etc.
Cudgel (or rack) one's brains See *Cudgel.*
Have something on the brain Be totally preoccupied with
something.
My son's got football on the brain.
Make one's brain reel Stagger one mentally. Applied to an almost
incredible statement or fact.
The number of stars now visible to astronomers makes one's brain reel.
Pick a person's brains Question a person (sometimes informally
or tactfully) to extract information, advice, etc., from him.
See *Crack, Hare, Scatter.*

Bran **Bran (or brand)-new** Absolutely new. [Or. Anglo-Saxon *brandoz* =
burning stick. Thus applied to metal goods taken straight from the
fire in which they were made.]

Branch **Branch out** Develop (into or away from) (as branches grow from
trees). Become independent.

19

The chip-shop is branching out into a café as well.
He's left the firm, to branch out on his own.

Brass **Brass farthing** Smallest possible amount.
I don't care a brass farthing (for) what he thinks.

Brazen **Brazen out** Defiantly defend, or deny.

Breach **Breach of the peace** (*strictly speaking,* **the Queen's peace**) Any action which breaches or breaks the law and may lead to violence and disturbance.

Breach of promise (*to marry*) Legal phrase for the breaking of a formal promise, usually but not always on the man's part, to marry.

Heal the breach Bring a serious or prolonged quarrel to an end.

Step into the breach Deputize.
The organist fell ill, but his assistant stepped into the breach at the last moment.

Bread **Bread-winner** The person whose earnings support the family.

Know which side his bread is buttered on Know where his interest, advantage, etc., lies.

Break **Break away** Free, or detach oneself, by a definite effort.
I broke away from the association ten years ago.

Break the back of Complete the most difficult or main part of.
I should break the back of this piece of work before the end of the week.

Break the bank 'Bank' in this case refers to a private or public gambling organization in which a gambler has a run of luck lasting long enough to cause the 'bank' to run out of funds, and to be compelled temporarily to stop the play.

Break down 1. Smash by force.
We shall have to break down the door to get in.
2. Cause to diminish and finally disappear.
It took a long time to break down his shyness.
3. Collapse under great pain or emotion.
When she heard he was dead, she broke down completely.

Break from (*or* **forth**) Escape from. Sound from.
Cheers broke from the crowd when the teams appeared.

Break new ground Begin something new or different.
We shall break new ground in the spring by opening a shop at Liverpool.

Break one's heart Cause profound distress.
It will break his heart to retire.

Break the ice Break an uncomfortable silence; put an end to formality or stiffness.

Break in 1. Enter a building by force.
2. Interrupt.
I could tell this story better if so many people didn't break in.
3. Train someone, usually an animal, in obedience.

I've spent nearly six months breaking in my pony.
Break a journey Interrupt it by stopping at some point on the way, and resuming the journey later.
We are breaking our journey at Chester for one night.
Break loose Escape.
The dog broke loose from its chain.
Similar to **break away.**
Break one's neck [MET] Be in a considerable hurry.
I broke my neck to arrive in time.
Break the news Pass on information. (Usually, startling or bad news, as tactfully and gently as possible.)
Break off End (suddenly, or temporarily).
We were discussing our plans, but had to break off when the telephone rang.
Break out 1. [LIT] Force one's way out.
He broke out of prison, but was caught again later.
2. [MET] Begin.
A roar of cheering broke out.
Break ranks Leave one's position (usually in disorder).
Break the record Surpass all previous performances.
James broke the record in our village by living to 105.
Break the thread Interrupt a story, a line of thought, etc.
I was telling the children a story, when the door-bell rang and broke the thread.
Break through Penetrate (the surroundings or impediment, etc.).
The sun broke through the clouds.
The crowd broke through the lines of police.
Break-through Successful development.
Break up [LIT] Break into small pieces. [MET] End, dismiss, destroy, depart.
Break with Have no further connection with.
Break one's word, *or* **promise** Fail to do what one has undertaken to do.
Make the break Similar to **break away (from).**
The weather breaks The weather changes. Hence **a break in the weather**: a change.

Breast **Make a clean breast (of)** Confess all.
Breath **A breath of (fresh) air** [LIT]
Let's go into the garden for a breath of air.
[MET] Someone or something invigorating, refreshing, delightful.
The new typist is a real breath of fresh air.
The breath of one's nostrils Vital; absolutely necessary.
In the same breath At the same time; simultaneously. (Usually in connection with two contradictory statements.)

Out (short) of breath Unable to breathe (because of exertion, illness, etc.).

Take away one's breath Leave one breathless through intense astonishment, delight, etc.

Your offer is so generous that it takes my breath away.

Under (*or* below) one's breath Very softly; almost in a whisper.

With one's last breath To the end of one's life; to the last. (Used metaphorically to add emphasis to a statement.)

I would maintain his innocence with my last breath.

See *Save, Waste.*

Breathe **Breathe again** Recover (from fear, inconvenience, etc.).

The floods subsided, and the villagers breathed again.

Breathe one's last Die.

Breathe (e.g. revenge, curses, blessings, *etc.*) Murmur; utter in low intense tones, or passionately.

Breathing-space Pause (for recovery or relaxation from effort).

Not to breathe a syllable Remain absolutely silent; keep secret.

I promised not to breathe a syllable about what he told me.

See **fire and brimstone.**

Brick **A brick,** *or* **a regular brick** [S] A thoroughly good fellow. [Old f.] [Or. The squareness, solidarity and general reliability of a brick (?)]

Brick up Fill up an opening in a building, etc., with bricks.

There was once a window there, but it has been bricked up for centuries.

Come down like a ton (*or* a hundred) of bricks [S] Blame severely and violently.

The manager came down on him like a ton of bricks for leaving the door of the safe open.

Drop a brick [S] Behave indiscreetly.

Make bricks without straw Make something without having the necessary materials. [Or. Biblical. The Israelites were commanded to make bricks without straw.]

Brief **In brief** In short. Concisely.

Hold no brief for Refrain from arguing in favour of.

Bright **Bright spark** Quick-witted person.

Bright idea Clever idea.

Brim **To the brim** [LIT] To the edge of any vessel made to contain fluid. [MET] To indicate absolute completion.

She was filled to the brim with happiness.

Bring **Bring about; bring to pass** Cause to happen.

It was gambling that brought about his ruin.

Bring to bear Apply (influence, etc.). Concentrate one's efforts with some special object.

She brought all her charm to bear.

Bring to book Detect someone in a mistake; bring a wrongdoer to punishment.

Bring (*or* call) into being Cause to exist.

Bring to a close End; conclude.

We are bringing our entertainment to a close with a firework display.

Bring down 1. Cause a penalty to fall on.

He'll bring trouble down on himself.

2. Lower.

Prices are being brought down.

3. Cause to end.

This controversy could bring down the Government.

Bring forth Produce; display.

Bring forward Introduce; initiate.

The Chancellor of the Exchequer brought forward a new scheme of taxation.

Bring home to one Cause one to realize, to feel, to understand. Convince one.

Bring the house down Cause uproarious laughter or applause. [Or. Theatre: house = theatre building.]

Bring off Succeed.

Bring on Start; cause to begin.

His troubles may bring on a serious illness.

Bring to mind Recall.

Bring into play Cause to operate.

Bring up the rear Follow at the end. [Or. Military.]

Policemen on horseback brought up the rear.

Bring oneself to Persuade oneself to.

He couldn't bring himself to apologize.

Bring out 1. Exhibit clearly.

Hardship sometimes brings out the best in people.

2. Publish.

The new edition will be brought out next year.

Bring round 1. Bring from a short distance.

Mrs Jones, who lives at No. 6, will bring round some apples.

2. Restore to conciousness. Also **bring to.**

We threw water over the woman to bring her round.

3. Persuade (to a point of view).

The strikers are taking a long time to be brought round.

Bring up 1. Refer to some matter requiring discussion (also **bring forward**).

Please bring up the matter at our next meeting.

2. Care for and educate.

He was very well brought up.

Bring word Convey information

Bristle **Bristle with** Be (unpleasantly) full of.
The whole plan bristles with difficulties.

Broad **It's as broad as it's long** Either alternative will lead to the same result.

Broadly speaking Speaking generally; stated in simple terms.
Broadly speaking, the English are reputed to be simple and friendly.

Broad-minded Tolerant.

Broken **Broken accents** Imperfect or hesitating speech.

Broken English Inaccurate and imperfect English.

Broken reed An ally or support who has proved useless or unworthy. [Or. A reed is a tall kind of grass which, although stiff, snaps very easily.]

See *Break.*

Brow **Lowbrow** Having to do with popular, undemanding forms of art, literature, music, etc.

Highbrow Having to do with highly developed, intellectual tastes in the arts.

Knit one's brows Frown (usually in thought).

Brown **In a brown study** In a reverie. Apparently thinking deeply; sometimes hardly thinking at all. [Or. A faulty translation of the French *sombre pensée*. *Sombre*, like *brun* (brown) = gloomy, melancholy. (?)]

Brush **A brush** A light, not serious, encounter.
He's out of sorts because he's just had a brush with a traffic-warden.

Brush up Renew one's memory of. Revise.
You can brush up your French by watching the TV programme.

Brute **Brute force** Physical force or strength.
The police had to use brute force to take her to the station.

Buck **Buck up** [S] Hurry. Become, or make, more vigorous, lively or cheerful.

Buckle **Buckle to** [S] Make an extra effort. Get to work vigorously. Set about.
We shall have to buckle to if we are to catch that train.

Buckle up Bend and collapse.
The iron supports of the bridge have buckled up.

Buff **In the buff** [S] Unclothed.

Build **Build upon** [MET] Rely upon.
He makes many promises, but it isn't safe to build upon them.

Buoy **Buoy up** Support; encourage. [Or. Nautical.]
He was buoyed up by the knowledge that his daughter would soon be arriving.

Burn **Burn one's bridges (*or* boats)** Make a change of plan impossible; make certain that the decision is final. [Or. If a general or sea captain wished to make his own retreat impossible, he burned the bridges he had crossed or the ships he had sailed in before the battle began.]

Burn the candle at both ends Fail to conserve one's energy. Work hard or for long hours, or live very energetically, usually with consequent exhaustion.

A burnt child dreads the fire See **once bitten twice shy**.

Burn one's fingers Suffer because of rashness, meddling or financial speculation.

Burnt-offering [LIT] The Jewish sacrifice to God of laying the body of an animal upon an altar, and burning it. [MET] A humble offering or sacrifice of any description. [Or. Biblical.]

Money burns a hole in one's pocket Money exists to be spent.

Burst **Burst into laughter (*or* out laughing) *or* tears** Suddenly erupt into laughter or tears.

Bury **Bury the hatchet** Forget past quarrels, and become friends. [Or. The custom of the American Indians of ceremoniously burying their war-hatchets after making peace with an enemy.]
See **pipe of peace** (under *Peace*) and **bygones be bygones**.

Bury one's head in the sand Obstinately refuse to accept or face facts. [Or. The legendary (and false) idea that ostriches bury their heads in the sand when in danger, believing that since they are unable to see their enemies, their enemies cannot see them.]

Business **The business end** [S] The effective end.
He sat down on the business end of a drawing-pin.
Go out of business Cease to trade; discontinue one's usual work.
Have no business Have no right.
Make it one's business to Assume personal responsibility for. Undertake to.
I'll make it my business to call on him.
Mean business Intend to take definite (and sometimes unpleasant) action.
There's a bull in the field, and I'm afraid he means business.
Mind one's own business Refrain from interfering.

Butt **Butt in** [S] Interrupt. Intervene. Interfere.

Butter **Look as if butter wouldn't melt in one's mouth** Appear demure, innocent.

Buttonhole Intercept and speak privately to. Detain a reluctant listener.

Buy **Buy in** Purchase at an auction-sale on behalf of the seller.
Buy out Pay person(s) to give up business, prosperity, etc.
Buy up Purchase the whole rights or interest in a business.
A good buy A bargain.

By **By and by** Soon; in the near future.
We'll meet again by and by.

C

By and large In general terms; comparing the advantages and disadvantages. On the whole.
By and large, the bus service is getting worse.
By him-(her-)self 1. Unaided.
The baby can now walk by himself.
2. Alone.
I spent all the afternoon by myself.
By the way See under *Way.*

Bygones **Let bygones be bygones** Let past quarrels or disagreements be ignored or forgotten. See **bury the hatchet** and **pipe of peace** (under *Peace*).

Byword **Become (or be) a byword** Become (be) notorious, proverbial.

C

Cake **Cakes and ale** A very enjoyable experience. Merry-making.
Have one's cake and eat it too Obtain two contradictory advantages from the same thing or by the same means. Similar to **have it both ways.**
Like hot cakes Very quickly.
A piece of cake [S] Something extremely easy.
Take the cake, bun *or* **biscuit** [S] Win the prize; be incredible. (Always used ironically in connection with some preposterous action or statement.)

Calculate **Calculated to** Likely to; tending to.
His conduct is calculated to offend people.
Calculate upon Expect; estimate.
We calculate upon a hundred people attending.

Call **Call to the bar** Admit as a barrister. [Or. Legal. Qualified law students are 'called' from the body of the hall to take part in legal proceedings. To be called *within* the Bar is to be made a Queen's (or King's) Counsel.]
Call for 1. Demand.
The present emergency calls for special measures to be taken.
2. Arrive to take away or accompany.
We will call for you on our way to the concert.
Call forth Bring out, develop good or bad qualities.
Call a halt End. Order to end.
The referee called a halt to the bout in the fourth round.
Call in Recall something that has been issued, e.g. coins or stamps.
Call to mind Recall; remember.
I can't call to mind where I've met you.
Call names Abuse.

26

She called him every name she could think of.

Call off 1. Order to cease. Cancel.

The search was called off at nightfall.

2. Change one's mind, and abandon plans previously made.

We were going to give a dance, but decided to call it off.

Call on 1. Visit.

2. Request.

The Chairman called on Mr Jones to address the meeting.

Call out 1. Raise one's voice; shout.

Call out the name of the winner.

2. Summon to keep public law and order.

Rioting began, and troops were called out.

Call over Read through a list of names aloud, in order to ascertain who are present. Also **call the roll.**

Call in question Express doubt about.

I call in question the accuracy of those figures.

Call a spade See *Spade.*

Call to account. See *Account.*

Call the tune Give the orders. Be in a position of superiority.

No call to No need to.

There's no call to be alarmed.

Camel **Break the camel's back** Go too far. See **last straw** under *Straw.*

Can **Carry the can** [S] Be blamed. Take responsibility.

Candle **Burn the candle at both ends** See *Burn.*

Not fit to hold a candle to Not fit even to assist; not good enough even to be compared with.

John isn't stupid, but he isn't fit to hold a candle to his brother.

Not worth the candle Not justifying the trouble, cost etc.

Betting is a game not worth the candle.

Cap **Put on one's thinking-cap** Give a problem some thought. [Or. A legendary magic cap worn by Eric XIV of Sweden which gave him special powers.]

I must put on my thinking-cap before I answer that question.

A feather in one's cap See *Feather.*

Cap and bells Part of the equipment of a professional jester or fool of the Middle Ages.

Cap in hand Humbly. Hence **go cap in hand**: solicit meekly; ask a favour.

If the cap fits (wear it) If something (e.g. a statement, remark) is appropriate or true (take note of it).

Set one's cap at Attempt. Also [Old f.] applied to a woman who is making a determined effort to persuade a man to marry her. [Or. The idea that she put on her most attractive cap to catch his attention.]

27

Take (send, pass) the cap round Make a collection of money by circulating some container among people.

To cap To go one better (e.g. **to cap a joke** : to tell a better one). Outdo.

Cards **House of cards** Unstable plan or operation.

On the cards [S] Possible; likely to happen.

It's on the cards that I may go to Australia.

Play one's cards (right *or* **well,** etc.) Act or plan, negotiate, etc. (sensibly).

If we play our cards right, we should get a good price for the house.

Put one's cards on the table Be absolutely candid, and conceal nothing.

Care **Have a care!** Be careful. [Old f.]

Care nothing for Take no interest in. [Old f.]

Take care of Protect.

Career **Chequered career** One including many changes; successes and failures. [Or. A 'chequered' pattern is one resembling a chessboard, with alternate squares of light and dark colours.]

Carpet **On the carpet(s)** Called in by one's superior for reprimand (the 'carpet' being the one in his office). In trouble.

See **haul over the coals** under *Coals.*

Carry **Carry all before one** Be overwhelmingly successful.

At college he carried all before him.

Carry away 1. Transport. 2. Deprive of self-control.

I'm sorry; I got carried away.

Carry conviction Be very persuasive.

His arguments don't carry much conviction.

Carry the day Reach final success; win.

Their greater skill eventually carried the day.

Carry off 1. Take away by force.

The invaders carried off many hostages.

2. Conduct oneself successfully (in a difficult situation).

He carried off the interview very well.

Carry on 1. Continue (e.g. one's work or recreation.) 2. Grieve. 3. Behave irregularly and badly.

Carry one's point Succeed in convincing one's opponent. [Or. Archery.]

Carry out Put into practice.

You mustn't expect him to carry out his threats.

Carry through Complete. Bring safely out of difficulties.

He seldom carries through what he begins.

Cart **In the cart** [S] In danger, disgrace or difficulty. In an awkward position. [Or. In olden times a criminal was driven in a cart to the place of execution.]

Put the cart before the horse Make two statements in reverse order of their importance; put the second and less important thing first; place the effect before the cause.

Case **As the case may be** Whichever of several things may happen.
Suppose your son becomes an artist, or a poet, as the case may be?
A case in point See under *Point.*
In any case Whatever may occur.
In any case I shall go.
In case Lest. In the event that.
Close the window in case it rains while we're away.
In case of In the event of.
In that case If that is true or should happen. That being so.
In the case of As regards. In the matter of.
In the case of Mary (or In my case) an exception was made.

Cast **Cast about** Seek for.
I've been casting about for some village in which I can spend a quiet holiday.
Cast aside Reject as worthless.
Cast aspersions on Comment unfavourably upon; decry. See **run down.**
Cast away Wrecked.
For five months they were cast away on an uninhabited island.
Cast a clout Discard one's winter clothing. [Or. Proverb: 'Cast not a clout till May be out.' Clout = piece of clothing.]
Cast down Depressed; unhappy.
Since he heard of his failure in the examination, George has been very cast down.
Cast an eye over Look at, usually quite casually. Similar to **cast a glance at.**
Cast (*or* throw) light upon Reveal; exhibit.
Pepys' diary casts a light on life in England in the seventeenth century.
Cast (*or* throw) in one's lot Decide to share the life, the good and bad fortunes, of another person or society.
Cast off 1. Unfasten the mooring ropes, chains, etc., preparatory to sailing.
The ship cast off from Plymouth in fine weather.
2. Repudiate. Throw away. 3. **Cast-off.** Unwanted. Used up.
Cast out Expel.
Cast pearls See *Pearl.*
Cast reflections on Similar to **Cast aspersions on.**
Cast sheep's eyes at See *Sheep.*
Cast a slur on Spoil; stain the reputation of.
Cast a spell over Bewitch; control by magic.
Cast up Flung up (from a depth).

C

The body of a whale was cast up by the sea.

Casting vote A vote given by the chairman of a meeting when the number of votes for and against any proposal is equal. It is the casting vote that then decides the matter.

Castle **Castle in the air** A dream building; a mere vision of happiness which has no basis in fact.

Castle in Spain The French version (*Château d'Espagne*) of the above.

An Englishman's home is his castle One's home is private, and may not be entered by force.

Cat **A cat may look at a king!** Whatever may be our (social) positions, one person is as good as another.

Cat-call Expression of disapproval (usually whistling) at theatre, etc.

Cat's concert A series of loud, discordant cries, resembling the noises made by cats at night.

Cat-and-dog life A life of continual quarrelling and fighting. Also **fight like cat and dog.**

Cat-and-mouse game Cautious manœuvring, bargaining, negotiation, etc.

Cat-nap Brief sleep.

Fight like Kilkenny cats Fight desperately with extreme fierceness. [Or. The legend of the two cats of Kilkenny (Ireland) who fought so furiously that presently 'instead of two cats there weren't any'.]

Have not a cat in hell's chance [S] Have no chance.

Let the cat out of the bag Allow a secret to escape.

Like a cat on hot bricks Restless. Fidgety. Uneasy.

Not room to swing a cat Confined space.

Put the cat among the pigeons Create a sensation, uproar, contention, by doing something, e.g. by taking some initiative in a given situation.

Rain cats and dogs Rain very heavily.

Which way the cat jumps What events indicate as a probability. *The Prime Minister will not announce anything yet: he is waiting to see which way the cat jumps.*

Similar to **which way the wind blows** (under *Wind.*)

Cat's paw One who is used merely for the convenience of a cleverer or stronger person. [Or. Æsop's fable of the monkey who, wanting to eat some chestnuts that were on a hot stove, but not wishing to burn himself getting them, seized a cat and holding its paw in his own, used it to knock the chestnuts to the ground.)

Catch **Catch cold** Become ill with a common cold.

Catch one's death (of cold) Become seriously ill (with a common cold) through exposure to inclement weather. (Jocular exaggeration.)

Catch fire (catch light; catch alight) Ignite; burn.

The spilt oil caught fire, and the house was burnt down.

Catch hold of Take a hold on. Take hold of.

Catch it [S] Receive punishment.

When your father discovers that you've broken his pipe, you'll catch it.

Catch someone napping [LIT] Discover someone asleep. [MET] Obtain an advantage through discovering someone being careless or ignorant.

Catch on [S] 1. Become fashionable or popular.

The new style of hairdressing seems to have caught on.

2. Understand.

I dropped some hints, but he didn't catch on.

Catch out Find out; expose. Discover someone making a mistake.

Catch penny Cheap, or superficially attractive, because purely commercial.

Catch a person's eye See under *Eye.*

Catch sight of, catch a glimpse of See for a moment.

Catch tripping Discover making a mistake.

Catch up 1. Snatch up; seize suddenly.

He caught up his briefcase and dashed out.

2. Become level with.

He ran so fast that he soon caught up with me (or *caught me up*).

Caught **Be caught bending** (*or* **napping** *or* **out**) Be put at a disadvantage by someone else's greater alertness.

Caviare **Caviare to the general** Something good which is beyond the appreciation or understanding of the general public. [Or. *Hamlet.* Caviare is an expensive preparation made from sturgeon's roe; it is highly popular in Russia.]

Chain **Chain reaction** A result which, in turn, produces an effect which, in turn, produces a similar result, and so on.

Chain store One of a number of precisely similar stores, controlled by the same company, and selling goods of the same type and price.

Chair **Take the chair** Occupy the chair, i.e. the seat of the chairman. Preside over a meeting as chairman.

Chalk **By a long chalk; by long chalks** [S] By a great deal; thoroughly. [Or. An ancient custom of recording merit by chalk marks.]

Thus **chalk up**: score.

The boy will win the race by a long chalk.

As different as chalk from cheese [S] Totally different.

The music of Strauss is as different from Bach's as chalk from cheese.

Chance **Chance one's arm** [S] Accept a risk.

I'll chance my arm, and offer £50 for the horse.

An eye to the main chance See under *Eye.*

Sporting chance A chance, though not a great one.
There's still a sporting chance that the horse will win.

Stand a good (*or* fair) chance of Be very (quite) likely to.
We stand a good chance of being late.

Taking no chances Taking no risks.
He has two bolts on every door, and an extra one on the window; he's taking no chance of burglars getting in.

The chances are The probability is.
The chances are that there will be a strike.

Change **Change hands** Change owners.
That shop has changed hands only once in a hundred years.

Get no change out of Fail to receive satisfaction from.
I complained to the manufacturers, but I didn't get any change out of them.

Ring the changes Do something in a variety of ways. [Or. Bell-ringing.]

Small change Coins of small value.
I had to give the conductor a pound note; I had no small change.

Chapter **Chapter of accidents** A series of accidents or misfortunes.

Chapter and verse. Exact authority for a statement; details by which the truth of a statement can be checked. [Or. the divisions of the Bible.]

Character **In character** In harmony with a person's known habits or temperament. Opposite: **out of character.**

Redeem one's character Cause one's faults to be forgiven; cancel a bad reputation.

Charge **Charge with** 1. Formally accuse of some crime. 2. Entrust with.
Charged with 1. Filled, loaded with. 2. Entrusted with.
In charge of Responsible for.

Charity **Charity begins at home** Kindness is due first to one's kith and kin. One should look after one's own interests, and those of one's relatives and friends, before showing kindness to strangers.

Cheap **Cheap as dirt; dirt cheap** Extremely cheap; a bargain.

Check **Check out** [S] [U.S.A.] Pay one's bill and leave.
Keep in check Restrain.

Cheek **Cheek by jowl** Close together, very near.
Have a cheek Be impertinent.
Have the cheek to Have the impertinence, effrontery, to.
I don't know how she's got the cheek to do it.

Cheer **Cheer up** Recover your cheerfulness!
Good cheer Good and rich food and drink.
The table was laden with good cheer.

C

Chest **Get something off one's chest** Say something (usually something one has been intending to say for some time).

Chew **Chew over** [S] Discuss. Think about. Reflect on.

Chicken **Chicken-feed** [S] [Or. U.S.A.] Something of small value, or use.
The cost will be chicken-feed in view of the benefits.
No chicken [S] No longer young (almost always applied to a woman).
Chicken-hearted Cowardly; easily terrified. [Or. Chickens run to their mother for shelter at the slightest danger.]
Count one's chickens before they are hatched Make definite plans about profits or advantages before it is certain that you will obtain them. [Or. Æsop's fable about the woman who, on her way to market, reckoned on how much she would get for her eggs and how she would spend the money, and in her excitement dropped the basket and broke them all.]

Chill **Cast a chill over** Have a depressing influence on.
If he comes, he'll only cast a chill over the proceedings.
Catch a chill Develop a cold.
Take the chill off Warm slightly.

Chime **Chime in** Add in support of something already said. [Or. The chiming of bells.]
Chime in with Harmonize with.
Those blue curtains will chime in with the carpet.

Chip **Chip off the old block** See under **Block**.
Chip in 1. Interrupt.
May I chip in for a moment?
2. Contribute.
All the staff chipped in to buy a farewell present.
Have one's chips [S] Be unsuccessful.
The pub's closed: we've had our chips.

Choice **Hobson's choice** No choice at all; the acceptance of what one is offered. [Or. The custom of a Cambridge stable-keeper named Hobson, who insisted on every customer who wanted to hire a horse taking the one nearest the stable door.]
Take one's choice Decide between several possibilities.

Chop **Chop and change** Frequently alter one's decisions or methods. Be inconsistent, vacillating, variable. (Emphatic form of 'change'.)

Chorus **Chorus of approval** (*or* **applause** etc.) General approval.

Chuck **Chuck away** Waste. Lose. Throw away carelessly.
Chuck out Expel. Throw out.
Chuck up Stop; abandon (in disgust).
I hear that Bill is going to chuck up his job.

Church **Broad church** A term applied to those who think the Church's religious belief should be broad-minded enough to include all variations of ritual.

High church comprises those who follow more elaborate ritual; those who give a 'high place' to the importance of the priests and bishops and have much in common with the Roman Catholic procedures and beliefs.

Low church is the term applied to those who follow simpler and less-formalized ritual. Protestant. Evangelical.

Circle **Vicious circle** Actions and consequences which make each other worse and worse.

Circumstance **Extenuating circumstances** Excuses; causes which make forgiveness possible.

In any circumstances Whatever may happen. Opposite **under no circumstances**: never.

In (under) the circumstances In the present condition or state of affairs; after consideration of what has happened.

Circumstantial **Circumstantial evidence** Evidence which gives no direct proof. Known facts which are hard to explain unless one accepts that they *appear* to constitute proof.

Clap **Clap eyes on** Catch sight of. See. (Usually used in negative.)
I haven't clapped eyes on him for some weeks.

Clap-trap Worthless, valueless talk, generally used in an attempt to become popular or appear learned. [LIT A trap to catch applause.]

Clean **Clean bill of health** [LIT] An official document certifying that a ship has left port with no case of infectious illness on board. [MET] Indication that there is no risk of infection, or, alternatively, that no illness, infectious or otherwise, exists.
He's recovered from his heart-attack and has a clean bill of health.

Clean away Similar to **clear away** (2).

Clean slate Freedom from commitments. Freedom from blame.

Make a clean breast of See *Breast*.

Make a clean sweep of See *Sweep*. See *Heel*.

Clear **Clear away** 1. Remove.
I'll clear away all this rubbish.
2. (*With* get) Escape completely.
The burglars got clear away.

Clear conscience Feeling that one is innocent.

Clear as crystal Obvious; absolutely plain. Also **crystal clear**.
Jack's reason for going to London is as clear as crystal.

Clear-cut Clearly defined.
The girl is pretty, with clear-cut features.

Clear the decks for action Prepare. Get ready. [Or. Nautical.

Before a sea battle or 'action' begins, the deck of each ship was cleared of all unneccessary or impeding objects.]

Our visitors are due in ten minutes, so we must clear the decks for action.

Clear of Free from.

The river is clear of weeds, and delightful to swim in.

Clear off Go away; depart.

Clear out 1. Make clean; remove impurities, etc.

The workmen are clearing out the tank.

2. Similar to **clear off.**

Clear the air Remove misunderstandings, quarrels, ambiguities, etc., which are impeding progress towards the successful outcome of a particular matter.

Clear up 1. Make plain and clear.

I am trying to clear up any misunderstanding.

2. Make tidy by removing or rearranging.

You'll have to clear up the things on the table before we have tea.

3. Become fine.

The weather has cleared up.

Clear the way Remove obstructions [LIT or MET].

This new law will clear the way for many educational improvements.

Clearing-house Office for the exchange of information.

The coast is clear No one is about to see or interfere.

Clinch **Clinch (an argument, a dispute, the matter,** *etc.***)** Settle finally and completely; conclude.

He clinched the dispute by producing new evidence.

Clip **Clip the wings of** [LIT] Cut the wing-feathers of a bird so that it is unable to fly at any height. [MET] Limit the powers or authority of a person.

Clipped speech Words uttered in short, staccato tones, with the final consonants sharply stressed.

Close **At close quarters** Near to.

Behind closed doors Privately; secretly.

We cannot report the discussion, as it took place behind closed doors.

A closed book Something unknown.

Archaeology is a closed book to me.

Close in upon Approach and surround.

Close with Grapple with; grasp violently.

Close season Period of time during which sporting events, etc., do not take place.

Close shave [S] A narrow escape; an event which just missed disaster. Also **a close call.**

The bus missed me, but it was a close shave.

Similar to **a near (***or* **close) thing.**

Closed shop See *Shop.*

C

Cloud **Every cloud has a silver lining** Every misfortune has its consolations. [Or. Proverb.]

In the clouds Day-dreaming, with one's thoughts elsewhere.

Under a cloud Regarded with disfavour and distrust; with an injured reputation.

Cloven **Cloven hoof** An evil or base personality suddenly revealed.

Clover **In Clover** In a condition of luxury; very well off.

Henry's new job is well paid, and the family are in clover.

Club **Club together** Join, combine together (usually to share payment).

Clutch **Clutch at a straw (or straws)** Eagerly seize any help, support, solution, etc., however flimsy it may be.

Coach **Drive a coach and four (or horses) through** Easily evade or make ineffective. The phrase is applied almost entirely to Parliamentary laws or to regulations which have loopholes in them.

Coals **Carry coals to Newcastle** Do something superfluous. [Or. Proverbial. Newcastle = important coal port.]

Haul over the coals Find fault; blame for some error. [Or. In the Middle Ages money was extorted by the King by hauling or pulling people over a slow-burning fire until they agreed to pay the amount demanded.]

I expect I'll get hauled over the coals for such a mistake.

Heap coals of fire on Return good for evil and kindness for unkindness, and so melt the heart of one's enemy and make him ashamed of his conduct. [Or. Biblical.]

Coast **The coast is clear** There is no enemy in view; no probability of interference.

Coat **Cut one's coat according to one's cloth** Limit oneself (or one's expenses) to the resources (or money) available.

Trail one's coat Seek to pick a quarrel.

Cock **Cock-a-hoop** Triumphant. Exultant. Boastful. [Or. The almost obsolete sport of cock-fighting. A winning bird erected his *houpe*, the feathered crest on his head.]

A cock-and-bull story A fantastic and unbelievable story.

Cock-eyed Having a squint. Crooked, not straight or level. Irregular.

Cock a snook at Express contempt for. Make a contemptuous gesture at. (Strictly speaking, placing thumb to nose with fingers outspread.)

Cock sure Aggressively sure and certain. Very self-confident. Also **cocky.**

Cock of the walk The chief; the dominant person. [Or. Walk = the name of the feeding-place of poultry, among whom there is always a cock who is master.]

Go off at half cock Succeed only partially, disappointingly. Proceed half-heartedly, with sense of anti-climax.

Because of the weather, the flower-show went off at half cock.

Live like fighting cocks Live on the best and richest food. [Or. Sporting. Fighting cocks were so fed in order to make them fiercer and stronger.]

Cockles **Warm the cockles of one's heart** Make one's body glow, as with wine. Be deeply moving, delightful. Be emotionally affecting.

Coin **Coin money** Produce riches very rapidly.

The shop at the corner is coining money.

Pay back in his own coin Retaliate or retort by the same method as the one he used. Similar to **give tit for tat.**

Cold **Cold comfort** Very slight satisfaction (the phrase is generally used ironically).

Give the cold shoulder to Avoid. Shun. Adopt an aloof manner towards.

In cold blood Deliberately. With premeditation.

Pour (*or* throw) cold water on Discourage. Behave very unenthusiastically towards (an idea, plan, proposal, etc.).

Colour **Colour-blind** Unable to distinguish colours correctly, though otherwise possessing normal sight.

Give (*or* lend) colour to Support; help to prove.

The cut on his cheek gave colour to his story that he had been attacked.

Off-colour Slightly ill.

Colours **In one's true colours** As one really is (as distinct from what is pretended, or supposed).

Nail one's colours to the mast Adopt a position from which one does not intend to budge. [Or. Nautical. Colours — flags. If nailed, they cannot be changed, or lowered to express surrender.]

Under false colours Falsely; pretending to be what one is not.

With flying colours Triumphantly.

He passed his examination with flying colours.

Come **Come about** Occur; happen.

I don't know exactly how it came about, but she promised to marry me.

Come across 1. [LIT] Cross.

He came across the road to speak to me.

2. [MET] Find casually, discover.

Yesterday, when tidying my desk, I came across some old letters of yours.

Come along Make haste.

Come to an arrangement Agree; mutually arrange.

Come away Leave. Become detached.

Come back Return. Recur to memory.

Come-back A return from obscurity to the prominence and success of the past.

He's far too old to stage a come-back to professional football.

2. [S] Repercussion. Reaction. Response.

You must take full responsibility for the consequences: I don't want to have to deal with any come-back.

Come to blows Proceed to fight.

Come by Acquire.

Where did you come by your new car?

Come clean [S] Confess fully. Similar to **make a clean breast** (see **Breast**).

Come down on Rebuke. Punish. Also **come down (on one) like a ton of bricks.** See *Ton.*

Come into existence Exist; be born; function.

The regulations came into existence on June 1st.

Come forward Present oneself.

Come to grief Suffer disaster.

He was learning to skate, but came to grief at the corner.

Come in for Receive; inherit. Encounter.

He came in for a good deal of praise for his action.

Come hell or high water [S] Whatever the circumstances.

Come it [S] Assume a superior or patronizing position.

Come it strong [S] Exaggerate.

Come into force Begin to operate.

Come of Become; result from.

I don't know what will come of all these developments.

Come off [LIT] Be removable.

I can't make the lid come off the saucepan.

[MET] [S] Reach a successful result.

The comedian did his best to amuse us, but it didn't quite come off.

Come off well, badly, *etc.* End with credit, discredit, etc.

For over an hour he was examined in court by the lawyer, and came off well.

Come on 1. Hasten! Move more quickly! Also **come along.**

2. Begin.

It came on to rain soon after midnight.

Come over 1. [S] Affect, overpower, master, with emotion or illness.

I don't know what came over me.

2. Sound. Project. Make an impression. Perform.

His speech on the radio came over very well.

3. Similar to **come round** (2).

Come right Prove itself to be correct.

I can't make this sum come right.

Come round 1. Recover (from a faint).

We splashed water on her face, and she soon came round.

2. Visit someone not far away.
Come round and see us when you've time.
3. Modify one's own account or accept another person's view.
I discussed the subject for an hour before he came round to my opinion.
Come the old soldier Attempt to impress by claiming a superior authority based on past experience.
Come to ; come to oneself Identical with **come round** (1).
Come to grief Encounter disaster.
Come to light Be revealed.
No further information has come to light.
Come to pass Happen.
Come to terms Reach a formal agreement.
We expect to come to terms about the house very soon.
Come true Actually happen.
If our hopes come true, we shall be married in the spring.
Come upon Encounter. Similar to **come across** (2).
Come up to Reach the level of [LIT and MET].
The water came up to the top of the bath.
This picture does not come up to the one you showed me yesterday.
Come up to scratch [S] See under *Scratch.*
Come up with 1. Draw level with.
We came up with the travellers at the top of the hill.
2. [S] Produce. Devise. Suggest.
Can you come up with a better way of doing it?
Come what may Whatever may happen in the future. Also [S] **come hell or high water.**
It comes (*or* amounts) to this Summarizing the situation; stated briefly.
Up-and-coming [S] [U.S.A.] Achieving prominence. Successfully ambitious.
He is an up-and-coming young politician.

Command   **At one's command** At one's service; available; capable of being used.
Word of command A formal order, spoken in public. [Or. Military.]

Common   **By common consent** By general agreement.
By common consent, the meeting was fixed for the following week.
Common origin An origin in common. The same beginning.
Many French and English words have a common origin—Latin.
Common parlance Plain, ordinary speech.
In common Shared; possessed by each (or all).
They should be very happy, for they have much in common.
In common with Together with.
In common with most people, I deplore violence of any kind.

C

Company **Be good company** Be a pleasant companion. Hence **in good company**.

In company with Together with.

Part company Separate; part.

The strain was so great that the links of the chain parted company.

Compare **Compare notes** Discuss impressions and opinions.

The American travellers were comparing notes on London.

Comparison **Comparisons are odious** Any comparison between two persons or things is almost certain to lead to dissatisfaction and trouble.

In comparison with When compared to.

Compliment **Complimentary tickets** Free tickets, given as a compliment to the receiver's position and importance.

Compliments of the season Traditional Christmas and New Year greetings.

Fish for compliments Speak deprecatingly of oneself in the hope of being contradicted.

Give (*or* pay) a compliment Express praise politely.

Give (*or* send) one's compliments Transmit an expression of formal greetings.

Return the compliment Repay a pleasant speech or a kindly action by another.

Concert **In concert** Unitedly; all together.

Conclusion **Arrive at (*or* come to) the conclusion** 1. Perceive; realize after considering all the facts.

I think you'll arrive at the conclusion that it is suitable for the job.

2. End.

The debate came to a conclusion soon after midnight.

Foregone conclusion An end so obvious that one is justified in assuming it.

When Peter came back to England, it was a foregone conclusion that he would be unsettled.

Jump to a conclusion Assume rashly and without justification.

Try conclusions Test by opposing; fight against. [Old f.]

Condition **On condition that** If. Provided that.

Out of condition In a poor state (e.g. of health, fitness, etc.).

Conduct **Line of conduct** Behaviour.

Confidence **Confidence trick** Swindle based on persuading someone to entrust money, etc., to one as a sign of confidence in his honesty.

In strict confidence Absolutely privately.

Confusion **Confusion worse confounded** Disorder and confusion made even worse than before. [Or. Milton's *Paradise Lost*.]

The Ministers tried to explain the Government's policy, but only made confusion worse confounded.

Conjecture **Hazard a conjecture** Guess.

Conjunction	**In conjunction with** Added to; together with.
	What you've told me, in conjunction with what I already know, fills me with confidence.
Connection	**In connection with** Relating to. Referring to. Regarding.
	He called in connection with the gas leak.
	In that connection As far as that matter is concerned.
	Miss the connection Miss a train, boat (etc.) which one's present mode of transport is intended to arrive in time for.
	My train arrived late at Crewe, and I missed the connection to Manchester.
Conscience	**Have on one's conscience** Feel guilty about. Also **have a conscience about.**
	In all conscience In any imaginable set of circumstance. (There is no exact and literal meaning for this idiom; it is almost entirely exclamatory.)
Consequence	**Of no consequence** Totally unimportant.
	Don't apologize for breaking the cup—it's of no consequence.
	Take the consequences Accept the results (usually of one's own behaviour, actions, etc.).
Construction	**Put a false construction on** Misinterpret; assume wrongly.
Contact	**Come in contact with** Meet; encounter.
	I don't often come into contact with them nowadays.
Contempt	**Bring into contempt** Cause to be despised.
	Their behaviour has brought their beliefs into contempt.
	Fall into contempt Become despised.
	Hold in contempt Regard with contempt or scorn.
Contradiction	**Contradiction in terms** A statement which contradicts itself.
Contrary	**On the contrary** The reverse; the opposite.
	I haven't finished. On the contrary, I've only just started.
	Contrary to expectation The reverse of what was expected.
	Contrary to expectation, he was not present.
	To the contrary To contradict. The opposite.
	Unless I hear to the contrary, I'll expect you to arrive on Sunday.
Convert	**Convert into** Change into.
	All the bank-notes were converted into cash.
Conviction	**Carry conviction** Convince; compel belief in.
	His excuse doesn't carry much conviction.
Cook	**Cook the books** Falsify statements (usually financial ones).
	Cook one's goose Create problems for one.
	Cook up Prepare. Concoct.
	Too many cooks spoil the broth One organizer is enough.
Cool	**Cool as a cucumber** Completely calm and unexcited.
	The boy was as cool as a cucumber throughout the examination.
	Cool customer (card, hand) A calmly audacious person.

Cool down [LIT] Become less heated. [MET] Become calmer.

Cool one's heels Wait. Be kept waiting (often as punishment, etc.).

Cost **At all costs** Whatever may be involved; whatever efforts or sacrifice may be needed.

Cost a packet [S] [U.S.A.] Be very expensive.

Count the cost Consider the risks before acting.

Cotton **Cotton on (to)** [S] Understand.

Counsel **Keep one's own counsel** Remain discreetly silent; say nothing of one's own plans.

Count **Count on** Rely on: be sure of.

We know we can count on your support.

Count one's chickens See *Chickens.*

Does not count Is immaterial; does not make any difference.

Personal friendship does not seem to count in politics.

Countenance **Keep one's countenance** Refrain from laughing. Maintain one's composure. Similar to **keep a straight face** (under *Face*).

Put out of countenance Confuse; disconcert. [Old f.]

Counter **Go (run) counter to** Be opposite to. Also **act counter to**: behave contrary to.

It is a philosophy which runs entirely counter to everything I believe in.

Courage **Dutch courage** Temporary courage created by drinking. [Or. In the seventeenth-century wars with Holland, Dutch sea-captains had barrels of brandy placed on deck from which the sailors helped themselves before beginning a fight.]

Have the courage of one's convictions Be brave enough to speak and act as one really believes.

Take one's courage in both hands Nerve oneself (to do something difficult).

Summon (*or* pluck) up courage Also **bring one's courage to the the sticking-point** [Old f.] Succeed in showing bravery in spite of fears.

Course **Adopt a course** Take a certain definite and considered action.

Change course Change direction.

In due course Eventually; ultimately; at the appropriate time.

In the course of During.

Embark on (*or* continue) a course Begin a connected series of actions or words. [Or. Nautical. The 'course' is the direction in which a ship travels.]

A matter of course The normal or expected procedure.

Of course Naturally.

Coventry **Send to Coventry** Disregard completely; refuse to associate with. [Or. The dislike the inhabitants of Coventry had at one time for soldiers. Any woman seen speaking to one was thereafter treated as an outcast and ignored.]

Cover **From cover to cover** From beginning to end (of a book, document, etc.).

Under cover 1. [LIT] (*a*) Sheltered.
We were under cover when the rain fell.
(*b*) Covered by a wrapping or envelope.
I am sending you a parcel under separate cover.
2. [MET] Concealed by a pretence.
Under cover of friendship, he betrayed their trust.

Cow **Till the cows come home** [S] For an indefinite period; for ever.
If we wait for him, we shall wait till the cows come home.

Crack **Crack-brained** Crazy. Similar to **hare-brained, scatter-brained.**
Crack of doom The Day of Judgement, the last day. Commonly used to indicate an infinitely future period.
This shed is built to last till the crack of doom.
Crack up Break; deteriorate. (Frequently used in connection with a person's health.)
I think Peter is beginning to crack up.
Crack the whip Show one's authority. Demand more effort (as of man driving a horse).

Creature **Creature comforts** The material things which make life comfortable—good food, warm clothing, etc.

Credence **Give credence to** Believe.

Credit **A credit to** A source of honour to or for.
The appearance of the book is a credit to the publishers.
Get the credit for Receive due praise for.
Give credit to Give praise where it should be given. Also **credit where credit is due.**
I must give my daughter credit for the decorations.
Redound to one's credit; reflect credit upon Be worthy of praise or honour.

Creeps **Give one the creeps** [S] Cause one to shudder with nervous fear. (Generally used less literally to express dislike.)
Make one's flesh creep Make one feel as if things were crawling over one's skin (as result of repugnance, fear, etc.).

Crop **Crop up** Appear unexpectedly (above the surface) [LIT] and [MET].
Weeds always crop up in our flower-bed.
I never expected that this problem would crop up again.

Cropper **Come a cropper** [S] Fall at full length. Meet with disaster.

Cross **Cross one's mind** Occur to one.
It never crossed my mind that he might be on holiday.
Crossed cheque Cheque marked with two parallel vertical lines signifying that it may only be paid through a bank.

Talk at cross purposes Discuss from incompatible points of view, owing to a misunderstanding.

Cross (*or* pass) the Rubicon Take any irrevocable step. [Or. The Rubicon was a small river dividing Ancient Italy from Caesar's territory, and when he and his army crossed it, he automatically invaded Italy.]

Cross as two sticks In an extremely bad temper. [Or. The cross formed when two sticks are placed one across the other. Thus pun on two meanings of the word 'cross'.]

Cross swords See *Sword*.

Crow **Crow's feet** The small wrinkles which age, ill-health or trouble cause to form at the corners of one's eyes.

As the crow flies In a straight line, regardless of obstructions. [Or. A crow flies in a straight line from point to point.]
The villages are ten miles apart as the crow flies, but nearly fifteen miles by road.

Crow over Boast about one's triumph over.

Cruise **Cruising speed** An economic travelling speed, less than full speed.

Crumb **Crumb of comfort** A tiny amount of comfort.

Crunch **The crunch comes** [S] The crucial, difficult moment arrives (usually when progress will be halted by an obstacle).

Crush **Have a crush on** [S] Be infatuated by.

Cry **Cry down** Decry; deprecate; speak slightingly about. [Old f.]
He cries down everything his wife does.

Cry for the moon Ask for the impossible.

Cry off Refuse, or cease, to share in or co-operate.
They said they were coming to the picnic, but cried off the day before.

Cry over spilt milk Express regrets too late, or when nothing is to be gained by expressing them.

Cry quits; call it quits Agree to end a dispute or transaction, and regard both sides as being equal.

Cry stinking fish Speak unfavourably about one's own profession, trade, family, endeavours, etc.

Cry wolf Cause excitement or anxiety by spreading false news. [Or. From Æsop's fable of the shepherd boy who shouted 'Wolf' and brought his neighbours from their work so many times that when a wolf really did attack his sheep no one paid attention to his cries.]

A far cry A long way. Very different.
Farm eggs are a far cry from the ones we get in the local shops.

Cudgel **Cudgel (*or* rack) one's brains** [LIT] Beat one's brains (a 'cudgel' is a stick) to compel them to work. [MET] Try to compel one's brain to function, and to understand or remember. Think hard.
I've cudgelled my brains, but I can't recollect where I put it.

Take up the cudgels Vigorously defend or support a cause.

Cuff **Off the cuff** Without prior thought, planning, preparation, etc.
I won't prepare a speech: I'll talk off the cuff.

Cup **One's cup (of happiness) is filled** One's happiness is absolutely complete. Opposite: **cup of bitterness.**
With his family around him and no fears for the future, his cup was filled.

Cup that cheers Tea. [Or. William Cowper's *Task*: 'The cups that cheer but not inebriate.']

In one's cups In the process of getting drunk. Intoxicated.

Cupboard **Cupboard love** Affection shown only in the hope of obtaining something in return.

Currency **Acquire (*or* obtain, *or* gain) currency** Circulate; become publicly discussed.
A rumour that the Prime Minister may resign has acquired currency.

Curry **Curry favour** Attempt by flattery, bribery, etc., to become popular.

Curtain **Curtains** [S] The end. [Or. Theatre.]
If we can't increase the membership, it'll be curtains for the society.

Customer **Ugly (awkward, tough, *etc.*) customer** A difficult or dangerous person to deal with.

Cut **A cut above** Rather better than.
This beer is a cut above the average.

Cut back Reduce. Also **cut-back.** Reduction.
Production at the factory has been cut back because of the strike.

Cuts both ways Has a second and compensating effect. Has an effect on both sides (of an argument, etc.).
Her refusal to live with him cuts both ways—he won't be responsible for maintaining her.

Cut the cackle [S] Be brief and to the point; talk less, and deal with the subject under discussion.

Cut capers Caper; dance fantastically about; waste time in irrelevant activity. (Also, incorrectly, **cut the capers**: stop wasting time.)

Cut and come again Help oneself freely and repeatedly. [Old f.]

Cut a dash, a figure [S] Exhibit oneself as a smart or fashionable person.

Cut down 1. [LIT]
He cut down a tree.
2. [MET] Reduce.
He has to cut down his expenses since he changed his job.

Cut and dried Already arranged or prepared.
His plans for leaving were all cut and dried.

Cut fine Allow little margin for accident, etc.

You may catch the train, but you are cutting it rather fine.
Cut in 1. Interrupt.
Simon cut in with an interesting suggestion.
2. Admit.
Shall we cut them in on the plans?
3. (Of a car, pedestrian, etc.) Obstruct, or nearly obstruct, by placing oneself in front of another after overtaking.
The taxi cut in very sharply, and I had to brake.
Cut the (Gordian) knot Take a quick and drastic method of ending a difficulty. [Or. The knot tied by Gordius, a peasant who, on being chosen King of Phrygia, dedicated his wagon to Jupiter and tied the yoke to the beam with a knot that no one could untie. Alexander, on being told that whoever untied it would rule the whole of the East, solved the problem by cutting the knot with his sword.]
Cut no ice [S] Fail to convince, or impress.
The salesman's arguments cut no ice at all.
Cut of one's jib [S] The face and general appearance. [Or. Nautical. The shape, or cut, of a ship's jib indicates to a sailor what type she is.]
Cut one's coat See *Coat.*
Cut one's losses Abandon any further attempts to continue a business or enterprise which has not been profitable, and limit one's losses to those already incurred.
Cut off 1. Sever; cut.
She is going to have all her hair cut off.
2. Separate. Also (of telephone) disconnect.
That remote village will entirely cut her off from her friends.
3. Hurry; hasten [S]. [Old f.]
Cut off and buy me some cigarettes.
Cut off one's nose to spite one's face Behave spitefully, damaging oneself.
Cut off with a shilling Bequeath nothing, or practically nothing, to a person. [Or. The custom of leaving an unpopular member of the family only a shilling in one's will—the shilling merely being to make it impossible for the recipient to plead that his or her name had been omitted by accident.]
Cut out 1. [LIT] Cut round, as with a pair of scissors.
2. [MET] Supplant.
The corner-shop has been cut out by the new super-market.
3. Designed for, suitable for.
I don't think you're cut out to be a soldier.
Cut (or wounded) to the quick Hurt intensely. [Or. Old meaning of 'quick' = 'living'; hence the part of one's nails which is below the skin, which still has feeling, is called the 'quick'.]

Cut and run [S] Hurry away; leave as quickly as possible.
You'll have to cut and run, if you want to catch the bus.
Cut and thrust Rapid exchange. [Or. Swordfighting.]
A barrister needs to be quick-witted to survive the cut-and-thrust of the court-room.
Cut short End abruptly.
The preacher cut short his sermon when the church caught fire.
Cut up 1. [LIT] Cut into small pieces. 2. [MET] Distressed, unhappy.
She was terribly cut up when she heard the news.
Cut up rough [S] Show excitement and anger.
When I tell Mary, she'll cut up rough.
Short cut See *Short.*

D

Daggers   **At daggers drawn** In a state of open and bitter hostility.
     Look daggers Look at fiercely and angrily.
Damn   **Damn with faint praise** Praise in so formal and limited a manner that it is an obvious cloak to adverse criticism or dislike. [Or. Quotation from Alexander Pope.]
Damp   **A damp squib** A squib is a small firework which sends out showers of sparks and finally explodes. If, however, it is not dry, it will do neither. Hence, anything which has failed is said to have 'gone off like a damp squib'.
Dance   **Dance attendance** Attend obsequiously to every whim or requirement of a person.
Darby   **Darby and Joan** An aged and devoted husband and wife. [Or. From an eighteenth-century ballad called 'The Happy Old Couple'.]
Dare   **Dare-devil** A daring and reckless person.
Dark   **A dark horse** A person whose qualities are not well known.
     In the dark In ignorance.
     I am completely in the dark concerning his plans.
     Keep it dark Keep it secret.
Dash   **Dash off** 1. Hurry away.
     He dashed off for help.
     2. Write in great haste.
     He dashed off a note to his wife.
     Dash one's hopes Abruptly destroy one's hopes.
Date   **Out of date** Obsolete; belonging to an earlier period.
     Your ideas about the rights of a husband are entirely out of date.
     Up to date Recent. Fashionable. Current.
Davy Jones   **Davy Jones' locker** The sea-bed. A 'locker' or box is one used by

seamen and others for their personal possessions. 'Davy Jones' (a corruption of 'Jonah', who was thrown into the sea) is a legendary character who lives at the bottom of the ocean. 'To go to Davy Jones' locker' is therefore to drown.

Day **All day (*or* night) long** Continuously; throughout the day (or night).

Broad daylight Full and complete daylight.
The house was robbed in broad daylight.

Call it a day [S] Consider work on any particular job ended for the day or for the present time.
We've worked till it's dark: we'll call it a day.

Carry the day See *Carry.*

Dark days Days of trouble and distress.

Day of doom Day on which some terrible or fatal occurrence takes place.

Daydream A reverie or flight of the imagination. Also used as a verb:
Cinderella was daydreaming over her work.

Day in, day out All day and every day.
Day in, day out they watched for the invaders.

Daylight robbery Any form of gross and obvious swindling or profiteering.
The price they are asking is daylight robbery.

Days (*or* hours) are numbered The end (e.g. death) is inevitable, and is approaching.
The revolution became less vigorous; it was plain that its days were numbered.

Days of old (*or* of yore) A long time ago; the remote past.
In days of yore people believed in dragons.

Days to come The future.

Fallen on evil days In misfortune.

The livelong day All day; the whole of the time. [Old f.]
She waited the livelong day, but he did not arrive.

Name the day Literally, the day which a girl nominates as her wedding-day. (But frequently used in the sense of 'consent to marry', no exact date being specified.)

The old (*or* olden) days The past.

One of these (fine) days Soon.

A rainy day An emergency, a period of misfortune for which money, etc., has been reserved.
He had £500 put aside for a rainy day.

See better days Be happier and more prosperous (almost always used in the past tense).
The woman had obviously seen better days.

D

Dead This word is commonly used in the sense of 'absolute' and 'absolutely', e.g. **dead centre, dead level, dead straight, dead certain, dead sure.**
Dead as a doornail (Emphatically) dead.
Dead beat Utterly exhausted.
Dead heat Event in which two competitors finish at exactly the same time.
Dead letter 1. Letters etc., which for any reason cannot be delivered go to the Dead Letter Office, which returns them to the senders. 2. A law or regulation which exists but is never enforced— e.g. the law compelling people to go to church on Sunday is said to to be a 'dead letter'.
Dead loss Complete or total loss. [S] A waste of time.
The ship broke up and became a dead loss.
(Waiting for a) dead man's shoes (Waiting for) an advantage that may be obtained when someone dies, or retires, or is promoted, etc.
(In) dead(ly) earnest Extremely seriously.
He spoke quickly, in low tones, and in deadly earnest.
Dead of night The darkest, most silent time of night.
Dead to the world Utterly exhausted; sleeping deeply; or unconscious for any other cause.
After working for two days and nights with only an hour's sleep, I was practically dead to the world.
Over my dead body Exaggerated expression meaning 'over-ruling my strongest wishes'.
If that dog comes into the house again, it will be over my dead body.
Deaf **Deaf mute** A person who is both deaf and dumb.
Deal **A raw deal** [S] Unfair or unduly harsh treatment.
Death **At death's door** On the verge of dying; desperately, almost hopelessly, ill.
In at the death Arriving in time to see the climax. [Or. Hunting.]
John will not see the beginning of the competition, but he will be in at the death.
Jaws of death Extreme danger; risk of death.
The firemen rescued the child from the jaws of death.
Pale as death As pale as though already dead.
A death-warrant [LIT] A legal warrant authorizing execution. [MET] State of being in serious difficulties, on the verge of extinction.
The defeat at Culloden was the death-warrant of the hopes of the Jacobites.
To the death Till one combatant is killed.
Deduction **Make a deduction** 1. Deduce.

From what the Chairman said, it was easy to make deductions about the future of the firm.
2. (With 'of' added.) Reduce by.
We can make a deduction of ten per cent.

Default **By default** As a result of failure to act or appear.

Deliver **Deliver under hand and seal** 'I deliver this under my hand and seal' is the phrase used when signing and sealing a legal document.

Demean **Demean oneself** Lower one's dignity.
I would not demean myself by apologizing.

Depend **Depend upon** Rely upon; have faith in.
You may depend upon our goods; they are of the best quality.
Depend upon it Be certain; have no doubt.
Depend upon it, we shall win.

Depth **Out of (or beyond) one's depth** Literally, one's 'depth' is the depth of water beyond which one's feet no longer touch the bottom, so that one must either swim or drown. Used as an idiom, 'out of one's depth' indicates a subject beyond one's knowledge or understanding.
The student was out of his depth in discussions on the Middle Ages.

Descend **Descend to particulars** Cease to talk about generalities, and discuss a subject in detail.

Deserve **Richly deserve** 'Richly' here means thoroughly, completely.

Despair **Yield (give away) to despair** Give up hope.

Devil **Between the Devil and the deep (blue) sea** Between two equally dangerous or unpleasant alternatives.
Devil-may-care A reckless person.
Devil's advocate One who makes unpopular suggestions without seriously believing them, i.e. simply to ensure that all sides of a case have been considered.
Give the Devil his due Admit good, even in someone of whom you disapprove.
To give the Devil his due, old Simpkins, mean though he is, has always been generous to me.
Hold a candle to the Devil (From fear or caution) assist someone of whom we disapprove. [Or. From the story of the old woman who lit one candle to St Michael and another to the Devil he was trampling underfoot, so that whether she went to Heaven or Hell she would have a friend.]
Needs must when the Devil drives If something must be done, then it must be done.
Play the very devil with Create disorder in.
Too much garlic plays the very devil with my digestion.
Talk of the Devil Applied (usually jocularly) to someone who

has been a topic of conversation and who then unexpectedly
arrives.

Die **Die away** Become more and more faint, until the sound cannot be
be heard at all.
The sound of her father's footsteps gradually died away.
Die down Subside; become calm after violence.
The die is cast An irrevocable decision has been taken.

Difference **Split the difference** Halve the amount in dispute.
*You ask twelve pounds; I offer eight. Will you split the difference and
accept ten?*

Dilemma **On the horns of a dilemma** In a position where a choice has to be
made between alternatives that are unpleasant in either case; in a
difficult position. (Or. 'Lemma', from the Greek, means taken for
granted, and dilemma is a double acceptance—*two* things accepted,
a bull with horns that will toss you whichever you grasp.]

Ding-dong **Ding-dong fight** One in which the opponents are fighting hard and
are fairly evenly matched. [Or. 'Ding' is Anglo-Saxon for 'bruise'.]

Dint **By dint of** Dint = effort, usually continued.
By dint of much saving, he succeeded in going to college.

Discount **At a discount** Not required, or not fully appreciated. (Also [LIT]
At a reduced price.)
Books about the war are at a discount just now.

Discretion See *Valour.*

Discussion **Open a discussion** Begin a discussion.
*The subject was 'Is Marriage a Failure?' and Mrs Smith opened the
discussion.*

Distance **Keep one's distance** Refrain from becoming familiar or intimate.
They have always kept their distance from the neighbours.

Divine **Divine right** A right supposedly received direct from God, applied
chiefly to the right of sovereigns to occupy their thrones regardless
of their suitability, or of their subjects' wishes, but also applied to
other situations.
He behaves as if has a divine right to be unpleasant.

Do 1. Be sufficient or suitable.
A small loaf will do for the family's breakfast.
2. Exert oneself.
I'll do all I can.
3. Swindle [S].
That man is a cheat—he'll do you if he has a chance.
4. Visit a theatre, etc., as part of a plan.
We did two concerts and the Royal Academy last week.
Do away (make away) with Dispose of, usually by destroying.
Abolish.
Do in [S] Kill.

Do to death Kill; murder. Also [MET] Repeat so frequently that all interest is 'killed'.
The whole subject has been done to death in the newspapers.
Do up Repair.
Doing Happening.
What's doing at the concert tonight?
Done Completely cooked.
The pudding is done.
Done in [S] Exhausted.
Have done with Cease to have any connection with.
I've done with hard work for the rest of my life.
Have to do with Have dealings, relationship with.
I refuse to have anything to do with that matter.
It isn't done It is socially forbidden; taboo.
You musn't pour your tea in the saucer to cool it—it isn't done.

Dog **A dog's chance** No chance at all.
He doesn't stand a dog's chance of getting the job.
A dog's life A very unpleasant existence.
Her poor husband leads a dog's life.
Dog-days (Traditionally July 3rd to August 4th.) The hottest weeks of the summer. So called because Sirius, or the dog-star, rising with the sun, combines to add his heat to it.
Dog doesn't eat dog See **honour among thieves.**
Dog-eared Applied to pages which, by constant handling, have become bent or curled at the corners.
Dog in the manger A person so selfish that he will not allow people to enjoy something he himself cannot enjoy. Also adjective: *A dog-in-the-manger attitude.* [Or. Æsop's fable of the malicious dog who barked and snarled in the manger containing the cows' hay, and refused to let them eat it, though he did not want it himself.]
Dog-watch A corruption of 'dodge' watch—two short watches introduced on board ship (from 4 to 6 and 6 to 8 in the evening) so that the same men should not be on duty at the same time every day.
Every dog has his day No one is always unlucky.
Go to the dogs Abandon or lose all standards, restraints, high qualities, etc. Be ruined.
That football team goes to the dogs whenever a goal is scored against them.
Hair of the dog that bit you A drink taken to cure the effects of too much drinking.
Help a lame dog over a stile Help someone who is in need of assistance, usually financial.

Let sleeping dogs lie Avoid any action leading to unnecessary friction or trouble; allow matters to remain as they are. [Or. Proverbial.]

Throw to the dogs Throw away, sacrifice, carelessly.

Under-dog One who is in a helpless or inferior position, who has no power to assert his wishes or authority.

Doldrums **In the doldrums** Depressed and miserable. [Or. Part of the ocean, near the equator, known as the doldrums, in which the wind is so slight that sailing vessels are frequently unable to proceed.]

Dole **Dole out** Distribute at intervals in small quantities, with a suggestion of charity.

Don Juan A dissipated and immoral character. [Or. A fourteenth-century Spanish nobleman, upon whose career Byron's poem 'Don Juan' is founded.]

Door **Show a person the door** [LIT] Escort him to the door. [MET] Order him to leave.

Dot **On the dot** Exactly. Precisely. Promptly.
The train arrived on the dot.

Double **Double-crossing** Tricking or betraying people who believed they were dealing with trustworthy friends.

Double-dealing Trickery and deceit.

Double-edged Possessing a double significance. Sarcastic. Ironical. [Or. A sword sharpened at both edges.]

Double-quick Extremely quickly. At the double.
I dashed to the door, double-quick, but was too late to catch him.

Double time Twice the normal amount of wages.
We earn time and a half on Saturday afternoons, and double time on Sundays.

Doubt **Beyond a doubt; without doubt** With absolute certainty.
The man is sincere beyond a doubt.

In doubt Uncertain; hesitant.
When in doubt, do what your conscience advises.

Have (make) no doubt Be quite sure; certain.
Note.—This idiom is used with two slight but definite shades of meaning:
1. Do what is necessary to make certain. [Old f.]
Make no doubt that the safe door is locked.
2. Accept as a fact about which there is no doubt at all.
He'll agree to our offer—have no doubt of that.

Shadow of doubt Very slight uncertainty. (Frequently in the negative to indicate complete certainty.)
The judge said he had no shadow of doubt of the prisoner's guilt.

Down **Down on one's luck** Temporarily unfortunate.

D

Down in the mouth Depressed-looking; miserable. Similar to **in the doldrums** and **in the dumps**.

Down and out In a state of complete destitution. [Or. Boxing. A boxer is said to be down and out when he has been knocked down and is unable to rise before he is 'counted out'.]

Dozen **Baker's dozen** Thirteen. [Or. A baker may be fined if his loaves are under the official weight. To ensure that this should not happen, he used to include an extra loaf in each dozen.]

Drag **Drag up** (*or* **in**) Talk about some subject which it is not tactful or necessary to discuss.

Draw **Draw a blank** Have no success.

The police searched all day, but drew a complete blank.

Draw aside. 1. [LIT] Draw, as one draws a curtain.

2. [MET] Separate a person from others.

At the end of the meeting, he drew me aside to discuss the situation.

Draw away Withdraw from; shrink from. Leave.

Draw back Withdraw from an undertaking.

Draw to an end Reach the end; finish.

I shall be glad when the concert draws to its end.

Draw in 1. Shrink; become shorter. (Applied especially to the period between summer and winter, when the hours of daylight decrease.)

After September the days seem to draw in very quickly.

2. Move to the side of the road, or stop entirely.

See **draw-up** (3).

Draw the line at Refuse to go as far as. Set limits beyond which one will not go.

I enjoy football, but I draw the line at flying to Vienna to watch the match.

Draw near Approach; come near.

Draw off 1. [LIT] Cause to flow away.

We must draw off the water from the tank.

2. [MET] Cause to depart, to lead away. [Old f.]

Draw out 1. Remove money from a bank or company.

I drew out a hundred pounds last week.

2. Encourage to talk.

The boy was very shy, but we succeeded in drawing him out about his hobbies.

Draw rein Pull at a horse's rein to compel it to stop.

Draw up 1. Arrange in correct order (applicable both to people and to legal documents).

He drew up an agreement.

The troops will be drawn up on the parade ground.

2. Raise; pull up.

The women used to draw up water from the well.

3. Stop; halt.

The taxi drew up at the station entrance.

Drawn game (or draw) Term applied to any match or competition which ends in both sides being absolutely equal. Similar to **dead heat.**

Dribs and Drabs Small quantities.

The landlady gave us our hot water in dribs and drabs.

Drive **Drive away, off** 1. Depart, in a vehicle.

I must drive away in five minutes.

2. Compel someone or something to leave quickly.

These flies are a nuisance; please drive them away.

Drive a bargain Arrive at an agreement, usually after forceful negotiation.

Drive home 1. [LIT] Hammer a nail, etc., as far as it can go.

2. [MET] Emphasize.

The message was driven home by frequent repetition in the course of his speech.

Driving (or getting) at [S] Implying; hinting.

Despite his embarrassment, I could see what he was getting at.

Drop **Drop** 1. Cease to be friends with (a person).

2. Abandon, cease to discuss (a subject).

I don't wish to discuss the matter further, so let's drop it.

Drop behind Be overtaken.

Drop a brick [S] Behave tactlessly; commit an indiscretion.

I'm afraid I dropped a brick when I asked if your uncle had ever been inside a prison.

Similar to **put one's foot in it.**

Drop in Call casually and informally.

Drop in for tea whenever you're passing.

Drop a hint See under *Hint*.

Drop a line Send a short letter.

Drop me a line when you are next in town.

Drop in the ocean (or bucket) A small and inadequate matter compared with the whole subject.

Why should I bother to vote? It would just be a drop in the ocean.

Drop off Fall asleep.

He closed his eyes, and soon dropped off.

Drop on 1. Select for questioning, etc.

The examiner may drop on George.

2. Blame.

I wasn't even there when the accident happened, so why drop on me?

Drop out Absent oneself; cease to compete.

Ten runners started, but three soon dropped out.

A drop too much [S] An intoxicating amount of drink. Similar to **one over the eight**; **dead to the world**; **half-seas over**; etc.

Duck **Duck** *(verb)* Jerk one's head downwards to avoid a blow.

Make a duck (*or* **duck's egg**) *(cricket only)* Be dismissed without scoring.

Make ducks and drakes 1. Send small flat stones skimming horizontally over the surface of the sea, a pond, etc. 2. Scatter one's fortune in extravagant living.

He soon made ducks and drakes of the money he had won.

Dumps **In the dumps** Thoroughly depressed. Similar to **in the doldrums**; **down in the mouth**.

Duress **Under duress** Compelled by moral or physical force.

He confessed, under duress, to several crimes.

Dust **Throw dust in the eyes** Hoodwink; mislead and confuse.

Not so dusty [S] Not so bad; tolerable.

Shake the dust from one's feet Leave.

Duty **In duty bound** Compelled by a sense of duty.

I shall make myself unpopular, but I'm in duty bound to do it.

Dye **Of the deepest dye** Of the most extreme type, usually unpleasant. [Old f.]

Dyed in the wool Permanently ingrained.

He's a Tory, dyed in the wool.

E

Ear **Box a person's ears** Administer a sharp slap on the side of the head.

If you don't go to bed at once I'll box your ears.

(Play) by ear 1. Without any technical knowledge, merely by a natural appreciation of the sounds.

She plays the piano entirely by ear.

2. Without preparation.

I haven't decided what to say when he comes; I'll play it by ear.

Come to (*or* **reach**) **one's ears** Be heard or known.

If the news should come to the old man's ears, it would break his heart.

All ears Very attentive.

When they came in, they were all ears.

An ear for A natural appreciation for.

Certain animals have an ear for danger.

Earshot Hearing distance.

Ear-splitting Deafening; distressingly loud and shrill.

He gave an ear-splitting yell.

Ears burning A sign that one is being talked about. (Used jocularly.)

'Frank was talking about you last night. Were your ears burning?'

A flea in the ear Truths, usually unpleasant.

A salesman came to the door, but I sent him away with a flea in his ear.

Give ear Listen to, and attend carefully. [Old f.]

Give one's ears Make almost any sacrifice to obtain.

I'd give my ears to visit Venice this spring.

Have one's ear to the ground [S] Be aware of what is likely to happen.

George knew of the proposals already; he always has his ear to the ground.

Have the ear of Be in a position to advise someone.

If you want to get anything done about it, you'll have to find someone who has the ear of the manager.

In at one ear and out at the other Without being appreciated or remembered.

Everything we try to teach the boy goes in at one ear and out at the other.

Prick up one's ears Listen with sudden attention to something heard unexpectedly. (Animals 'prick up' or raise their ears at an unfamiliar sound.)

Turn a deaf ear Refuse to listen.

The gambler turned a deaf ear to all advice.

Earnest **In earnest; in dead (*or* good) earnest** Serious; the reverse of joking.

I am in earnest when I say that we are ruined.

Earth **Go to earth** Disappear from the places in which one is usually seen. [Or. Hunting. A fox 'goes to earth' when it vanishes into its 'earth' or burrow.]

Ease **Put (*or* set) at ease** Make unembarrassed and socially happy by friendliness.

He has a knack of putting visitors at their ease.

Ill at ease Uncomfortable. Anxious.

Easy **In easy circumstances** Financially comfortable; rich enough to be able to live without worrying.

The old man has retired; he is in easy circumstances.

Easy money 1. One from whom money is easily obtained.

Try borrowing from Simon. He's easy money.

2. Money which is easily earned.

I'd like George's job. It's easy money.

Eat **Eat away** Penetrate and use up.

The sea had eaten away much of the shore.

Eat one's cake See under *Cake.*

Eat one's heart out Grieve continuously.

She is eating her heart out because Jim never writes.

Eat humble pie Behave meekly, apologetically. [Or. 'Umbles', the inferior parts of a deer, which was served as a pie to the servants of a medieval household, while the host and guests received the better portions.]

He began by blustering, but when I explained the position he ate humble pie.

Eat into Similar to **eat away**.

Eat one's head off Eat very large quantities.

Eat out of house and home Eat so much that one would have to sell one's house to pay for food. (Often used jokingly of hungry children.)

That boy will eat you out of house and home.

Eat one's words Completely and ignominiously withdraw a statement.

Edge **Edge away** Move gradually away (as a boat moves very slowly from the edge of the shore).

Have an edge on one's appetite Be hungry.

On edge In a state of nervous tension.

We were all on edge to know the news.

Effect **In effect** Stated briefly and in other words.

He drank too much, and neglected his wife and children, and was, in effect, a failure.

Take effect Operate; function.

The medicine will soon take effect.

Egg **As sure as eggs is eggs** [S] Stated with absolute certainty.

As sure as eggs is eggs it will rain tomorrow.

A bad egg [S] See under *Bad*.

A duck's egg *(cricket)* See under *Duck*.

Don't teach your grandmother to suck eggs Don't offer advice to people who are more experienced than you are.

Put all one's eggs in one basket Invest all one's resources, financial or otherwise, in a single enterprise.

He's put all his eggs in one basket, and bought a hotel.

Eke **Eke out** Make just sufficient by adding to.

The widow eked out her little income by selling flowers from her garden.

Elbow **Elbow one's way** Push forward by thrusting with one's elbows. Frequently used metaphorically:

They're trying to elbow their way into the tennis club committee.

Elbow-grease [S] Physical effort and energy.

You'll never clean the floor properly unless you put more elbow-grease into your work.

Elbow-room Space in which to move.

We're moving to an office in which we shall have more elbow-room.

Element **In one's element** In a congenial atmosphere and surroundings.
Jim is entirely in his element among a crowd of girls.
Out of one's element In an uncongenial atmosphere or surroundings. Similar to **a fish out of water.**

Eleven **The eleventh hour** The latest possible time before it is too late.
The crew were rescued at the eleventh hour.

Embargo **Lay (place) an embargo on** An embargo is a legal prohibition. The phrase is also loosely applied to any definite impediment.
The new taxes will lay an embargo on the company's future prosperity.

Embark **Embark on** Begin.

End **At a loose end** Unoccupied.
Give me a ring if you're at a loose end tonight.
At one's wits' end Mentally desperate, and unable to find a solution. Also used jocularly (as an exaggeration) to mean simply 'in a state of confusion', or 'unable to think clearly'.
To the bitter end To the extreme end, whatever may happen.
I intend to see this matter through to the bitter end.
No end [S] Greatly; very much.
I was pleased no end when I heard of my promotion.
No end of a [S] Superlatively good.
We went to Brighton, and had no end of a time.
Ends of the earth [LIT] The most distant parts of the world. [MET] A considerable distance.
She swore that she would follow him to the ends of the earth.
The end of one's tether The limit of one's endurance or patience. [Or. Tether = the rope or chain by which a horse or other animal is secured.]
We had been walking all day, and were at the end of our tether.
Go off the deep end [S] Become suddenly and violently angry. [Or. The deep end of a swimming-pool.] Similar to **fly off the handle.**
In the end Finally.
Make (both) ends meet Make one's income enough for one's expenses. (More frequently used in the negative.)
I cannot make ends meet on my salary.
On end Continuously.
The rain has been falling for days on end.
Put an end to Finish; terminate. (Applied to something which has already existed for some time.)
The King decided to put an end to the barons' quarrels.
To no end (*or* purpose) Without effect or result.
The priest tried to put the fire out, but to no end.

E

Enemy **How goes the enemy?** How is the time (the enemy of man) going? What time is it?

English **Murder the Queen's English** 'Queen's English', or 'standard English', is the English language as spoken by educated people. To 'murder' the Queen's English is to use it incorrectly or to speak it with a very bad accent.

Enough **Enough and to spare** Ample; more than is needed.
Ten yards of carpet will be enough and to spare.
Enough to wake the dead Very loud, noisy.
The racket at the party was enough to wake the dead.
Oddly enough Unexpectedly; surprisingly. ('Enough' here is equivalent to 'in the circumstances', 'considering the conditions', etc.) Similarly, **curiously, strangely, remarkably enough,** etc.
We met by chance in Egypt, and a year later, oddly enough, in New York.

Enquiry **In the course of enquiry** While enquiries were being made; during an investigation.
In the course of an enquiry, it was discovered that he had never been in the Army.
Searching enquiry Close and thorough enquiry.
The Government promise a searching enquiry into the whole matter.

Enter **Enter into** 1. Comprehend; understand.
We can enter into your feelings of relief.
2. Occupy oneself with.
We cannot enter into details at present.
The two old men entered into (or upon) a long discussion.
Enter into an agreement Agree; undertake.
The firm will enter into an agreement to supply five thousand pairs of shoes.
Enter a protest Complain. Register a protest.
Enter up Make an entry.
Please enter up these figures in the account book.
Enter upon Begin.
We are entering upon a new epoch in the history of civilization.

Entry **Make an entry** 1. Record in a book.
The secretary made an entry in the diary.
2. Enter formally or ceremoniously a town, etc.
The troops made an entry into the city.

Esteem **Hold in (high) esteem, honour,** *etc.* Regard as deserving.
The young man was held in high esteem by the neighbours.

Estimate **Form an estimate** Judge in a general way.
You can form an estimate of her charm when I tell you that her portrait has been painted at least a dozen times.
Rough estimate A rough calculation; an approximation.

At a rough estimate, he must have walked twenty miles.

Even **Even so** In spite of, even after the circumstances have been considered.
George is a wealthy man, but even so, there is no reason for him to show it so blatantly.

Be even with Be revenged upon; pay back an injury.
He beat me, but I'll be even with him next time we play.

Event **At all events** Nevertheless; yet.
Our landlady may be a bad cook, but at all events she does her best.
Similar to **at any rate**.

Coming events Events which are expected or planned.
Coming events in the village include a flower-show and a treat for the schoolchildren.

Course of events A succession of events; a number of events that followed.
The course of events made it necessary for him to go to America.

In any event Whatever may happen.
I hope to go tomorrow; in any event I shall go before Saturday.
Similar to **in any case; in any circumstances; happen what may**.

In the event of If a specified event should take place.
In the event of fire, ring the alarm-bell.

Prophesy after the event State that something was certain to have happened after it has already happened.

Be wise after the event State what should have been done to avert a disaster when it has already occurred.

Ever Widely used as a form of emphasis.
Did you ever hear such nonsense. Come as quick as ever you can.
Whatever will he do next?

For ever and a day [LIT] Always; eternally. [MET] For a long time.
We won't reach agreement if we sit here for ever and a day.

For ever and ever Similar to **for ever and a day**.

Ever so; ever so much, many [S] 'Ever so' is a popular (but not recommended) form of emphasis, equivalent to 'extremely' or 'greatly'.
Thank you ever so much for inviting me.

Every **Every other** Every alternate. 1. [LIT] 2. [MET] (Applied only to the singular.)
1. Every other man carried a lighted torch.
2. She asks questions every other minute.

Example **For example** To quote as an example.
Some English poems are extremely long—'The Faerie Queene', for example.

Make an example of Inflict punishment on an individual who has done wrong as a warning to others who might behave in the same way.

Exception **Take exception to** Object. Feel offended by.
I take exception to your statement that I am bad tempered.
The exception that proves the rule An action which draws one's attention to the fact that most people (as a rule) behave very differently, and that the action in question is an exception to the rule.

Execution **Put into execution** Do something already planned or arranged. Similar to **carry out.**
They wanted to sell the house and go abroad, but realized that it would be some months before they could put their plan into execution.

Exercise **Exercise power** Exert power or influence.
The Queen cannot exercise political power, though she frequently offers advice.

Expense **At one's expense** 1. [LIT] Causing financial expense to one.
2. [MET] Causing inconvenience, embarrassment, discredit, etc., to one.

Explain **Explain away** Remove uncertainty by persuasive and reasonable explanations.
I didn't believe her at first, but she managed to explain away my doubts.

Extent **To a certain (considerable, large) extent** To a limited (considerable, large) degree; partially.

Eye **Apple of one's eye** Loved and prized intensely.
Her son was the apple of her eye.
A black eye The result of being struck so violently in the face that the flesh surrounding the eye is bruised and blackened.
Catch someone's eye Meet the gaze of a person for a brief time.
The schoolboy caught the teacher's eye, and stopped talking.
An eye for Ability to appreciate (visual).
He has always had an eye for a bargain.
See also **an ear for; a taste for.**
An eye for an eye Revenge. Retaliation.
To eye To glance at, usually with suspicion.
Have an eye to the main chance Be alert for opportunities of personal profit.
Have one's eyes about one Be observant and alert.
A big-game hunter must have his eyes about him.
Have (keep) one's eyes skinned As above.
In the eyes of Regarded by.
In the eyes of our grandfathers, Picasso's paintings would have seemed absurd.
Keep an eye on Watch; devote some attention to.

Keep an eye on the children while I go to the shops.
Eye of the law See under *Law*.
Make eyes at Ogle. Look amorously, provocatively or seductively.
She makes eyes at every man she meets.
In one's mind's eye Mentally; as a mental vision.
In my mind's eye I can still see my old home.
Run an (the) eye over Glance over; survey quickly.
Do you mind running your eye over these accounts.
See eye to eye Regard in the same way; agree.
I hope we shall see eye to eye in this matter.
See with half an eye Realize easily, and at once.
One could see with half an eye that he was a gentleman.
Up to the eyes, *or* **eyebrows, in** [S] Immersed; completely occupied with.
I found George up to the eyebrows in business.
With an eye to With a definite object in one's mind.
I bought the barn with an eye to converting it into a cottage.
With one's eyes open Fully aware of the circumstances.
He was a sick man, but June married him with her eyes open.
Eye-witness One who actually sees an incident, etc.
According to an eye-witness, it was the car-driver's fault.

F

Face **Face; face up to** Accept and meet a situation without flinching.
We are lost, and must face up to the fact.
Face about Turn in the opposite direction.
The troops were ordered to face about.
Face to face Directly opposite; confronting one another.
The brothers came face to face in a crowd.
Face the music Accept the unfortunate consequences.
We were in the wrong, so we'll have to face the music.
Face it out Meet a situation.
He knew he was in the wrong, but was determined to face it out.
Face value Nominal or superficial value.
The face value of the stamp was a penny, but it was worth fifty pounds.
Fly in the face of Commit an act which is obviously rash, foolish or provocative.
It would be flying in the face of Providence to go out in this weather without a coat.
Have the face (the nerve) to Have the effrontery or impertinence to.
I'm surprised that you have the face to ask again.

Keep a straight face Remain serious.

George was so funny that it was impossible to keep a straight face.

Similar to **keep one's countenance.**

Lose face Be humiliated. Lose some of one's credit or reputation, etc.

Make faces Twist and contort one's features, usually in contempt or dislike, or to make someone laugh.

On the face of it As it appears; judging from what has been stated.

On the face of it, you have been very badly treated.

Pull a long face Look miserable and depressed.

We've lost a good deal of money, but it's no use pulling a long face about it.

Put a good (*or* brave *or* bold) face upon it Behave cheerfully, and as though there was nothing wrong.

Joan Smith has run away from home, but her family are putting on a brave face.

Put a new face on Alter.

Moon-landings have put a new face on our scientific knowledge.

Set one's face against Oppose.

Show one's face Appear.

Fact **In fact** Stated exactly or briefly.

He will not come; in fact, I think he never intended to.

Stubborn fact A fact which cannot be denied or ignored.

The stubborn fact remains that the man is incompetent.

Fag **Fag-end** The latter, the final remaining part. [LIT] The rough end of a piece of cloth.

We spent the fag-end of our holiday on the river.

Fair **All's fair in love and war** In any competition, the competitors must fend for themselves (*or* have equal conditions).

Fair copy A neat copy, unspoilt by corrections.

Fair deal A transaction which is fair and just to both sides.

My house for your farm would be a fair deal.

Fair game A suitable object of amusement and ridicule.

(By) fair means or foul (In) any way possible.

Fair play Correct and courteous treatment between opponents; justice according to accepted rule.

Fair sex Women. [Old f.]

Fair and square Just; openly honest.

The terms of the contract are absolutely fair and square.

In a fair way to Likely to; behaving so that a certain event is probable.

Fair-weather friend One who is a friend only during prosperity, and who ceases to be one when trouble comes.

Fair words butter no parsnips Polite and friendly speeches are of no practical value unless accompanied by kind actions. [Or. Proverb.]

Faith **Bad faith** Treachery; dishonesty.
It was an act of bad faith to betray his friend.
Breach of faith A dishonourable action; a broken promise, given or implied.
It was a breach of faith to reveal the information I gave you.
In (all) good faith Honestly believing. With honest intention.
Even though he was wrong, he acted in good faith.
Pin one's faith to (*or* on) Place one's entire faith in; believe in.
I pin my faith on that horse winning the Derby.
Shake one's faith Make one doubtful of one's previous beliefs.
What you tell me shakes my faith in human nature.
Shatter one's faith Destroy one's belief completely.

Fall **Fall apart, asunder** Break up in separate pieces.
Fall into arrears Fail to pay a sum due at regular intervals.
Fall astern Go more slowly, till instead of being level one is behind. [Or. Nautical.]
Fall away 1. Diminish; dwindle.
Trade always falls away during the summer.
2. Separate from; desert.
All his old friends fell away from him.
Fall back 1. Retire; retreat.
The crowd fell back to let the ambulances through.
2. Make use of in an emergency.
One can always fall back upon condensed milk.
Fall (*or* drop) behind 1. Be passed by; be overtaken.
2. Similar to **fall into arrears.**
Fall between two stools Attempt to combine two plans, and succeed with neither.
Fall flat 1. [LIT] Be prostrate.
The man staggered, and fell flat on the floor.
2. [MET] Fail to amuse or interest; end in an anti-climax. ('Flat' here is used as the reverse of 'sparkling', a term applied to effervescent drink which has been spoilt by exposure to the air.)
What was meant to be a funny story fell completely flat.
Fall for [S] Become an admirer of; yield to the attractions of.
My son has definitely fallen for your daughter.
Fall foul of [LIT] Collide with; crash into. [MET] Quarrel with. Be in a state of dispute with.
He has a knack of falling foul of everyone he meets.
Fall into a habit Form or acquire a habit.
He's fallen into the habit of coming to tea every Sunday.

F

Fall in place [LIT and MET] Take up the proper and logical place or position.
When he told me his story, all the facts I had known before fell into place.
Fall in with Encounter. Meet and accompany. Agree with. Coincide with.
It would be very convenient if you could fall in with my plans.
Fall on evil days Be in misfortune.
Fall on one's feet Be successful as the result of good fortune or luck.
Arriving in London penniless, John, as usual, fell on his feet, and met a friend who offered him a job.
Fall off Deteriorate.
The quality of his paintings has fallen off greatly.
Fall out 1. Disagree; quarrel.
If we talk politics we are bound to fall out.
2. Happen; occur. [Old f.]
It may never fall out that we meet again.
Fall short Be less than, or below.
My income falls short of my expenditure by five hundred pounds.
Fall through Collapse; fail to happen.
All his plans fell through.
Fall to one's lot Happen to one.
It will probably fall to my lot to die a bachelor.
Fall to pieces Break up completely.
The chair was made so badly that it fell to pieces the first time I sat on it.
Fall upon Attack.
The wolf fell upon the lamb and devoured it.
Fall upon a person's neck Embrace [Or. Biblical, now used only facetiously].

Fancy **Catch the fancy of** Please. Attract.
It caught my fancy and I bought it without thinking.
Fancy free Not in love. Hence, carefree. [Or. Shakespeare, *A Midsummer Night's Dream.*]
Fancy price High cost.
Flight of fancy (or imagination) Something visualized which is entirely imaginary; unconnected with actual events.
Take a fancy to Be attracted by.
On second thoughts, I've rather taken a fancy to the idea.
Tickle one's fancy Amuse; divert. Attract.
Do you see anything in the shop which tickles your fancy?

Far **As far as in one lies** As much as one is capable.
Far and away, *or* **by far** To a much greater extent or degree.

I was far and away happier before I changed jobs.

Far and wide; far and near Many places, both near and distant.

People came from far and wide to hear him.

A far cry A remote connection only; distant or slightly connected.

It is a far cry from selling cabbages to lecturing on agriculture.

Far be it from me An apologetic phrase for interfering or criticizing.

Far be it from me to instruct the nurse in her duties, but the patient has fallen out of bed.

Far-fetched Exaggerated and over-elaborate.

Far gone In a dangerously critical condition.

I'm afraid he is so far gone that there is no hope.

In so far To the extent or degree.

I am able to help you, in so far that I can arrange an appointment.

So far as one can As much as one can.

Fashion **After a fashion** In an amateurish and ineffective way.

He cooked the dinner after a fashion.

Fast **Fast dye** 'Fast' here is equivalent to 'fixed'; immovable. Dye which will not wash out.

Play fast and loose Act irresponsibly, and without regard to one's duties.

If you think you can play fast and loose with the agreement we made, you are mistaken.

Fasten **Fasten on** 1. [LIT] Attach.

I can't fasten this lid on.

2. [MET] Pick out for a particular purpose, or as the person responsible.

Someone must have broken the plate, but why fasten on me?

Fat **Fat in the fire** [LIT] The splutter and flames made when fat splashes from a frying-pan into the fire. [MET] General excitement, anger, etc., when a sensational piece of news is made known.

The fat of the land The best and most expensive (food, etc.) obtainable.

Though they haven't much money, they seem to live off the fat of the land.

Fate **The irony of fate** An ironic coincidence. An event, frequently tragic, which defies or defeats what has been intended.

Fault **At fault** Wrong; inaccurate.

You were at fault in thinking that.

Find fault with Grumble at; complain.

His wife is constantly finding fault with him.

Favour **In high favour** Extremely popular.

I hear you're in high favour with the boss.

Feather **Birds of a feather** People of a particular type. [Or. Proverb: *Birds of a feather flock together.*]

F

A feather in one's cap An honour; something to be proud of. [Or. The custom of American Indians adding a feather to their headdress for every enemy that they killed.]

It's a feather in John's cap to be chosen captain of the cricket team.

Feather one's nest Gradually acquire extra money, honestly or otherwise, during one's employment. [Or. The habit of birds lining their nests with feathers.]

Feathered friends Birds in general.

Show the white feather Behave like a coward. [Or. The old English sport of cockfighting. No pure-bred gamecock has a white feather in its plumage.]

Fed **Fed up** [S] Utterly bored, having had too much of something. Also **fed up to the back teeth**.

I'm fed up with London and want to go back to Sheffield.

Feel **Feel for** Feel pity for; sympathize with.

All of us feel for you in your great trouble.

Feeler **Put (*or* throw) out feelers (*or* a feeler)** Find out by surreptitious or gentle question or hint.

Why not put out a few feelers to see what the rest of the staff think?

Feeling **Fellow-feeling** The sympathy and understanding felt for a sufferer by one who has been through similar trials.

Fellowship **The hand of fellowship** The right hand of a friend, clasped as a sign of goodwill and peace.

Fence **Fence with a question** Give a non-committal answer to avoid the question.

Sit on the fence [S] Refrain from giving one's support to either side; remain entirely neutral (usually from motives of cowardice or discretion).

Fettle **In fine fettle** In good condition (applied to person or animal). In good spirits.

Wrong (right) side of the fence In these and similar expressions, 'fence' means 'dispute'.

Few **Every few days** Once in every group of a few days.

Few and far between Rare, scarce. [Or. Abbreviated quotation from the poet Campbell, 'Like angel visits, few and far between'.]

My holidays are few and far between.

A good few A reasonable number.

Field **Open field** Many (or unlimited) opportunities.

There's an open field for new industry in this area.

Take the field Enter a playing-field to begin a competition.

Manchester United took the field to the accompaniment of deafening cheers.

Fifty **Fifty-fifty** Equal shares. Halves.

The proceeds of the event will be split fifty-fifty between two charities.

Fight **Fight shy of** Avoid, keep away from.
Peter fights shy of women : he says they frighten him.
Fight to a standstill Fight until both sides are too exhausted to make any further effort.

Figure **Cut a figure** Become prominent (often for being conspicuously well dressed). Make an impression.
Figure of fun Ridiculous; absurd.
Unless Colin changes his ways, he's in danger of becoming merely a figure of fun.
Figures of speech Literary forms such as the metaphor, simile, hyperbole, allegory, etc.
Figure out [S] [U.S.A.] Estimate. Reckon.

File **In Indian file; in single file** Singly, one behind another. [Or. The American Indians used to mislead their enemies as to their number by each man stepping exactly in the footsteps of the man in front of him.]
The path was so narrow that we had to walk in Indian file.

Fill **Fill the bill** Suffice.
I haven't any gin; would whisky fill the bill?
Fill an office Occupy a position or post.
Mr Charles filled the office of general manager for twenty years.
Fill out Enlarge.
Fill up (*or* in) documents Add details which are required.
If you require a passport, will you please fill up this form.
Drink (take) one's fill Take enough to satisfy, all that one is capable of taking.
We took our fill of the sunshine and fresh air.

Filthy **Filthy lucre** Money. Wealth. [Old f.] [Or. Biblical.]

Final **Final touch** The last detail; that which completes the work.
As a final touch to her costume, she pinned a red rose in her hair.

Find **Find oneself in** Supply oneself with.
We can let you have tea and sugar, but you'll have to find yourself in milk.
All found Everything provided.
We are paying five pounds a week, all found.
Find guilty The legal phrase used when an accused person has been tried, and it has been 'found' that he committed the crime.
Find one's feet Obtain and develop the use of one's abilities.
After a year in the job, I'm beginning to find my feet.
Find in one's heart Be firm enough. Be inclined.
I couldn't find it in my heart to refuse her request.

Fine **In fine** Stated exactly or briefly.
In fine, you will have to stay in bed till we know what is the matter with you.

Fine distinction A difference perceptible only with difficulty.

One of these fine days Some day (used in prophesying).

I'll do something about it one of these fine days.

With a fine-tooth comb Very carefully, with minute attention to detail.

I've been through my bank-statement with a fine-tooth comb.

Fingers **Fingers are all thumbs** Fingers are clumsy, awkward. Also **all fingers and thumbs**: clumsy.

Burn one's fingers Suffer as a result of some action.

If you buy that business, I think you'll burn your fingers.

Have a finger in the pie [S] Be concerned with, or mixed up with some affair.

Lift (stir) a finger Make the smallest effort.

At one's finger-tips Immediately available. (Applied to information, knowledge, etc.)

Work one's fingers to the bone Work very hard (usually, with one's hands).

Fire **(Breathe) fire and brimstone** (Utter) angry threats.

Fire away [S] Begin.

He hesitated for a time, but I told him to fire away and tell me what happened.

Strike fire Arouse enthusiasm.

Take fire [LIT] Become ignited. [MET] Become excited, indignant or enthusiastic.

Through fire and water Through any kind of suffering or discomfort.

I would go through fire and water to make her happy.

First **At the first blush (*or* glance)** Superficially; before examining closely.

At first blush it seems an excellent plan.

First class Top quality. Best available.

First things first A proper order of priorities.

From first to last From beginning to end; all the time.

From first to last, he never treated his family as he should.

Fish **A fish out of water** One out of his natural element or surroundings.

During my first weeks in the new job, I felt like a fish out of water.

Fish in troubled waters Interest oneself in affairs that are likely to lead to trouble and danger.

The man who interferes in South American politics is fishing in troubled waters.

Neither fish nor fowl See under *Flesh.*

Other fish to fry Other business to occupy the time.

I can't discuss the matter any longer—I've other fish to fry.

Pretty kettle of fish A thoroughly unsatisfactory state of affairs;

F

general upheaval and excitement; a mixture of muddle and trouble. [Or. 'Kettle' is a corruption of 'kittle', which in turn is a corruption of 'kiddle', a basket arranged in river water to catch fish.]

A queer fish An eccentric person; an unusual type.

Fit In a suitable condition to work, in good health. [Also **fighting fit.**)

Fit in with Co-ordinate with.

Your visit tomorrow will fit in with my cousin's arrival.

Fit to wake the dead Very loud.

Fit up (*or* out) Prepare an expedition, etc.

The Government is fitting up a new expedition to the North Pole.

In fits and starts Irregularly, in a series of spurts.

He does his work in fits and starts.

Throw a fit; have a thousand fits [S] Be extremely agitated.

Mother would throw a fit if she saw me in these clothes.

Fix **In a fix** In difficulty.

Flame **Add fuel to (*or* Fan) the flames** Add fresh causes for anger.

An old flame A sweetheart in past days. [Old f.]

Flare **Flare up** 1 As a verb: give way to a sudden burst of anger.

You need not flare up merely because I mentioned your unpunctuality.

2. As a noun: a violent quarrel.

Flash **Flash in the pan** A brief display producing no useful result. [Or. Military. The 'flash-pan' of the old-fashioned gun was the place at which a small quantity of powder was exploded to fire the larger quantity in the barrel. If it failed to do this, it merely 'flashed' in the pan.]

That brilliant poem he wrote when young was a mere flash in the pan; he has produced nothing since.

In a flash, quick as a flash Very quickly indeed.

Flat **Flat denial, contradiction, *etc.*** Flat (adjective) (or flatly, adverb) is here in the sense of 'complete' and 'absolute'.

He flatly denied that he had stolen the coat.

Flat as a flounder (*or* pancake) Completely flat. [Or. A flounder is a flat fish. A pancake is a thin cake made of batter and fried in a pan.] See **fall flat.**

That's flat Let there be no doubt about that.

Flea **Sent off with a flea in one's ear** [S] Dismissed, after receiving a sharp rebuke.

If anyone wakens me up, he'll get a flea in his ear.

Flea-bite, a mere A trivial quantity or sum.

He is a rich man; five thousand pounds is a mere flea-bite to him.

Flesh **Neither flesh (*or* fish), fowl nor good red herring** With no definite qualities; not worth classifying.

71

He is extremely vague about his profession; he seems to be neither fish, fowl nor good red herring.

Flesh-pots (*of* Egypt) The good things of life; rich food, etc. [Or. Biblical.]

Make one's flesh creep Horrify; shock; frighten with some ghastly story or sight.

More than flesh and blood can stand Utterly intolerable.

One's own flesh and blood Near relation. Close family.

Flight **Take flight** Retreat; flee away rapidly.

At the first sight of a policeman, all the spectators took flight.

Fling **Have one's fling** Indulge freely in one's pleasures.

Float **Float a company** Organize a public company and issue shares in it.

Flog **Flog a dead horse** [S] Waste one's energy. Work very hard for little or no result. Persevere with a doomed endeavour.

Flood **Flood tide** Highest degree of success, misery, etc.

Floor **Wipe the floor** [S] Reduce to helplessness or ignominy; completely overwhelm.

Flown **The bird has flown** The person wanted has escaped.

Flowing **Flowing with milk and honey** Filled with all good things to eat and drink. [Or. Biblical.] [Old f.]

Flutter (Applied to playing card games, betting, etc.) A brief period of amusement.

I had a flutter at Epsom, and lost nearly £30.

Cause a flutter Cause excitement, as when a flock of birds is disturbed. (Similarly **flutter the dovecotes**: cause excitement in a society or community.)

Fly **Fly a kite** Do something tentatively (in words or deeds) to test people's reactions to an idea or plan.

Fly at Attack violently, physically or verbally.

The dog flew at the milkman.

Don't fly at me because I mentioned lunch.

See **fly off the handle.**

Fly-by-night Unreliable person. Similar to **here today and gone tomorrow.**

Fly in the ointment The flaw, inconvenience or impediment in an arrangement.

Fly off the handle [S] (As the iron head of a hammer flies off when loose.) Suddenly lose one's temper.

Don't contradict him, or he's sure to fly off the handle.

Similar to **go off the deep end,** under *End.*

Fly (*or* go) off at a tangent Abruptly abandon one subject for another.

Let fly Throw. Discharge a missile. Use strong, violent or abusive language.

I managed to keep calm for a long time, but finally I just had to let fly at them.

Make the fur fly [S] Create a violent quarrel or disturbance, as animals make the fur fly when fighting.

Foam **Foam with rage** [LIT] To foam at the mouth, as mad dogs do. [MET] Indicate a state of extreme and ungovernable anger.

Fob **Fob off** Persuade someone to accept a substitute.
I asked for butter, and will not be fobbed off with margarine.

Follow **Follow one's bent** Follow one's inclination; act in accordance with one's abilities and desires.
John became a clerk, but if he had followed his bent he would have been a sailor.

Follow the dictates of one's heart Obey one's inward desires and feelings.

Follow one's own devices Amuse or divert oneself as one wishes. Similar to **go one's own way.**

Follow suit Behave similarly; do the same thing. [Or. Card-playing.]
The conductor missed a beat, and the orchestra followed suit.

Follow up Continue a process already begun.
The horse kicked furiously and followed this up by trying to bite me.

Follow-up (noun and adjective.) Continuation.
When the survey is complete, we shall keep a follow-up check on the people we questioned.

Fool **Fool away** Waste (as a fool wastes).
Don't fool away your time in gardening.

Fool on, play the fool Act stupidly.

A fool's errand A useless journey.

Fool's paradise An entirely false conception; a state of happiness unjustified by the actual facts.

Fool-proof So simple and strong that even a fool cannot use it wrongly or break it.

Fools rush in (where angels fear to tread)
It is unwise to be over-hasty. [Or. Proverb.]

Make a fool of Cause someone to appear ridiculous or contemptible. Similar to **take a rise out of.**

Foot (feet) **Feet foremost (or first)** An elaborate evasion of 'dead'.
I shan't leave this house until I'm carried out feet foremost.

Foot the bill Pay whatever charge is involved.
If the Government grants higher pensions, the people themselves will have to foot the bill.

Have feet of clay Be weak, and liable to overthrow.
He may be a dictator, but his feet are of clay.

Miss one's footing Slip; stumble.

Obtain (*or* gain) a footing Obtain a status or position ('footing' is constantly used in this sense).

On a firm footing On a sound and stable basis.

Since its reorganization, the business is on a much firmer footing.

On a friendly footing On friendly terms; friends with.

I like to be on a friendly footing with my neighbours.

One foot in the grave So old or diseased that life is nearly finished.

On foot Walking or running.

Put one's foot down Take firm and determined action.

When the girl wanted to stay out until past midnight, her father put his foot down.

Put one's best foot forward Proceed as quickly as possible.

We shall have to put our best foot forward if we are to reach London tonight.

Put one's foot in it Make a blunder; a *faux pas*. Similar to **drop a brick**.

Set foot on Step on to.

My father has never set foot on foreign soil.

Set on foot Initiate; begin any process or action.

The Government intends to set on foot an enquiry into euthanasia.

Set on his (*or* her) feet Help a person to regain a lost position or lost health.

Force **By force of circumstances** Compelled by events.

Come into force Operate; function.

The new laws come into force next month.

Force a man's hand Compel him to show his intentions, or to take definite action. [Or. Card-playing.]

I did not want to sell the car, but a financial crisis forced my hand.

Join forces Become associated with, or partners with.

The two explorers joined forces, and continued their journey together.

Foreign **Foreign soil** A foreign country.

Foreign substance *or* body Any improper and injurious substance —dust, dirt, etc.

The boy was half-blinded by some foreign substance which the wind had blown into his eye.

Forfeit **Forfeit the good opinion of** Lose the good opinion of a person by bad or foolish conduct.

Fork **Fork out** [S] Pay.

You'll have to fork out a pound for your dinner.

Forlorn **Forlorn hope** Hope that is very unlikely to be fulfilled. A final effort. [Or. Corruption of the Dutch 'Verlorenhoop'—lost troop.]

I'll try again, but I think it's a forlorn hope.

Forty **Forty winks** [S] A slight, brief sleep. [Or. 'Forty' formerly implied an indefinite number, meaning 'a few'. Shakespeare and the Bible so use it.]
Mother always has forty winks after lunch.
The roaring forties Applied to latitude 40 degrees south, where strong winds blow throughout the year.

Foul **Foul play** Unfair, unsporting; frequently applied to criminal action.
The sailor was never seen again; the police suspected foul play.

Fountain **Fountain-head** Starting-place; source.
The fountain-head of all these stories is Miss Jones, the village gossip.

Four **Four-square** [LIT] Facing squarely in four directions. [MET] Facing the world firmly and without fear.

Fraught **Fraught with** Laden with; bearing.
This whole matter is fraught with hazards.

Fray **Thick of the fray** Where the fighting is fiercest.

Free **Free and easy** Unconventional; not arranged according to any formal plan.
Free-hand *(one word, or with hyphen)* Applied to drawing in which no mechanical help from instruments is employed.
Free hand *(two entirely separate words)* Complete freedom of action.
I have been given a free hand in arranging the concert.
Free-handed, *or* **free** Generous.
He is extremely free-handed with his advice.
Free fight *or* **free for all** A general and indiscriminate dispute in which anyone may join.
Someone in the audience threw a cabbage at the speaker, and the meeting ended in a free fight.
Free-lance Self-employed person, or one who works for a number of organizations, instead of being regularly employed by one employer only. Usually applied to a limited number of trades, e.g. musician, journalist, photographer, artist.
Free translation *or* **rendering** A translation which is not literal, but which conveys the general meaning and effect.
Scot free [LIT] Tax free. [MET] Without any punishment or penalty. [Or. Legal. Scot = tax.]
Set free Release.
I opened the cage door, and set the birds free.

Fresh **Fresh as (new) paint** Entirely fresh and unspoilt.
In spite of the party last night, Mary looks as fresh as paint this morning.

Friend **Bosom friend** A specially close and intimate friend.
Friend at court Someone with private influence.
Through a friend at court, he was able to obtain confidential information.

Make friends *(plural only)* Form friendships; become friendly.
Peter never made friends easily.

Fry **Out of the frying pan (into the fire)** Out of one difficulty into another equally or more serious.

Full **Full well** Very well (adverb only).
He knew full well.
See *Speed.*

Fur **Make the fur fly** Create a disturbance.

G

Gaff **Blow the gaff** [S] Reveal or betray a secret.

Game **Make game of** Similar to **make fun of (**under *Make***).**
The game's up Further effort is useless. Similar to **all up.**

Gate **Gate-crashing** Entering uninvited to a dance, entertainment, etc.
Gate-crasher—one who so enters.

Gauntlet **Running the gauntlet** [LIT] Driven between a row of persons each provided with sticks, ropes, etc., with which to strike the offender. [Or. Gauntlet = corruption of the French *Gauntelope*, itself of Swedish derivation, a passage between two rows of soldiers facing one another.] A former punishment for sailors, also employed by schoolboys. [MET] Subjected to criticism or attack from an organized body of people.
He ran the gauntlet of criticism from every doctor in the country when he published his book.
Throw (fling) down the gauntlet Applied to any act of defiance or challenge. [Or. The Middle Ages, when a knight who wished to fight with another threw down his gauntlet (or hand-armour) as a challenge.]
Take up the gauntlet Accept the challenge.
After the speech of the Leader of the Opposition, the Prime Minister took up the gauntlet on behalf of the Government.

Get **Get at** 1. Contact; reach.
I should like to get at some of the papers in Uncle Joe's safe.
2. [S] Influence.
If he's changed his mind, it can only be because someone's been getting at him.
Getting at Implying, hinting, inadequately communicating.
He spoke so vaguely that I couldn't understand what he was getting at.
Get away Escape.
I caught three mice, but one got away.
Get away with Succeed in what one is trying to do.
Get away with murder Succeed by dint of effrontery, or luck.

Get away with you Jocular term of dismissal or refusal.

Get one's goat; get one's monkey up; get one's rag out [S] Make one angry; exasperate one.

That girl's incompetence always gets my goat.

Get going Make a beginning, a start.

It's past seven—we must get going.

Get the hang of [S] Comprehend; understand the working of.

The machinery is quite simple: you'll soon get the hang of it.

Get hold of Grasp [LIT and MET].

I'll explain, and you'll soon get hold of the idea.

Get off [S] Become friendly and intimate with.

Get off to Begin with.

The performance got off to a rather shaky start.

Get on 1. [LIT] Mount; climb on to.

The boy was too small to get on his pony without help.

2. [MET] Agree; be friends with.

I hope Jack and his cousin will get on with each other.

Similar to **hit it off.**

3. [MET] Progress satisfactorily.

Jane works so hard at her job that she is certain to get on.

4. Continue.

I'll get on with cleaning the car.

Get on with you! Expression of disbelief.

Get out of Escape from.

Get out of hand Become out of control.

Get out on the wrong side of the bed [S] Get up in the morning in a bad temper.

Get over 1. Recover from.

He soon got over the shock.

2. Overcome by persuasion, etc.

He got over her objections to the marriage.

Get rid of Dispose of something not desired or needed.

We're going to get rid of our old car.

Get up 1. Arrange. Begin.

Our cricket club is getting up a concert.

2. Rise from one's bed.

At what time do you get up in the morning?

3. Study for a special purpose.

I have to get up Milton's poems for the examination.

Get oneself up Dress smartly or strikingly.

Dorothy has got herself up in a new outfit.

Get wind of Hear rumours of.

Get the wind up Become apprehensive.

Ghost **Ghost of a chance** The slightest, the least chance.

That horse hasn't a ghost of a chance of winning the race.

Gift **Gift of the gab** [S] The ability to speak fluently and convincingly. [Or. 'Gab' is both Scots and Danish for 'mouth'.]
There is no doubt that our Headmaster has the gift of the gab.

Gilt **Take the gilt off the gingerbread** Take away the charm or advantage (sometimes the artificial attractiveness). [Or. In the Middle Ages small gilded gingerbread cakes were sold at fairs.]
The fact that I've got to return to the office in the middle of my holiday takes the gilt off the gingerbread.

Gilt-edged investments Investments—mortgages, debentures. etc.—in which there is no risk of losing one's capital.

Gird **Gird up one's loins** Prepare for an ordeal or combat. [Or. Biblical.] [Old f.]
We must gird up our loins for the long journey tomorrow.

Give **Give a brass farthing (*or* a damn)** Care in the slightest. (Usually used in negative.)
I don't give a damn what the price is.

Give a person (*or* thing) the go-by Ignore; treat as non-existent.
I shall give the whole scheme the go-by.

Give away 1. Distribute. 2. Reveal a secret or expose a person.

Give oneself away Unintentionally reveal one's intentions or emotions.

Give in Surrender.

Give it to [S] Punish, reprimand (usually mildly).
I'll give it (to) you if I find you opening my desk again!

Give notice Make an announcement (often formally, or in writing, etc.) of one's intention. ('Notice' often = statement of intention to quit job.)
Half of the cleaning-staff have given their notice.

Give out 1. Issue; distribute (information, verbally or in print). 2. Be finished, all used.
You can't have a hot bath—the water has given out.

Give over [S] Stop; cease.
Give over teasing the cat.

Give (*or* yield) place to Be replaced or superseded by someone or something else.
In the nineteenth century gas gave place to electric light.

Give rise to Cause; create.
The Ambassador's disappearance is giving rise to concern.

Give and take Mutual allowances and concessions.
With a little give and take, we can soon come to an agreement.

Give up 1. Abandon.
I shall give up smoking.
2. Surrender; cease to fight.

Give it up Cease to attempt.
The puzzle is too difficult; I shall give it up.
Give oneself up Surrender to authority.
Give up the ghost Die; expire. [Or. The ghost or spirit of man is supposed to leave his body at the moment of death.] The idiom is also used (facetiously) in connection with inanimate things.
My old bicycle ran into a lamp-post today and gave up the ghost.
Give way 1. Yield.
Mary refused at first but she gave way in the end.
2. Break; collapse.
The railings gave way, and he fell over the cliff.

Globe **Globe-trotter** One who travels extensively.
Glory **Glory in** Take great pride in.
Gloss **Gloss over** Try to minimize by ignoring or excusing.
The lawyer tried to gloss over his client's bad record by saying that his parents neglected him.
Glove **With kid gloves** Gently.
The whole matter needs handling with kid gloves.
See *Velvet.*

Go *(noun)* [S] Turn, according to a prearranged plan.
It's my go to throw the ball.
Go after Follow.
Go ahead 1. [LIT] Go in front, or before.
You go ahead and tell him that we're coming.
2. [MET] Proceed at once.
If you think you can solve the problem, go ahead.
Go all out [S] Make every possible effort.
We shall have to go all out if we are to succeed.
Go along with Agree with.
Go back on Reverse a previous promise or undertaking.
He said he would help us, and then went back on his promise.
Go-between One who acts as a link between two people or groups of people; a negotiator.
Go-by See under *Give.*
Go by the board Be ignored. Be finished with. [Or. Board = side of a ship, so the expression means 'fall overboard'.]
Caution went by the board as the match neared its conclusion.
Go down [S] 1. Be believed; be acceptable.
That argument won't do down with him.
2. (With **with**.) Be struck by, afflicted with.
He's gone down with chicken-pox.
Go fifty-fifty Receive fifty per cent each; share equally.
We'll go fifty-fifty with the profits.
Go for [S] Attack.

I saw your dog go for our cat.

Go for nothing Be without value; have no effect.

All the efforts we have made will go for nothing.

Go-getter Ambitious person.

Go halves Same as **go fifty-fifty.**

Go in for Undertake seriously, as a profession or hobby.

I hear he's gone in for gardening.

Going strong Persisting vigorously.

My grandfather is ninety and still going strong.

Go on 1. An expression which may mean, according to circumstances, an injunction to hurry *(Go—we shall never get there!)*; an expression of disbelief *(You saw a ghost? Go on!)*; a request for further information *(Please go on with the story).*

2. Use as guidance.

We have no information to go on.

3. Continue.

If we can't find a hotel, we shall have to go on.

Go one better Improve upon; prove more skilful, etc.

Henry's ambition is to be a schoolmaster, but George wants to go one better, and become a professor.

Go out of one's way Incur extra trouble.

This hotel-keeper goes out of his way to make his guests happy.

Go over Revise.

Go over the ground Examine the facts, survey.

It is a difficult problem, and I should like to go over the ground again.

Go through fire and water Make any sacrifice; endure any sufferings.

Go through with Continue to the end.

He has begun to study for a degree, but I don't think he'll go through with it.

Go to the wall Be pushed on one side, passed by; be ignored.

Go under 1. Succumb. Fail.

If a supermarket opens here, the small grocers will go under.

2. Be known by.

On the stage, she goes under a different name.

Go without Be without; lack.

I'm afraid you'll have to go without milk in your tea.

Go without saying Be obvious; self-evident.

No go [S] Impossible; futile; unworkable.

I've tried to persuade your father to come, but it's no go.

On the go [S] Active; continually busy.

My mother is on the go all day long.

G

Going **Going to happen; occur,** *etc.* 'Going to' here is used in the sense 'will'.
I don't know what is going to happen when Father hears the news.
(Make) heavy going Difficult progress. [Or. Horse-riding. A wet or muddy race-track.]
This book is rather heavy going.
While the going is good While the circumstances are favourable.

Golden **Golden mean** The ideal 'middle course'; that which pleases most people because most moderate.
Golden rule The recommended way, because it has been well tried.
The golden rule for frying sausages is to do it slowly.

Good **As good as** Equal to.
This coat is as good as new.
Be so good as to Will you please.
Be so good as to open the door for me.
For good, *or* **for good and all** Permanently; always.
You may keep it for good.
Good-for-nothing Wastrel.
Good for nothing Valueless. Useless.
Good wine needs no bush Things of good quality need no advertisement.
Make good 1. Repair. See *Make.*
2. Reclaim the past. See *Make.*
A good Samaritan One who helps a needy person. [Or. Biblical. The Parable of the Good Samaritan, St Luke x. 30–37.]
He acted as a good Samaritan, and took the woman to hospital.
On good terms On friendly conditions; in a friendly way.
We parted on good terms.
A good turn A kindness; a friendly action.
My wife is always ready to do a good turn for a neighbour.
To the good 1. Profit.
I am a pound to the good after my day at the races.
2. General advantage.
Peace is all to the good.

Goodness See *Wish.*

Goose **Goose-flesh** A cold and roughened condition of the skin, resembling that of a plucked goose, caused by cold or fear. People are said to 'go all goose-flesh' when they are terrified.
Say 'boo' to a goose Show courage. (*Note.*—This idiom is always used in the negative.)

Got **Have got to** Must.
I have got to finish this sewing before I go out.

Grace **With a good grace** Cheerfully; without protesting.

81

The traffic-warden listened to my arguments with a good grace.
With a bad grace The reverse.
In one's good graces Popular with.
I must keep in his good graces if I want to borrow his lawn-mower.
See **in one's good books** (under *Book*).

Grade **Make the grade** [S] Succeed in some specified object. [Or. American. The literal meaning of 'grade' is a railroad incline which the engine driver is required to 'make' or climb.]
He's working very hard for his exams, but I'm afraid he won't make the grade.

Grain **Against the grain** Against one's inclination or wishes. [Or. The grain or fibre of wood.]

Grass **Grass widow** A woman whose husband is away for a prolonged period.

Grate **Grate on the ear** Sound harsh and unpleasant.

Grave **Turn in one's grave** Expression used of something which the deceased person referred to would have very strongly resented.
That production is enough to make Shakespeare turn in his grave.

Grease **Grease a man's palm** Bribe him.

Greek **All Greek to me** Incomprehensible. Unintelligible. [Or. Shakespeare, *Julius Caesar*.]

Green **Green-eyed monster** Jealousy. [Or. Shakespeare's *Othello*: 'Beware of jealousy, it is a green-eyed monster.']
Green room The general reception room of a theatre; it is said that such rooms formerly had their walls coloured green to relieve the strain on the actors' eyes after the stage lights.

Grief **Come to grief** Meet with misfortune.
The yachtsman came to grief when the wind got up suddenly.

Grievance **Air a grievance** See under *Air*.

Grin **Grin and bear it** [S] Endure as well as one can.

Grips **Come (get) to grips with** Try to deal with (in a workmanlike or vigorous fashion).

Grist **All's grist that comes to the mill** Everything that is received can be used. [Or. 'Grist' is all corn, etc., which is to be crushed in a mill at one time.]
The author writes on any subject; everything is grist to his mill.

Groove **Run (Be) in a groove (or rut)** Function in the same limited and narrow way, or by the same methods.
He was a man of simple tastes, and his whole life ran in a narrow groove.

Ground **Cut the ground from under one's feet** Anticipate and/or negate one's plans, arguments, etc., by having unexpected information, skill, etc.
Gain ground Advance; progress.

He wanted to be more friendly with the girl, but did not seem able to gain ground.
Stand one's ground Keep to one's position.

Grow **Grown up** Adult.
Young John looks quite grown up.
Grow on one Gradually impress its charm and personality.
You may not like Brighton at first, but you'll find it grows on you.

Grudge **Bear a grudge** Retain resentful feelings because of a previous dispute.

Grundy **Mrs Grundy** A severely conventional character in a play called 'Speed the Plough'. 'What will Mrs Grundy say?' = 'What will Society and our neighbours think of this?' 'To offend Mrs Grundy' is to commit some social crime, though she is usually a figure of fun.

Guard **Catch off one's guard** Take advantage of someone when he is temporarily distracted or forgetful.
On one's guard Alert; prepared.

Gun **Big guns** [S] Important and influential people.
George is one of the big guns of his profession.
Blow great guns Blow tremendous winds; a gale.
It was blowing great guns when the ship left harbour.
Stick to one's guns Firmly maintain one's standpoint.

H

Hackles **Make one's hackles rise** Make one angry.

Hail **Hail from** Come from.
O'Reilly hails from Ulster.
Hail-fellow-well-met Person on familiar and friendly terms with everybody one meets. (Also adjective.)

Hair **Hair standing on end** Indicative of extreme terror and astonishment. [Or. There is a legend of one prisoner whose long grey hair rose and stood stiffly upright, and then gradually sank down.] Also used more jocularly.
His impertinence is enough to make your hair stand on end.
Hair-raising Frightening. Very surprising.
Splitting hairs Arguing or disagreeing over extremely trivial matters. (Also **hair-splitting.)**
(Not) turn a hair Show (no) signs of fear or embarrassment.
Hair's breadth A minute distance. E.g., a hair's-breadth escape is a very narrow escape, an event which only just missed disaster.

Halcyon **Halcyon days** A time of happiness and prosperity. [Or. An ancient belief that the kingfisher, called in Greek 'halcyon', laid and hatched its eggs on the sea just before the coming of winter (mid-December), when the waves were smooth and unruffled.]

Half **By half** Expression of exaggeration, e.g. **too clever by half; too cheeky by half.**

Half-baked [S] Half-witted; silly. Not fully prepared or thought out.

Half-and-half Divided into two equal parts or portions.

Half-hearted Without energy or enthusiasm.

Half-seas over [S] Intoxicated.

Halfway house Half the distance.

His socialism is a halfway house to toryism.

Hallmark [LIT] The official marking (after testing) of all gold and silver goods with the 'hall' or standard mark as a guarantee of purity. [MET] A sign of good quality (in conduct, manners, ability, taste, etc.).

A deep chest is the hallmark of a real athlete.

Hammer **Hammer and tongs** With much noise and/or vigour and enthusiasm.

He may have no skill as a golfer, but he certainly goes at it hammer and tongs.

Hammer out Arrive at a decision or solution by examining and discussing every detail of the subject.

We spent all day hammering out our plans for the holiday.

Under the hammer By public auction. [Or. The auctioneer's hammer (technically a 'gavel') with which he raps on his table each time an object is 'knocked down' to a buyer.]

Hand **All hands to the pumps** Assistance from everyone available. [Or. Nautical. When a ship is leaking so badly that she is likely to sink, all 'hands' (members of the crew) are summoned to work the pumps.]

They'll need all hands to the pumps if the business is to be saved.

(At) first hand Directly; straight from the person concerned.

I heard the story of the match first hand from the captain.

At hand; close at hand Near; available.

I want you to be at hand during my interview.

At the hands of Under the control or direction of.

High-handed Insolent. Overbearing. Supercilious.

Change hands Pass from the ownership of one person to that of another.

The property has recently changed hands.

Clean hands Innocently; honestly; without fraud.

Give one's hand to Marry (used of females only). [Old f.]

Hand in glove In partnership; intimately associated.

Road and rail transport ought to work hand in glove.

Hand in hand [LIT] Clasped hands. [MET] In close association.

The two firms work hand in hand.

Hand to hand One person to another.

The document was passed from hand to hand.

Hand to mouth From day to day, without any provision for the future. Also **hand-to-mouth** (adjective).

Hand over Surrender; give to someone else. Similar to **turn over.**
He handed over the business to his son.

Hand over (hand, *or*) fist Rapidly. [Or. Nautical.]
He's overtaking us, hand over fist.

Have a hand in Take a part or share in.
George would like to have a hand in arranging the entertainment.

Have one's hands fúll Be completely occupied, very busy.
We shall have our hands full when the visitors arrive.

Have on one's hands Be responsible for; have to dispose of.
When the house is sold I shall have the furniture on my hands.

In hand, *or* well in hand 1. Under one's control.
There was a little rioting, but the police soon had the situation well in hand.
2. In one's possession.
When all our debts are paid, we shall have over £10 in hand.

In the hands of Being dealt with by.
The contract is in the hands of my solicitor.

Keep in hand Retain; keep under control.
We are keeping £10 in hand.

Lend a hand Help.
All the packing has to be done; perhaps you'll lend a hand?

Lift (*or* raise) one's hand against Strike; attack; threaten to hit.
A gentleman would never lift his hand against a woman.

Off-hand See *Off.*

An old hand A person with considerable experience.
Let me help—I'm an old hand at chopping wood.

On all hands; on every hand Universally.
It was agreed on all hands that the evening was a success.

On hand Same as **at hand.**

On one's hands As one's responsibility.
I've a lot of work on my hands at the moment.

On the other hand Otherwise; alternatively.
We may leave London; on the other hand, we may remain.
Similar to **on the contrary.**

Out of hand Uncontrollable; beyond restraint.
The crowd became so excited that it was soon completely out of hand.

Out of one's hands No longer in one's control.
The matter is now out of my hands.

Show one's hand Reveal one's real intentions. [Or. The 'hand' of cards held by a player.]
If he asks you to name a price, don't show all your hand at once.

Sleight of hand See under *Sleight.*

Stay one's hand Refrain from action.

Take a hand Share; play a part in.

The State ought to take a hand in building new houses.

Similar to **have a hand.**

Take in hand Take immediate charge of; assume responsibility for.

The State will take in hand the problem of juvenile crime without further delay.

The upper (*or* whip) hand The chief power; the real control.

Grumbling is useless; we no longer have the upper hand.

Throw in one's hand Abandon any further effort. [Or. Card-playing.]

I'm so disgusted with the whole thing that I'm going to throw in my hand.

Try one's hand at Attempt; test one's powers.

Have you ever tried your hand at cooking?

Wash one's hands of Have no further connection with; refuse to accept any further responsibility for.

Handle Deal with; direct.

I think the plumber is the best man to handle this.

A handle to one's name A title.

I knew Sir John long before he had a handle to his name.

Handsome **Do the handsome, *or* handsome thing; come down handsome** [S] Treat liberally. [Old f.]

Hang **Get the hang of** Understand.

Hang about Loiter.

Hang back Hesitate to proceed; show reluctance to agree or assist.

Hangdog Untrustworthy. (Sometimes used as noun, meaning 'a suspicious-looking person'.)

Hang fire Fail to produce results when expected. Wait. [Or. A gun or pistol in which the cartridge fails to explode 'hangs fire'.]

Hang in the balance Be undecided.

The future of this school hangs in the balance until the Council next meets.

Hang heavy Pass slowly. (Usually applied to time.)

Hang on [S] 1. Cling to; persevere in spite of discouragements.

The business hasn't paid yet, but we mean to hang on till Christmas.

2. Wait.

Hang on a minute.

Hang one's head Appear embarrassed and ashamed.

Hang out [S] Live; lodge.

I hang out in North London.

Hang by a thread Be in an extremely delicate and precarious state.

[Or. The story of the sword of Damocles, which see under *Sword*.]

The negotiations are hanging by a thread.

Hang together Collaborate closely; support one another. Be a unified whole.

The plan needs more details if it is to hang together.

Hang upon Depend upon.

Whether we can come hangs upon our getting a baby-sitter.

I'll be hanged Expression of annoyance or astonishment. (Also **hang it all!**) See *Blow*.

I'll be hanged if I'll pay that much for a pair of shoes.

Hanky-panky [S] Fraud; dishonest and untruthful dealing.

Happen **Happen what may** Whatever may occur. [Old f.]

Happy **Happy-go-lucky** Careless; gaily reckless; relying on good luck for help out of difficulties.

Hard **Go hard with** Involve punishment or suffering for.

It will go hard with Mary if John leaves her.

Hard and fast Strict. Rigidly organized.

In view of the weather, we'd better not make any hard and fast arrangements.

Hard bargain One without concessions.

Don't let him drive too hard a bargain.

Hard by Near. [Old f.]

Hard cash Real money, not cheques, promises, etc.

Hard drinker One who drinks beer, wine, etc., frequently and in large quantities.

Hard facts Indisputable ones.

We have to face the hard fact that we can't afford it.

Hard-featured Severe-looking; grim.

Hard-headed Tough. Practical, not sentimental.

Hard-hearted Unfeeling. Unsympathetic.

Hard lines (*or* luck) Harsh; undeservedly severe.

Hard nut to crack Difficult person, problem, situation, etc., to deal with.

Hard times Difficult circumstances to bear.

These are hard times for the unemployed.

Hard up With insufficient money.

Hard words See *Word*.

See also **plain speaking** (under *Speak*) and **not to mince matters** (under *Mince*).

Hare **Hare-brained** (= **scatter-brained**) Foolish and irresponsible.

It was hare-brained to spend the night on the mountain.

Mad as a March hare See under *Mad*.

Harness **In harness** Actively engaged in regular work.

H

Harp **Harp on; harp on the same string** (*or* **subject,** *etc.*) Talk about the same subject until the listener becomes bored or irritated.

Hash **Make a hash of** Make a muddle of.
Colin made rather a hash of trying to lay the carpet.
Settle one's hash [S] See *Settle.*

Hat **Eat one's hat** Expression used to add emphasis.
If the train arrives on time, I'll eat my hat.
Perform the hat-trick In cricket, a bowler is said to do this when he dismisses three consecutive batsmen in three consecutive balls. Loosely used in connection with any similar triple success.
Take off one's hat to [MET] Express unusual approval of some action of another's.
I don't expect him to succeed, but I'll take my hat off to him if he does.
Talk through one's hat [S] Talk nonsense.

Have **To have anyone** [S] To deceive or swindle.
If you paid a pound for that, you've been had.
Have anything (*or* **nothing**) **to do with** Be (not) concerned or connected with.
He's the kindest person I've ever had to do with.
If I were you, I'd have nothing to do with that laundry.
Have done Finish; stop.
Have you done with the washing-up?
Have it out 1. Have extracted.
I'll have this tooth out tomorrow.
2. Discuss a subject (usually a dispute) openly and frankly.
I am going to have the whole thing out with the garage.
Have on 1. Wear.
Are you sure you had gloves on when you arrived?
2. Deceive. Trick.
If he said he was a first-class snooker-player, he was having you on.

Hay **Make hay of** Ruin; render confused and muddled.
This new plan of yours will make hay of our arrangements for the holiday.
Make hay while the sun shines Take advantage of a good opportunity, or a specially suitable occasion.

Haywire **Go haywire** [S] Become confused, tangled, excited, etc.

Hazard **Hazard an opinion** (*or* **guess**) Risk expressing an opinion or view.

Head **Come** (*or* **enter**) **into one's head** Occur to one.
The idea had just come into my head.
Go to one's head Excite; intoxicate; make irresponsible.
Hang one's head See under *Hang.*
Have a head on one's shoulders Possess intelligence and common sense.
Have his head Go his own way without any interference. [Or.

Riding or driving a horse. To let a horse 'have his head' is to allow him to travel at his own speed unrestrained by the reins.]
He's the sort of man who works best if you let him have his head.
Have one's head screwed on the right way Be intelligent and shrewd.
Head and shoulders above Far above or superior to.
He's head and shoulders above the rest of the candidates.
Head off Intercept; prevent escaping. Divert.
Similar to **cut off.**
Head on Directly; frontally.
The two cars collided head on.
Head-over-ears *(in love, debt, etc.).* Utterly and completely.
Head-over-heels Turned upside down; complete inversion.
Similar to **topsy-turvy.**
Heads or tails A coin is frequently 'tossed' (or thrown in the air) by one person to decide which of two alternatives shall be followed. The other competing person 'calls' either 'heads' or 'tails'; if what he calls falls uppermost, he is considered the winner. If not, the one who tossed the coin succeeds.
Heads I win, tails you lose An arrangement which ends in the challenger remaining the winner, whatever happens; a hopelessly unfair agreement.
See **heads or tails.**
Keep one's head above water Live within one's income; avoid bankruptcy. Just manage to avoid difficulty. [Or. Swimming.]
It's a very difficult book, but I'm just managing to keep my head above water.
Lose one's head Momentarily lose self-control; behave wildly and senselessly.
Make head or tail of Understand; comprehend. (Always used in the negative.)
I cannot make head nor tail of the argument.
Off one's head Mentally weak; unbalanced; mad; so excited as to be entirely irresponsible.
Old head on young shoulders Wisdom or experience unexpected in so young a person.
On one's own head One's own personal responsibility. (The phrase is generally used as a warning.)
If you insist, it will be on your own head.
Standing on one's head Very easily.
He can repair car-engines standing on his head.
Put into one's head Suggest.
The boy says he wants to be a sailor; our seaside holiday must have put it into his head.

Put (or lay) our heads together Consult together; discuss.
If they would only put their heads together, I'm sure they could reach an agreement.
Take into one's head Take a sudden and unexpected action.
The boy took it into his head to play truant.
Toss one's head Raise it with a jerk of pride or contempt.
Turn one's head (or brain) Render one vain, self-conscious, irresponsible, etc.
The attention the pop-group received completely turned their heads.
Two heads are better than one It is an advantage to have a second person's opinion; collaboration is valuable.
Over one's head 1. Beyond one's comprehension.
Most of his speech went over my head.
2. In preference to one having a prior claim.
He was appointed manager over his boss's head.

Headway **Make headway** Progress; go forward.
They made considerable headway up the mountain.

Heap **Struck all of a heap** [S] Overcome; overwhelmed.
I was struck all of a heap to see Phyllis pushing a pram.

Hearing **Hard of hearing** Partially, but not completely, deaf.
You'll have to shout—the old lady is hard of hearing.
Lose one's hearing Become completely deaf.
Out of hearing Too far away to be heard.

Heart **After one's own heart** Such as one could like and appreciate. In accordance with one's tastes.
He is a man after my own heart.
Break one's heart Cause one extreme distress or disappointment.
Do one's heart good Make one happy and pleased.
It did my heart good to see the children's delight.
Find it in one's heart Be firm or hard-hearted enough (usually used in the negative).
I could not find it in my heart to refuse the boy's request.
Have a heart Be personally concerned or interested in.
Her parents naturally have the girl's happiness at heart.
Have one's heart in one's boots [S] Be intensely depressed.
Have one's heart in one's mouth Be in a state of extreme nervousness.
My heart was in my mouth when I sat the exam.
Have the heart to See **find it in one's heart.**
Heart in the right place In spite of imperfections, possessing good and sensible ideas. Well-meaning.
He's rather unapproachable, but his heart is in the right place.
Heart's content Complete satisfaction; as much or as long as one desires.

We can swim in the river to our heart's content.

Heart of the matter The essence, or most vital part, of something.

There are many explanations for his behaviour, but the heart of the matter is his wife's ill-heath.

Heart-rending Extremely distressing.

Heart-strings Deepest feelings or affections.

Christmas cards always tug at my heart-strings.

Heart-to-heart Frank and intimate.

We had a heart-to-heart talk.

Know (off) by heart Know, literally and every word.

I knew the verses off by heart.

Learn (off) by heart Memorize.

Lose heart Become too depressed to continue.

Don't lose heart; there's still a chance of winning.

Lose one's heart to Fall in love with; be charmed.

Set one's heart upon Desire intensely.

My mother's set her heart on new wallpaper.

Take heart Be encouraged.

We may take heart from the fact that the illness isn't getting any worse.

Take to heart Take very seriously.

Wear one's heart on one's sleeve Exhibit one's intentions for all to see; be completely frank. [Or. The old custom of a lover tying a ribbon given him by his sweetheart on his sleeve.]

He's not a man to wear his heart on his sleeve.

Win the heart of Gain the affection of.

Heat **In the heat of the moment** During a brief time of confusion, anxiety, excitement, panic, etc.

Heavy **Make heavy weather of** Find great difficulties in.

You seem to be making heavy weather of that job.

Heel **Heel of Achilles** See **Achilles' heel.**

Clean pair of heels Superior speed.

Come to heel Obey humbly and completely, as a dog comes obediently to the heels of his master.

Down-at-heel Shabby and untidy, like one whose shoe-heels are worn down.

Kick one's heels Waste time.

I had to kick my heels for an hour before he would see me.

Similar to **cool one's heels** and **twiddle one's thumbs.**

Left to cool one's heels Kept waiting, usually by a superior.

On the heels of Immediately behind, or very soon afterwards.

George arrived on the heels of William.

Show a clean pair of heels Run away from and escape.

H

91

H

Take to one's heels Run away.
The boy broke the window and took to his heels.
Turn on one's heel Turn sharply away.
She turned on her heel, and disappeared in the crowd.

Hell **All hell broke loose** A tremendous uproar, a riot, ensued.
Someone opened a bottle of whisky, and all hell broke loose.
Hell for leather At full speed.

Help **Help oneself to** Select and take away without formality or waiting to ask permission.
The guests helped themselves to the refreshments at the buffet.

Helter-skelter Hurriedly and in confusion.
They dashed helter-skelter out of the room.

Hem **Hem in** Restrain; restrict.

Hen **Hen-pecked** Constantly faulted, nagged, scolded, etc., by one's wife.

Here **Here and there** Scattered; distributed. In various places.
They looked down upon fields and woods, with a farmhouse here and there.
Here today and gone tomorrow Merely temporary; staying for a short time in any place.
Neither here nor there Immaterial to a discussion, etc.
I would rather stay, but that's neither here nor there.

Herod **Out-Herod Herod** To be excessively wicked. [Or. Shakespeare, *Hamlet*.]

Hide **Hide one's light under a bushel** Conceal one's merits because of modesty. [Or. Biblical: 'Neither do men light a candle and put it under a bushel.'] The phrase is generally used in the negative.
He was never one to hide his cleverness under a bushel.

High **High and dry** Stranded.
High and mighty Arrogant.
Highbrow Of cultured tastes.
Highdays, holidays and bonfire nights An old-f. facetious phrase applied to celebrations in general.
High-falutin' High-flown; absurdly elaborate and fantastic (generally applied to speech).
High-flyer Ambitious person with the ability to succeed.
High-handed See *Hand.*
High jinks [S] A gay time.
They tell me you had high jinks at the pub last night.
Highlight Most prominent part.
Highly (probable, *etc.*) To a great extent.
He was highly annoyed at her skill.
Highly strung Tense. Unusually sensitive.
High-sounding Pompous; magnificent.

He's talking a lot of high-sounding nonsense.

High spot Outstanding attraction.

The high spot of the evening was the firework display.

High table The end table, usually at right-angles to the others and raised, at which the masters and other important personages of a college dine.

High tea An early evening meal which combines meat or some similar extra dish with the usual tea.

High time Fully time; applied to an event already due, if not overdue.

Look at the clock; it's high time you went to bed.

Highway **Queen's highway** All public roads and thoroughfares along which the public has a right to travel (but, legally, only to travel, not to linger upon, or to obstruct).

Hinge **Hinge upon** Depend on.

The whole play hinges on the success of his performance.

Hint **Broad hint** A stressed, an obvious hint.

The salesman received a broad hint that we did not want him to call again.

Drop (*or* throw out) a hint Hint in a casual manner.

I still haven't received the boss's reply; will you drop a hint to his secretary?

Hit **Hit it off** Agree.

It is unfortunate that the two tenants don't hit it off with each other.
Similar to **see eye to eye** and **get on.**

Hit the (right) nail on the head Guess or judge correctly.

Hit upon Discover (usually unexpectedly).

I've hit upon a new method of extracting salt from sea-water.

Hither **Hither and thither** Here and there; in this direction and in that direction. [Old f.]

We searched hither and thither, but could not find her.

Hoary **Hoary age** Age when one's hair has turned white, or hoary; very old.

He died at the hoary age of ninety.

(*Note.*—Hoary is frequently used as the equivalent of very old in connection with other matters, e.g. *a hoary joke.*)

Hobby See *Horse.*

Hobson **Hobson's choice** See *Choice.*

Hocus-pocus The words traditionally uttered by a conjuror as he performs a trick; hence, a cheat, a swindle. [Or. Obscure. Perhaps the name of a famous French conjuror, Ochus Boshus, or the Welsh *Hocca pucca.*]

Hog **Go the whole hog** Go to the fullest possible extent. Complete a matter.

If we're going to the cinema, why not go the whole hog and have a meal out as well.

Hoist **Hoist with one's own petard** Beaten with one's own weapons; caught in one's own trap. [Or. The medieval 'petard', an engine designed, when filled with gunpowder, to blow in a city gate. There was extreme risk of those who fired it being destroyed too.]

Hold **Hold aloof** Remain deliberately apart; isolated.

Hold cheap Regard as having little value.

Hold down [S] [U.S.A.] Retain.

I can't understand how he manages to hold down that job.

Hold the fort [LIT] Defend a fortress. [MET] Remain on duty, in charge, at work, in supervision, etc.

Hold forth Discourse; orate.

Hold good Remain unaffected and unaltered.

My promise to visit you next summer holds good.

Hold (or stand) one's ground Not yield.

Despite the Opposition's abuse, the Minister stood his ground.

Hold (oneself) in Restrain (oneself).

Hold on 1. [LIT] Continue one's grasp. 2. [MET] Wait.

If you can hold on a little longer, I'll ask her to come to the telephone.

Hold one's own Maintain successfully one's opinion, argument, or position.

George can generally hold his own when discussing politics.

Hold out 1. As **hold on** (1). 2. Extend, offer.

I can hold out no hope of an improvement.

Hold over 1. Keep back; reserve.

I have some more news, but I will hold it over for my next letter.

2. Use some knowledge as a threat.

Hold together Remain undivided; not separated.

I've tied up the parcel with string, but I am afraid it won't hold together.

Hold up Delay.

The train was held up for an hour by the bad weather.

Hold water See *Water.*

Hold with Concur; agree with.

I don't hold with allowing children too much freedom.

Hole **Be in a hole** Be in an awkward situation.

Hole-and-corner Furtive; secret.

Their meeting was a hole-and-corner affair.

Pick holes in Find fault with.

Homage **Pay (or give) homage to** Show respect and reverence.

They came to pay homage to the old musician on his birthday.

Home **At-home** An evening party, usually informal.

Bring a thing home to a person Compel him to realize it.

Perhaps the accident will bring home to him his stupidity in driving so fast.

Make oneself at home Behave informally, as though the house was one's own.

Do sit down and make yourself at home.

Honour **A debt of honour** A debt which cannot be legally enforced—e.g. a gambling debt, or one which is purely moral.

She was very kind to me when I first came here, and I consider it a debt of honour to help her now.

Do the honours Act as host (or hostess).

Honour among thieves Mutual help or trust even among people normally considered incapable of either. Similar to **dog doesn't eat dog.**

In honour bound Compelled by one's sense of duty or correctness.

A point of honour Conduct arising from one's own particular sense of self-respect.

It was a point of honour with the old man to walk a mile every day.

Hook **By hook or by crook** By any method, right or wrong; without scruples.

Hook, line and sinker Completely and utterly. [Or. Parts of a fishing-rod.]

I put the plan a different way, and they fell for it (swallowed it) hook, line and sinker.

Off the hook Out of a difficulty. [Or. Fishing.]

It's his own fault for getting himself into this situation, but we'll have to think of a way to get him off the hook.

Sling one's hook [S] Depart. [Old f.]

Horizon **On the horizon** [MET] Likely to occur in the remote future.

Horn **Draw in one's horns** Withdraw, alter or abandon (plans, etc.). [Or. A snail's 'horns', which are drawn in if it senses danger.]

Owing to shortage of money, the architect has had to draw in his horns considerably.

Hornet's nest **Stir up a hornet's nest,** *or* **put one's hand in a hornet's nest** Create trouble by interfering unwisely.

Horse **A dark horse** A person whose qualities and possibilities are unknown. [Or. Racing.]

Simon is very frank and friendly, but Richard seems to be a dark horse.

Hobby-horse 1. Favourite notion or private idea which one is constantly referring to.

The foreman's been riding his hobby-horse about efficiency again.

2. Abbreviation **hobby.** Spare-time occupation. Pastime. [Or. Wickerwork horse worn round waist of folk-dancers. Child's toy: stick with horse's head. Both are 'ridden'.]

Look a gift horse in the mouth Examine too critically anything which is a present. [Or. The proverb, 'Never look a gift horse in the mouth.' A horse's age is judged by the condition of its teeth.]

On one's high horse Assuming a haughty or superior attitude. Also **trying to ride the high horse.**

Take a horse to the water Only go so far. [Or. Proverb, 'You can take a horse to the water, but you can't make him drink.']

Hot **Hot air** Excited, boastful, meaningless talk.
Take no notice of him : he talks nothing but hot air.

Hot favourite Very popular. Strongly recommended.

Hot stuff [S] Exceptionally brilliant; daring; unconventional, etc.

Hot water See under *Water.*

Hour **Improve the shining hour** Take advantage of an opportunity. [Or. Abbrev. quotation from child's poem, 'How doth the little busy bee improve each shining hour.']

Keep regular hours Always go to bed and get up at the same times, usually early ones.

The small hours The early hours of the morning, i.e. between 1 and 4 a.m.

The witching hour Midnight. [Or. The time when witches are said to exercise their powers.] [Old. f]

House **Bring down the house** Give a tremendously popular performance, not necessarily in a theatre, of any type. [Or. Theatrical, to receive so much applause that the building shakes.]

House-warming A dinner-party, etc., given to celebrate the settling down in a new house, a return after a long absence, or any similar occasion.

Keep open house Welcome visitors, without invitation, at any time.

Like a house on fire Vigorously.
She was typing away like a house on fire.

How **How are you?** Same as **how do you do?**

How comes it?; how is it? How or why does it happen?
How comes it that you are always late on Monday?

How do you do? The usual formal greeting. [Or. 'Do' = 'du', from the Anglo-Saxon 'dugan', 'to go'.]

How goes it? [S] How are you and your affairs progressing?

How is ——? Abbrev. for How (= in what state) is the health of ——?
How is the invalid this morning?

Hue **Hue and cry** Noise of pursuit. Outcry (**against**). [Or. Old legal name for official cry when calling for assistance, e.g. in pursuit of escaping criminal. Old French = *huer*, to shout.]

Some M.P.s are raising a great hue and cry about the amount of money being spent on defence.

Hum **Hum and haw** Hesitate; procrastinate.
He hummed and hawed so long that I finally gave up.

Hunt **Hunt down** Find after careful search.
Hunt up Search for.
You'll have to hunt up the word in the dictionary.

Hurl **Hurl defiance** Openly and loudly defy. Frequently used facetiously.
The small kitten hurled defiance at the big dog.

Hurly-burly Tumult; the noise and struggle of crowds.

Hurry **Hurry on with; hurry up** Hasten.
Hurry up, or we shall miss the train.
In a hurry Hastening. Not reluctantly.
We won't go to that restaurant again in a hurry.

Husband **Husband one's resources** To 'husband' is to take care of, to use economically. 'Resources' are all the means one has.

I

Idea **What's the big idea?** What folly have you in mind?

Ilk **That ilk** The same name. The same nature.

Ill **Ill-assorted** Incompatible; badly matched.
Ill-at-ease Uncomfortable; in a state of embarrassment.
The boy was ill-at-ease in the presence of the headmaster.
It's an ill wind that blows nobody good It is a specially disastrous matter if nobody whatsoever derives any benefit from it.

Image **The image; the very image; the spit and image** (incorrectly **the spitting image**) Exactly alike.
The baby is the image of his father.

Imagination **Flight (*or* stretch) of imagination** Imaginative effort.
By no stretch of the imagination can I see George as a successful shopkeeper.

Impression **Give (*or* create) a false impression** Mislead by a statement or action.
The story she has told gives a totally false impression of what really happened.
Make a good impression Behave in a manner which will create admiration and respect.
He made a very good impression when he applied for the job.
Under the impression Having the notion or (vague) belief.
I was under the impression that today was Friday.

In **In for it** [S] Involved. Destined for trouble.

When I saw the look on her face, I realized that I was in for it.
In with On intimate or friendly terms with.

Inch **Every inch** Completely; entirely.
John looks every inch a golfer.
Inch by inch See **little by little.**

Incline **Be inclined to** Have a tendency to; be in favour of.
I am inclined to forgive him because of his youth.

Incumbent **Incumbent upon one** An essential duty for one.
It is incumbent upon you to provide for your parents.

Inference **Draw an inference** Assume; infer.
From his manner, we drew the inference that he was satisfied with the results of his visit.

Influence **Under the influence** In full, 'under the influence of intoxicating liquor'.

Iniquity **Sink of iniquity** Any place with a bad reputation. (Frequently used facetiously.)
If you're going to the Club to play bridge, I'll join you in that sink of iniquity later on.

In-laws The relations of one's husband or wife—**mother-in-law, sister-in-law,** etc.
Three of my in-laws are visiting us next week.

Ins-and-outs **The ins-and-outs** All the details.
I haven't heard all the ins-and-outs of the story yet.

Instance **For instance** As an example; to explain or elaborate one's meaning.
What would you do if you met a wild animal—a lion, for instance?
Similar to **for example.**

Intent **To all intents and purposes** Apparently. As far as one can see.

Interim **In the interim** From now until some specified event occurs.
We leave next week; in the interim we shall be visiting friends.

Interval **At intervals** At irregular periods of time.
The dicussion continued; at intervals the speakers stopped for refreshment.

Iota **One iota** The smallest possible quantity. [Or. The iota is the smallest letter of the Greek alphabet.]
I don't care an iota what the result may be.
(*Note.*—This idiom is always used in the negative.)

Irons **Irons in the fire** Matters of interest or importance which may prove profitable.
Even if I don't get the job, I have other irons in the fire.
Strike while the iron is hot Act promptly, and while the conditions are in one's favour.

Issue **Confuse the issue** Confuse the final analysis or result; bring forward irrelevant arguments.

To talk about politics is merely to confuse the issue.
Force an issue Compel a decision to be reached.
I don't want to force the issue, but I do think the meeting ought to end soon.
Join issue (with someone) (on something) Proceed to argue.
Take issue Disagree.
I shall have to take issue with the newspaper-boy over the noise he makes every morning.

J

Jack **Jack of all trades (and master of none)** One capable of undertaking a variety of jobs (but who is expert at none of them).
Before you can say Jack Robinson [S] Extremely quickly.
He knocked, and before you could say Jack Robinson the door opened.

Jaundice **View with a jaundiced eye; take a jaundiced view of** Regard with jealousy, envy, suspicion or distrust. [Or. Jaundice is a disease which turns the skin temporarily yellow, and yellow is the colour associated with jealousy.]

Jiff(y) **In a jiff(y),** *or* **half a jiff(y)** Very soon; almost immediately. Also *Moment* and *Tick*.

Job **Job's comforter** One who comes nominally to console and comfort a person, but who actually adds to his distress by being pessimistic and reproachful. [Or. Biblical.]

Jog **Jog along** To 'jog' is to proceed at a slow, regular pace. Used almost always metaphorically to indicate quiet, routine and unexciting progress.
How's life? Jogging along as usual?
Jog-trot Progress as above.
Jog a person's memory Remind, in order to prevent something being forgotten.

Joke **Crack a joke** Make a joke; tell a humorous story.
They seem to spend most of their time cracking jokes.
It's no joke It is a serious matter.
Practical joke Trick played on a person to gain a laugh at his expense.

Jot **Jot or tittle** 'Jot' is a corruption of 'iota' (which see); 'tittle' also means something tiny. (The expression is always used negatively.)
I don't care a jot or tittle what you think of my tie.
Jot down Note briefly and quickly.
I will jot down all your instructions.

Judgment **Sit in judgment on** Judge.

Jump **Jump at** Take a quick advantage of; seize an opportunity.

The house is a bargain, and you should jump at the offer.
Jump down one's throat Speak with unexpected violence to one.
I only asked him if I could use his telephone, and he jumped down my throat.
The high jump Serious trouble.
When David comes back home, he's for the high jump.

Justice **Do justice to** Treat justly or fairly; appreciate fully (used frequently in reference to food).
Our guests did justice to my wife's excellent cooking.
Do oneself justice Show one's abilities to their good advantage.
Did you do yourself justice in the driving-test?

K

Keep **Keep abreast of** Keep level with.
We do our best to keep abreast of modern improvements.
Similar to **keep pace with.**
Keep aloof Remain distant from, physically or in manner.
Keep at Persist or continue with.
You'll never learn to paint unless you keep at it.
Keep back Conceal. Slow down the progress of.
Keep company Associate with.
A man is known by the company he keeps.
Keep cool Remain calm.
Keep dark Conceal; refrain from mentioning.
I'm going into hospital next week, but please keep it dark.
Keep one's counsel Remain silent and reticent.
Keep one's distance (Originally) Maintain one's correct and formal attitude. (Now more frequently) Remain away from.
The dog's rather wild, so I should keep your distance.
Keep one's end up Not slacken. Acquit oneself well.
Keep an eye on Watch; act as temporary guardian to.
I would be glad if you'd keep an eye on the children while we're away.
Keep at arm's length Avoid familiarity with.
She's very indiscreet, so I should keep her at arm's length.
Keep going Continue (at one's work or routine, etc.).
He looks terribly ill; I don't know how long he'll be able to keep going.
Keep guard Watch; act as sentinel.
Keep one's hair on [S] Remain calm.
Keep one's hand in Continue to practise, in order to retain one's skill.
I've retired from journalism, but I still write an occasional article to keep my hand in.

Keep one's head Not allow oneself to become flustered.

Keep house Act as the manager of a household.

When his wife died his sister went to keep house for him.

Keep in with Remain on good terms with, usually with some definite motive.

Keep it up Continue in the same manner.

I've been working twelve hours a day, but I won't be able to keep it up.

Keep on Persist in; repeat one's present actions.

Don't keep on asking silly questions.

Keep out Refuse admittance to.

Keep out of the way Absent or efface oneself.

When father's practising his trumpet, we keep out of his way.

Keep pace with Move at the same speed as.

1. [LIT]

My horse couldn't keep pace with the rest of the field.

2. [MET]

I can't keep pace with all the changes in tax law.

Keep the peace Maintain peace.

The mother did her best to keep the peace between her sons.

Keep secret Similar to **keep it dark**.

Keep to oneself Remain alone.

Keep something to oneself Fail to disclose or share something.

Keep a stiff upper lip Not allow one's lip to tremble with emotion; be firm and brave.

Keep in touch with Remain in communication with.

Keep track of Follow the progress of.

Keep up Continue.

We wrote frequently at first, but I hadn't enough time to keep up the correspondence.

Keep up with Similar to **keep pace with** [LIT and MET]

I can't keep up with you—you walk too fast.

It is difficult to keep up with all these new inventions.

In keeping with (negative form = out of keeping with) Appropriate to; suitable to.

Drinks all round would be in keeping with the spirit of the occasion.

Kick **Kick the bucket** [S] Die.

Kick over the traces Be insubordinate. Act independently.

Kick up a fuss (*or* **row, shindy** *or* **rumpus**) [S] Cause a violent disturbance; quarrel.

Kill **Dressed** (*or* **got up**) **to kill** Dressed in a manner designed to attract maximum attention.

Kill two birds with one stone Achieve two purposes with a single act.

Kin **Next of kin** Nearest relations.

K

Kindness **Kill with kindness** Overwhelm with too much kindness.

Kith **Kith and kin** Acquaintances and blood relations. (Used loosely to refer to members of same race.)

Knight **Knight errant** In medieval days, an armed knight who roamed about the countryside, prepared to defend oppressed and helpless maidens. The phrase is today applied to any chivalrous man who, without expecting reward, helps and protects a weak or helpless person.

Knit **Knit one's brows** Frown; regard in a puzzled way. ('Knit' in this idiom means to draw towards one another.)

Knock **Knock about** 1. Wander, gaining experience in the process.
I've knocked about the world for forty years.
2. Injure physically. Treat roughly.
I got knocked about a bit playing football yesterday.
3. **Knock-about** *(adjective)* Noisy, boisterous, rowdy.

Knock down Strike a person so violently that he falls.

Knock-down prices The cheapest possible. The best available (as in an auction. See **knock down to**).

Knock down to Sell to a person who has made a final bid at an auction sale. (An auctioneer gives a sharp rap with his hammer when the highest and final bid has been made, and the article or 'lot' is then legally the property of the bidder.) See **under the hammer** (under *Hammer*).

Knock into a cocked hat Defeat easily. Be very much superior to.
Manchester United can knock any team into a cocked hat.

Knock off [S] 1. Cease work for the day.
We knock off at one o'clock on Saturday.
2. Steal.

Knock on the head 1. [LIT] Kill [Oldf.]
2. [MET] Destroy.
We'll soon knock his scheme on the head.

Knock out *(verb)* Render incapable of further fighting. [Or. Boxing.]
He was knocked out in ten minutes.
(Noun and adjective (with hyphen)) 1. [LIT] The blow which officially ends a fight.
He received the knock-out in the fifth round.
2. [MET] [S] Something astonishing or startling.
Jenny's new flat is a knock-out.

Knock over 1. [LIT] Overturn; upset. 2. [MET] [S] Completely overwhelm.
The family was knocked over at the news.
Also **knock all of a heap** [S].

Knock together Create hastily.

I'd better knock a few things together for lunch.
Knock up Rouse from sleep by knocking at the door.
Take a knock 1. Receive a slight injury. 2. Suffer (slightly).
My bank account has taken a few knocks recently.

Know **I don't know him from Adam** Exaggeration for 'I don't know him'.
Know the ropes See under *Ropes.*
Know a thing or two [S] Be shrewd; possess worldly wisdom.
Bert is a smart lad; he knows a thing or two.
Similar to **know all the answers.**

Knuckle **Knuckle down** Work hard. Begin to work.
If I can get a chance to knuckle down to it, I'll soon finish painting the bathroom.
Knuckle under Surrender. [LIT] Kneel for pardon. ('Knuckle' here means the knee.)
Rap on the knuckle See *Rap.*

L

Labour **Labour of love** Work performed from affection or regard, and without expectation of payment.
Labour a point Over-stress a point in one's argument.
I realize that—you need not labour the point.
Labour under an affliction Suffer from some handicap or inconvenience, usually permanent.
Labour under a delusion (*or* **illusion)** Be influenced by some false idea.
If he thinks I'll do it for him, he is labouring under a delusion.

Lady **Lady Bountiful** A generous and kindly woman; now often applied derogatorily to a person who is too prominent in works of charity. [Or. Character in Farquhar's *Beaux' Stratagem.*]
Ladies' man One who makes special efforts to charm or please women.

Laid **Laid up** 1. In bed through illness or accident.
I've been laid up all the week with influenza.
2. Nautical. In harbour for repairs, etc.

Lamb **Like a lamb** Without resistance.
He accepted the whole idea like a lamb.

Land **See how the land lies** Discover the state of affairs; make discreet enquiries.

Landslide (*political*) A sudden complete change of political popularity and, as a result, political power in an election. (Hence **Landslide victory.**)

L

Lap **Lap of luxury** Extreme richness.
This flat is hardly the lap of luxury, but it suits us.

Large **At large** 1. Free after escaping. 2. In general.
Two lions from the Zoo are at large.
Similar to **at liberty.**

Last **At last** Eventually; after a long time has passed.
At last we are together again.
At long last As above, but more emphatic.
At one's last gasp In an utterly exhausted, or almost dying, condition.
Last but not least Last to be mentioned, but not last in importance.
On one's last legs Almost, though not quite, exhausted. (The idiom is also applied to any affair, etc., which is on the verge of failing.)
Their business is on its last legs through bad management.
The last straw See *Straw.*
The last word 1. The final contribution to an argument.
He's a difficult man to negotiate with—always insists on having the last word.
2. [MET] The culminating achievement, than which nothing can be better. (Usually exaggeration.)
This is the last word in electric cookers.

Laugh; Laughter **Convulsed with laughter** Laughing so excessively that one is practically helpless.
Laugh away *or* **off** Dismiss (or conceal) something by laughing.
Laugh on the other side of one's face Be the reverse of amused; be depressed or unhappy.
You'll laugh on the other side of your face if your wife hears about this.
Laugh up one's sleeve Be amused secretly; hide one's laughter in contempt.

Launch **Launch out** Depart from one's normal habits or occupation.
He launched out on a new career at the age of fifty.

Laurels **(Win) laurels** (Acquire) honour. [Or. The Roman custom of crowning a victor with laurel wreaths.]
Look to one's laurels Beware of losing one's place.
Rest on one's laurels Cease to strive further.

Law **Arm of the law** Criminal law, personified by the police.
The eyes (or eye) of the law A legal stand-point.
In the eyes of the law, you are now an adult.
Have the law on [S] Prosecute in a court of law.
If your trees drop leaves in his garden, he's the sort of man who'll have the law on you.
A law unto himself One who follows his own inclinations, regardless of custom.

George is a law unto himself where gardening is concerned.
Law-abiding One who obeys the law.
Lay down the law Speak very firmly; use one's authority; insist on proper observance.
The doctor laid down the law, and told me to eat less.
Take the law into one's own hands Ignore the legal method of obtaining justice, and act entirely as one considers suitable and just.

Lay **Lay about one** Strike out violently in every direction.
Lay (or put) aside; lay by 1. Abandon, usually for a short time.
2. Put away for future use.
I've laid aside £20 for the wedding.
Lay a bet Place a bet or wager.
Lay at one's door (or to one's charge) Place the blame or responsibility on one.
The death of the patient was laid at the hospital's door.
Lay down the law Make any statement with an air of authority and as one who does not expect to be contradicted.
Lay one's hands on Find. Obtain possession of.
I can't lay my hands on my umbrella.
Lay in (or lay up) Store for future use.
We'd better lay in some candles in case there's another electricity strike.
Lay on thick [S] Exaggerate greatly (usually blame, or praise).
I know the boy was to blame, but I do think you laid it on a bit thick.
Lay oneself open (to) Expose oneself (to); lead to an unfavourable assumption.
If this party goes on much longer, we'll lay ourselves wide open to complaints from the people next door.
Lay out 1. Spend. 2. Present to view. 3. [S] Render unconscious.
I'm going to lay out £500 in fittings for my shop.
Lay stress (weight, emphasis) on Emphasize.
The Chancellor laid stress on the need for economy.

Lead **Lead a dance** [S] Cause considerable trouble and trivial activity.
The chicken led us a dance before we caught it.
Lead astray Mislead. Encourage to do wrong.
Lead by the nose [S] Control a person as completely as if he were a horse being led by a rope.
Lead off Act as the leader in beginning any function (dancing, singing, etc.); start.
Lead on Encourage to go further than was intended.
He's normally a well-behaved boy, but sometimes others lead him on.
Lead the way Similar to **lead off,** but also frequently used in the literal sense of going first to point the way.
Lead up the garden path [S] Mislead; deceive.
Lead up to Progress gradually towards.

What are you trying to lead up to?

Swing the lead [S] *(pron. 'led')* Exaggerate; invent stories. Use pretence (lies, etc.) to evade truth or avoid responsibilities.

Take the lead (*or* leading part) Act the most important part. Show initiative.

Someone will have to take the lead in forming a committee.

Leaf **Take a leaf out of a person's book** Copy; take as an example.

I wish you'd take a leaf out of Peter's book, and get up early.

Turn over a new leaf Alter; change; make a fresh and better beginning.

She has promised to turn over a new leaf, and be more punctual.

Leap **By leaps and bounds** With extreme rapidity.

National prosperity is increasing by leaps and bounds.

A leap in the dark An action the result of which is uncertain or unknown.

Learn **Learn by heart** Memorize. Similar to **commit to memory**.

Least **At least** As the minimum.

If we can't afford a new car, at least we can get the old one repaired.

Least said, soonest mended The less one says, the better.

To say the least of it To minimize; express as mildly as possible.

His bluntness was, to say the least of it, unlikely to make him popular.

Leave **Beg leave** Ask permission. [Oldf. Formal.]

May I beg leave to remind you that it is nearly noon.

Leave alone Do not interfere with.

Leave behind 1. Forget.

John has left his spectacles behind.

2. Deliberately discard.

I've left my umbrella behind; it isn't going to rain.

Leave in (*or* out in) the cold Ignore; take no notice of, or interest in.

Leave in the lurch Abandon in circumstances of danger and difficulty. [Or. The card-game called cribbage, in which the 'lurch' is a hopeless position.]

The car ran out of petrol and left me in the lurch.

Leave off 1. Cease to wear a garment.

I've left off my overcoat.

2. Cease; stop what one is doing.

The children are making too much noise; tell them to leave off.

Leave out Omit.

Leave over Defer.

I can't do it now; I'll leave it over till tomorrow.

Leave a person to it Leave a person alone to continue in his own way.

If you think you can finish it on your own, I'll leave you to it.

Leave at the post See under *Post*.

Leave it at that [S] Say or do nothing further.
Leave one cold Fail to excite, interest, etc.
That sort of book just leaves me cold.
Leave to oneself Leave in solitude, without interference.
If you leave him to himself, he'll be quite happy.
Similar to **leave a person to it**.
Leave word Leave a message, verbal or written.
Take French leave Abandon one's work or post without obtaining the necessary permission from one's superior.
Take leave Venture.
I'm afraid I must take leave to disagree.
Take leave of one's senses Go mad.
Take one's leave Depart; say farewell to.

Leeway **Make up leeway** Compensate for time which has been lost. [Or. Nautical. 'Leeway' is the distance which a ship has drifted from the position in which she should have been.] Also, escape from a difficult position. 'Leeway' is often used to mean 'room for manœuvre'.
The train was late, and we had an hour's leeway to make up.

Left **Left-handed compliment** One which is the reverse of complimentary.

Leg **Give a leg-up** [S] [LIT] Help a person to mount his horse. [MET] Help generally.
We'd better give Tom a leg-up with his work, or it won't be finished.
Not a leg to stand on Having nothing effective in support of an argument.
George is sure that England will become a republic, but he hasn't a leg to stand on.
Pull one's leg Deceive jocularly. Trick. Befool.
He takes everything so seriously: I can't resist pulling his leg.
Stretch one's legs Take a walk for exercise.

Length **At great length** For a long time.
She spoke at great length about nothing at all.
At length After considerable time; eventually.
Go to any lengths Ignore every impediment that may get in one's way.

Lesson **Teach one a lesson** Do something which will act as a reprimand to one and show him his fault.

Let **Let alone** 1. Refrain from interfering with.
Let that bottle alone.
2. In addition to being (or having).
Let be Same as **let alone** (1).
Let the cat out of the bag Reveal a secret (usually accidentally). Create trouble (usually by tactlessness).
Let down Betray; fail to support when support was needed.

My brother promised to give me a lift, but he let me down.
Let fall *(applied to speech)* Remark casually.
He let fall a hint of trouble.
Let fly 1. [LIT] Propel swiftly.
2. [MET] Abandon control.
He lost his temper, and let fly.
Let go Release one's hold.
He let go of the rope, and crashed to the ground.
Let one's hair down [S] [U.S.A.] Behave informally. Relax. Have an enjoyable time.
Let someone in 1. Admit.
John knocked, and I let him in.
2. Involve a person without his knowledge or consent; make responsible for.
His tactlessness lets me in for a lot of embarrassment.
Let loose Release.
Let off 1. Allow to go free and unpunished.
The prisoner was let off with some good advice.
2. Explode.
We let off fireworks on November 5th.
Let on [S] Tell; make public.
I'm going out to buy her a birthday present—don't let on.
Let oneself go Give way to one's impulses, enthusiasms, etc.
Let out 1. Release; set free.
I'll open the cage and let out the bird.
2. Disclose; reveal.
I'll tell you a secret, but you mustn't let it out.
Let pass Ignore.
What the newspaper said isn't at all accurate, but let that pass.
Let sleeping dogs lie Avoid anything (usually people) which might stir up trouble.
Let slip Inadvertently release (e.g. a remark). Miss (an opportunity).
Let well alone Refrain from interfering, because it may do more harm than good.
Let up [S] Refrain. Stop. Become less severe.
If he has a job to do, he won't let up until he's finished.
Let-up Diminution. Relaxation.
I've been writing letters since lunch-time, without any let-up.
Letter **To the letter** Exactly; precisely.
His report was correct to the letter.
The letter of the law Exactly in accordance with the rules and regulations of the law.
Level **Do one's level best** Do one's utmost; use all one's efforts.

I'll do my level best to be at the concert.
Keep a level head Remain calm and sensible.
In these exciting times, it isn't always easy to keep a level head.
On the level Truth(fully), honest(ly).

Liberal **Liberal education** One planned on broad principles. The phrase is entirely non-political, 'liberal' here meaning 'ample, abundant'. The opposite of a specialized education.

Liberty **At liberty** Free; unrestrained. Permitted. Invited.
You are at liberty to wander anywhere in the park.
Take the liberty Act as though one possessed a right which in fact one does not; presume.
I have taken the liberty of switching off your car-lights.
Take liberties Go beyond the normal limits of convention or good manners. Be unduly familiar **(with).**

Lick **Lick into shape** Make efficient or presentable. Mould [Or. The licking by its mother of a new-born bear or similar cub.]
The garden's a jungle, but we'll soon lick it into shape.

Lie **Give the lie to** Completely deny; disprove.
His story will give the lie to the rumours we have been hearing.
Lie at one's door Become one's reponsibility.
Lie up Lie in bed as the result of an illness or accident. See *Laid.*
Mother has strained her back, and has had to lie up.
White lie A harmless lie told only with the object of helping or comforting someone.

Lieu **In lieu of** Instead of; in place of.

Life **As large as life** [LIT] In person. [MET] Prominent. Unmistakable.. (This idiom is used in a general rather than an exact and literal sense, as emphasis.)
There stood George, as large as life.
Breath of life Absolutely essential.
Liberty is the breath of life to every Englishman.
Come to life Become alive; give an indication of being alive.
I seldom come to life before mid-morning.
For the life of me. For dear life. [LIT] 'Even if what I am saying meant the loss of my life.' Used merely for emphasis.
For the life of me I can't understand what you're worrying about.
Have the time of one's life [S] Enjoy oneself thoroughly.
Life and soul A vivacious person.
Dominic is always the life and soul of the party.
New lease of life Fresh possibilities of continued existence.
Since he got back from holiday he's taken on a new lease of life.
Prime of life The most fully developed period of life (usually supposed to be about forty).
To the life Exactly; with complete realism.

L

The boy can imitate the milkman to the life.

Lift **Lift a finger** Make a slight effort. (Usually used in negative.)
He never lifted a finger to help me.
Lift one's hand against Strike.

Light **Come to light** Be revealed, exposed.
His marriage came to light after his death.
In a good light Favourably.
In the light of In view of. With the help given by.
Light-fingered Thievish.
Light upon Discover by chance.
In an old bookshop I happened to light upon a volume belonging to my grandfather.
Make light of Treat as of little consequence.
He has always made light of his deafness.
Shed (*or* throw) (a flood of) light on 1. [LIT] Light brilliantly.
2. [MET] Make clear and plain. Help to explain.
The article in the paper throws some light on the position in China.
Strike a light Ignite a match.
The lighter side The more enjoyable or amusing aspect.

Like **Like; The like** A similar object; anything strongly resembling another of the same class.
Apples, pears, and the like.
Nothing like 1. Emphatic form of 'unlike'.
That picture is nothing like him.
2. Not nearly.
There were nothing like as many people as we expected.

Likelihood **In all likelihood** Very probably.
In all likelihood the missing boy has run away to sea.
Similar to **in all probability**.

Likely **Likely enough** Fairly probable.
It is likely enough we shall meet at the station.

Limit **The limit** [S] As far as one can go. (Used idiomatically as an expression of exasperation or disgust.)
His latest idea is the limit!

Line **All along the line** In every way. [Or. Military, the 'line' being the line of battle.]
I agree with you all along the line.
Come into line Agree. Co-operate.
In one's line Within one's knowledge, experience or interests.

Lion **The lion's share** The greatest or most valuable portion.
The comedian received the lion's share of applause.

Lips **Lick one's lips** Express pleasure in anticipation of something.

Little **Little by little, inch by inch,** *etc.* A small amount or distance, repeated until a large total is reached.

Little by little the truth is being made public.

Live **Live down** By good conduct, etc., enable people to forget some past failure.
If I fail, I shall never live it down.
Live and learn Way of greeting some new fact or piece of knowledge, etc.
Live and let live Be sympathetic to the failings of others.
Live up to Prove oneself worthy of.
These are magnificent furs; I must try to live up to them.

Lo! **Lo and behold!** An exclamatory introduction. ('Lo' is a shortened form of *loke*, Anglo-Saxon for 'look'.)
And lo and behold, he changed his mind.

Lock **Lock, stock and barrel** Entirely; wholly. [Or. Military. A gun or pistol consists of three principal parts—the lock, containing the mechanism; the stock, or wooden portion; and the barrel.]
I've finished the whole business, lock, stock and barrel.

Loggerheads **At loggerheads** Disagreeing; quarrelling.
Arthur and his brother are always at loggerheads.

Long **In the long run** At the end; after a number of other things have happened.
In the long run, honesty is always the best policy.
Long ago A long time ago; in the distant past.
Long arm of coincidence Applied to coincidences in general, the 'long arm' referring to the surprising and abnormal way in which they occur.
I hadn't seen him for years, but by the long arm of coincidence we met on a train journey.
Long-drawn (out) Long continued or sustained.
A long-drawn cry sounded across the sea.
Long duration (or short duration) A long (or short) period during which some event continues.
Their journey was not, however, of long duration.
Long odds Unfavourable chances; an improbable event. [Or. Betting.]
It is long odds against Peter's winning the prize.
The long and the short of it The whole position or situation briefly stated.
The long and the short of it is that he can't cope.
Long shot See *Shot.*
Long-standing Existing for a long time.
I am keeping a long-standing engagement this evening.
Long-suffering Patient and enduring.
Long-term plans Plans which extend a long way into the future.
Long-winded Verbose; wearingly talkative.

He is one of the most long-winded people I have ever met.

Look **Look about (*or* around) one** Study one's surroundings and prospects.

I want to look around for a month or two before I start at university.

Look after Take care or charge of.

We promised to look after the cats while the family was abroad.

Look alive, lively *or* **sharp** [S] Hurry ; hasten.

Look alive, or we shall miss the train.

Look back Contemplate the past.

If we look back, we realize the changes war has made.

Look before you leap Take care before committing yourself to action.

Look daggers Regard fiercely and bitterly ; look at with fury and hatred.

Look down upon (one's nose at) Scorn ; regard with contempt.

Look for 1. Search for.

She looked for the missing money.

2. Expect.

I look for a number of improvements when the Government changes.

Look for a needle in a haystack Look for a small object in a large place, or for one person among many, etc.

Look forward to Regard some future event with pleasure.

I look forward to your visit next week.

Look a gift horse in the mouth See under *Horse.*

Look into Examine ; scrutinize.

He promised to look into my complaint.

Look on the bright side Regard cheerfully ; see the best in any situation.

However bad his luck may be, Edward always looks on the bright side.

Look small Appear insignificant.

Look the other way [LIT] Turn one's head. [MET] Refrain from noticing.

Look out! *(exclamation)* Beware ; be careful !

Look out, or you'll be run over!

Look out; keep a sharp lookout for Watch for.

Look out for Simon, or we shall miss him.

Look-out *(with hyphen)* Affair ; concern ; business.

Joan has decided to go to South America. What happens there is her own look-out.

Look over 1. [LIT]

He looked over the wall.

2. [MET] Scan ; examine.

I'd be glad if you'll look over these letters.

Look to it Note ; take careful action.

Look up 1. Refer to books, etc., to ascertain some fact.
I'll look it up in the encyclopaedia.
2. Visit an acquaintance whom one hasn't seen for some time.
It's time I looked Colin up again.
3. Improve; appear more cheerful.
The business is beginning to look up.
Look up to Regard with awe or respect.

Loose **(Play) fast and loose** (Enjoy oneself) vigorously
On the loose [S] Unattached, and in search of enjoyment, with no particular object in view.
John has gone out on the loose, and won't be back till late.
At loose ends; at a loose end Idle; having no definite object.

Lord **Lord it over** Behave arrogantly, as a person of importance.
The head of the department lords it over the assistants.

Lose **Lose face** Be humiliated. Lose reputation or credibility. Hence **loss of face.**
Lose ground Suffer, by degrees, loss of reputation, health or position.
Lose one's hearing Become deaf.

Loss; Lost **At a loss** 1. For less than the cost price.
I sold the goods at a loss.
2. Temporarily unable to act or reply; undecided.
I was at a loss to answer him.
Meet with a loss Lose; be deprived of.
He met with a heavy loss; over a hundred pounds was stolen from his shop.
A lost cause A movement, project or agitation, etc., which has no longer any chance of becoming effective.
Lost in admiration So overcome with admiration that one cannot express one's emotions.

Lot **Throw (or cast) in one's lot with** Decide to join, or to share the fortunes of.
Draw lots or cast lots Decide by throwing dice or by some similar method of chance.

Love **Calf-love** Adolescent love; a young man's first love affair, usually not very serious.
Labour of love Work done out of love for someone or something, rather than for money.
For love or money By any means.
I've tried all the shops, but I can't get any cream for love nor money.
No love lost Dislike, unfriendliness.
There's no love lost between the two sisters.

Low **At a low ebb** [LIT] A condition existing when an ebbing tide has left the water in a river at its lowest point. [MET] Feeble, almost exhausted.

Our cheerfulness, like our money, was at a low ebb.
In low spirits Depressed.

Luck **Run of luck** A series of lucky events. Used also in the opposite sense—**a run of bad luck**. [Or. Gambling].

Take pot luck Accept impromptu hospitality without a definite invitation. Dine on whatever happens to be cooking in the pot. Take any sort of risk.
I haven't booked a hotel; we'll have to take pot luck on finding somewhere to stay.

Worse luck Exclamation meaning 'Unfortunately'.

Lump **A lump in one's throat** A sense of pity, producing a desire to weep.

Lump it [S] Endure; suffer.
If you don't like it, you can lump it.

Lump sum The whole amount at once.
They paid him in a lump sum all that was owing.

Lump together Merge.
If we lump all our money together, we shall have over £5.

Lying **Refuse to take something lying down** Object strenuously to something. Resist something strongly.

Lynx **Lynx-eyed** Having especially keen sight, such as the lynx is supposed to possess.

M

Mad **Drive (*or* send) mad** Cause to become mad.
The noise of that gramophone is driving me mad.

Like mad [S] With tremendous energy.
He ran like mad.

Mad as a march hare Utterly and completely mad. [Or. Hares are supposed to be particularly wild and shy during March, their mating-season.]

Mad on Extremely or wildly interested in.
My daughter's mad on dancing.

Maiden **Maiden name** The surname of a woman before she was married. (Fr. *née*.)

Maiden speech The first speech made in Parliament by a member.
Maiden voyage The first voyage made by a vessel in the sea or air. (*Note* that in all the above cases 'maiden' is used in the sense of 'first'.)

Maiden over An 'over' (or six consecutive balls) in which no runs have been made. [Or. Cricket.]

Main **In the main** Chiefly.

M

The letters, in the main, were from her mother.
Main chance; have an eye to the main chance Be alert to one's own interests.

Majority **Attain one's majority** Reach the age at which one is legally regarded as an adult.

Make **Make after** Follow quickly.
Make as if Pretend.
The troops will make as if to retire, and then suddenly attack.
Make-believe Pretence.
The man's anger was only make-believe.
Make the best of it Accept misfortune or discomfort cheerfully.
We have got soaked to the skin, but we must make the best of it.
Make a clean breast See under **Breast.**
Make a clean sweep See under **Sweep.**
Make do Use as the best substitute available.
We hadn't time for lunch, but we made do with sandwiches.
Make eyes at Gaze at lovingly or longingly.
Make fast Secure; fasten firmly.
They made fast the boat to the pier.
Make for 1. Set out, usually quickly, in a particular direction.
The ships made for the harbour because of the storm.
2. Help to make or maintain.
The minister's speech does not make for peace.
Make free with Use freely, without asking permission.
Make fun of Ridicule; joke about.
Make a fuss of Treat with unusual and excessive courtesy and kindness,
The family made a tremendous fuss of John when he came back from his year abroad.
Make good 1. Repair; put back something that has been destroyed; restore.
The carpenter will make good the broken chair-leg.
2. Recover a lost reputation.
The young man has learnt a lesson, and will make good.
Make headway (or head) (against) Proceed, usually in spite of any difficulties or obstructions. [Or. Nautical.]
The building has made considerable headway, though workmen were difficult to obtain.
Make head or tail of See under **Head.**
Make it up Become friendly again after a quarrel, or agree after a dispute.
Make light (or little) of Treat as something of little importance.
The athlete made light of his injury.
Make the most of Put to the best use possible.

115

We must make the most of the fine weather.

Make much of Make special efforts to please; treat with conspicuous kindness and respect.

Very similar to **make a fuss of.**

Make no bones Show no hesitation or fear of the consequences.

Make nothing of 1. Treat as trivial or of no importance. Similar to **make little of.** 2. Completely fail to understand.

I can make nothing of these figures.

What do you make of it? What do you deduce from it? Do you understand it?

Make off Run away (usually as the result of some guilty act).

Make oneself scarce Disappear quickly; efface oneself.

We decided that it would be tactful to make ourselves scarce.

Make out 1. Comprehend; decipher.

I can't make out these letters.

2. Inscribe, write.

Please make out a bill for these goods.

3. Imply; indicate.

The scoundrel tried to make out that I had swindled him.

Make over Make a formal gift of property.

I have made over the farm to my son.

Make so bold as to Take the liberty of. [Slightly formal and oldf.]

May I make so bold as to suggest a compromise?

Make a splash See under *Splash.*

Make up 1. Invent; originate.

He made up the story he told you.

2. Complete.

He made up his set of Dickens' works.

3. Compensate for.

I gave the child a chocolate to make up for his disappointment.

See **make it up.**

Make-up Cosmetics.

Make up to Flatter, attempt to please, in order to obtain favours.

Make a virtue of necessity Treat something one is obliged to do as if it were being done from choice.

Make way for Move away to allow something else to fill the place.

Makeshift **Makeshift** Inferior or temporary; substitute.

We will put up a makeshift roof till the other is mended.

Man **Every man-jack** [S] Everyone.

A man of letters An author; one whose profession is that of a writer.

A man of straw A worthless person.

A man of his word One who is truthful and trustworthy, who does not break promises.

A man of the world One with worldly knowledge and experience.

To a man Everyone, without exception.

The regiment fought bravely, to a man.

Manner **By no manner of means** See under *Means*.

In a manner of speaking So to say. As it were.

To the manner born As if naturally or instinctively fitted for a position, etc.

My young son has taken to the clarinet as to the manner born.

Many **Many a long day** A long time.

I have not seen him for many a long day.

Mare's nest Something which does not exist; a mere effort of the imagination. (A mare—female horse—has obviously no nest.)

Mark **Beside the mark** Unconnected with the subject being discussed.

Your comments are beside the mark.

Make one's mark Establish an outstanding reputation.

Peter is a boy who will make his mark.

A marked man One who has become notorious through his connection with some particular incident.

Mark my words Take particular note of what I am saying.

Mark time Deliberately wait, without progressing. [Or. Military. At the command 'Mark time' soldiers raise and lower their feet as if marching, but do not move forward.]

We shall have to mark time at the factory until we receive definite orders from the Government.

Up to the mark In a normal state of health; well.

Hilary isn't looking up to the mark this morning.

(This idiom is generally used in the negative.) See also *Par.*

Wide of the mark Very inaccurate.

His guesses were all wide of the mark.

Master **Master mind** *(noun)* Chief planner, thinker or originator.

Master-mind *(verb)* To be in control as master mind.

Master of oneself Capable of self-control; able to think and act coolly and logically.

Master-stroke An exceptionally shrewd or clever action.

Matter **Matter of course** An affair of normal routine; regularly.

He reached his office as a matter of course at nine o'clock.

Matter of fact Something which is established as truth (as opposed to opinion). Hence **as a matter of fact**: emphatic phrase stressing truth of an expression.

As a matter of fact, I saw him only yesterday.

Matter-of-fact *(adjective)* Commonplace; ordinary.

M

He spoke in a matter-of-fact voice, despite the emotion he must have been feeling.

A matter of life and death Of vital and extreme importance.

The matter in question The affair being discussed or referred to.

No matter 1. In spite of.

I shall go, no matter what the weather may be.

2. Immaterial; having no importance.

I had something to say, but it's no matter (it doesn't matter).

What's the matter? What is concerning or occupying you?

Meal **Square meal** A full, complete meal.

We haven't had a square meal for a week.

Mealy **Mealy-mouthed** Applied to one who is a hypocrite or coward, and is afraid to speak honestly.

Means **By all means** 1. Indication of cordial assent.

Shall I ask him to come in? By all means.

2. By exerting every effort.

Try by all (or every) means to persuade him to come.

By all (or no) manner of means Indicating emphatic assent (or dissent).

Are you calling at the house? By no manner of means.

By fair means or foul In any way possible.

By no means; not by any means Elaborated forms of 'not'.

He was not by any means difficult to get on with, but his wife was by no means happy.

By what means? By what method? How?

By what means are you going to travel tonight?

Mean well Possess good intentions.

Means to an end An action merely leading to one's real object.

Meantime; meanwhile **In the meantime; meanwhile** The period during which an event has occurred; while this was happening; during the intervening time.

Wellington began the battle of Waterloo; in the meantime Blücher was marching to help him.

Similar to **for the time being** (under *Time*).

Measure **In some measure** To some extent.

I agree with you in some measure.

Measure one's length Fall flat.

He staggered, and measured his length on the pavement.

Take measures to Take suitable action to.

Measure up to Reach the level or standard of.

Does the scenery measure up to your expectations?

Meet **Meet with** 1. Receive.

He met with great kindness in Scotland.

2. Be received with.

118

The President hoped his plans would meet with approval.
More than meets the eye Something suppressed or hidden.
Ther's more in this than meets the eye.

Melt In the melting-pot Under reconsideration, and likely to be completely changed.
The organization of secondary education in this country is in the melting-pot.
Melt down Reduce to a single mass by heating until it becomes fluid, and then allow to harden.
The gold candlesticks were sold and melted down.

Memory Burden one's memory Cause to become a weight or burden on one's memory.
I don't want to burden your memory with too many instructions.
Commit to memory Similar to **learn by heart** (under *Heart*).
Within living memory During the lifetime of people now alive.

Mention Not to mention In addition to; distinct from.
I've all these apples to carry, not to mention some pounds of potatoes.
Don't mention it A polite dismissal of apology or thanks.
'I am sorry to have troubled you.' 'Don't mention it'

Mercy At the mercy of Dependent upon; controlled by; in the power of.
The ship was at the mercy of the waves.

Merry Make merry Rejoice.
Make merry at Make fun of. Laugh at.
Merry-making Rejoicing and festivities upon some special occasion.

Mete Mete out Distribute; give out. (Frequently applied to justice, punishment, etc.)

Mettle On one's mettle Roused to the use of one's best efforts; prepared to do one's utmost.

Midsummer Midsummer madness [LIT] Temporary madness, brought on by the conjunction of the full moon at midsummer and the heat of the season. [MET] Applied to any sort of crazy idea or plan.

Midway Halfway; half the distance.
He started to cross the road, but stopped midway.

Might Might and main All one's powers or strength.
He struggled with might and main to escape.

Mildly Put something mildly Make a deliberate or ironic understatement.
When the telephone rang in the middle of the night, I was rather irritated, to put it mildly.

Mile A mile away (off) [S] Easily.
You could see a mile off that the accident would happen.

Milk Milk-and-water Feeble; weak.
Also *Wishy-washy.*

Milk of human kindness Genuine and natural kindness towards one's fellow-creatures.

Mill **Go (be put) through the mill** Undergo any rigorous experience, usually at someone's hands.

My driving instructor certainly puts me through the mill.

Mince **No to mince matters (*or* words)** Not to speak tactfully or politely; to be plain and direct.

I told him, without mincing matters, that I wasn't satisfied.

Make mincemeat of [S] 'Mincemeat' consists [LIT] of ingredients chopped (or minced) into very small pieces for cooking. The phrase is used [MET] to indicate the destruction of arguments, plans, etc.

The Professor made mincemeat of the young man's theories.

Mind **Apply (*or* give) one's mind to** Consider carefully; concentrate one's attention upon.

She will never succeed until she gives her mind to her work.

Bear (*or* keep) in mind Retain in one's memory; remember.

Please bear in mind the advice I've given you.

Call to mind Recollect. Remember.

Cast one's mind back Recall the past.

If you cast your mind back, you will remember that an oak-tree used to grow here.

Go out of one's mind 1. Forget.

I'm afraid that the date of his birthday went right out of my mind.

2. [LIT] Go insane. [MET] Become intensely irritated, confused, etc.

Give one's mind to See **apply one's mind.**

Give a piece of one's mind Blame; express one's opinion candidly (and, usually, critically or adversely).

I shall give him a piece of my mind when I see him.

Have half a mind to Be strongly disposed to do something, but unlikely to do it.

In one's right mind Sane. Generally used negatively, an alternative being **out of one's mind.**

John couldn't have been in his right mind when he wrote this.

Know one's own mind Have clear and fixed opinions.

Mary always knows her own mind.

Make up one's mind Come to a decision.

Mind 1. Take into one's care or charge.

The mother asked the girl to mind the baby for an hour.

2. Show care about; be careful of.

Mind the wet paint.

3. Regret; object to.

I hope you won't mind my going out.

Mind one's eye [S] Be specially careful; cautious.

Mind one's own business Do not concern oneself in other people's affairs.

Mind one's P's and Q's [S] Be especially careful and exact in one's behaviour. [Or. of this idiom is doubtful, but one suggestion is that it arose from the custom in alehouses of marking up 'p' for pint and 'q' for quart in keeping customers' accounts.]

A mind to A liking or desire to.

I've a good mind to complain to the manufacturers.

Of one (*or* the same) mind Having the same opinions.

Most of the electors seemed to be of one mind.

One-track mind A mind, or personality, exclusively committed to one preoccupation (e.g. money, work, sex, etc.).

Out of one's mind See **in one's right mind.**

Presence of mind Mental alertness and an immediate response to an emergency.

Prey on one's mind Cause deep and prolonged mental distress.

Set one's mind on Wish to attain.

She's set her mind on learning Italian.

To my mind In my opinion. According to my judgment.

Mint **Mint of money** A very large sum of money. [Or. The Royal Mint is where English coins are made.]

Mischief **Make mischief** Intentionally cause discord and unhappiness.

Mistake **And (*or* make) no mistake!** An idiom used entirely for emphasis.

It will rain this afternoon, and no mistake.

There's no mistaking It is impossible to mistake.

Moment **At the moment** At present.

Half a moment (*abbrev.* **half a mo**) [S] A very short time.

In a moment In a short while.

Unguarded moment A moment in which one has forgotten to be careful in speech or action.

Money **Hush-money** Money paid to prevent a secret being revealed.

Money is no object The shortage of money is no hindrance.

Money's no object in film-making these days.

Money for jam (*or* old rope) [S] A profit made by little or no effort.

Pin-money Money supplied for minor pleasures and amusements. [Or. Pin-money was the term originally applied to money supplied to women to purchase the very elaborate and beautiful pins that jewellers were allowed to offer for sale on the first two days of the year.]

Pocket-money Small sums given to children, usually each week, for their personal expenditure.

Month **Month of Sundays** [S] A long and indefinite period.

I expect we shan't meet again for a month of Sundays.

Moon   **Moonshine** Unreal, fantastic and untrue statement, ideas, plans, etc.

Moon-struck Dazed, incapable of thought.

Morning   **Morning coffee** Coffee drunk halfway through the morning, i.e. about eleven o'clock.

Morning dress Official and formal clothing worn by men during the day (as opposed to evening dress), i.e. black coat with short 'tails', black waistcoat and dark grey trousers.

Morning tea Tea drunk in one's bedroom before dressing in the morning.

Most   **At the most; at most** At the highest; as the limit.

You'll get £5, at the most, for that bicycle.

For the most part In most circumstances; usually.

For the most part, we go away at weekends.

Mother   **Mother of pearl** The shining inner lining of oyster and similar shells, extensively used for ornamental purposes.

Mother-tongue The language spoken in one's native land.

Mount   **Mount up** Increase; accumulate.

I'm afraid our expenses are mounting up rather fast.

Mountain   **Mahomet and the mountain** Several expressions include these terms: Mahomet = person who can't get his own way; mountain = something inevitable, unavoidable, fixed.

Make a mountain out of a molehill Make much out of very little; greatly exaggerate.

Mouth   **By word of mouth** By speech; orally.

We received the news by word of mouth.

Down in the mouth Depressed; despondent.

Make one's mouth water Create pleasurable sense of anticipation.

Take the words out of someone's mouth Say what someone was about to say.

Move   **Get a move on** [S] Take immediate action; proceed at once.

We'd better get a move on if we are to reach Manchester tonight.

Make a move Go.

Move heaven and earth Make every possible effort; use every available means.

Joe is moving heaven and earth to come home for Christmas.

Move off Depart.

Move on Change one's position.

Mow   **Mow down** Cut, with wide sweeping strokes, as wheat, etc., is cut with a scythe. Gunfire is frequently said to 'mow down' advancing troops.

Muddle   **Muddle through** Achieve one's objectives without showing very much skill in doing so.

Muscle **Muscle in(to)** [S] [U.S.A.] Thrust one's way into, usually with some vigour and unpopularity.
We were having a sensible discussion till the landlord muscled in.

Must **It must needs be** It will inevitably be. [Old f.]
It must needs be some weeks before we receive a reply from Australia.
Needs must when the Devil drives If this is inevitable, I must accept it as such.

Muster **Pass muster** Be accepted as adequate.

Mustard **Keen as mustard** Very eager.

N

Nth **To the *n*th degree** To any extent, without number. [Or. *N* in mathematics stands for number, *any* number.]
I believe in him, and I'll support him to the nth degree.
N times Very many times.

Nail **Hard as nails** Very tough. (Applied to people.)
Hit the nail on the head See under *Hit*.
Nail in one's coffin Something that will shorten life—drink. anxiety, etc.—or destroy one's reputation.
Nail one's colours to the mast Publicly demonstrate one's allegiance. Refuse to surrender or modify one's opinions or principles. [Or. Naval. During a battle the colours, or flag, of a ship were in the past frequently nailed to the mast to make it impossible to lower them as a signal of surrender.]
On the nail [S] Promptly; immediately.
He pays his debts on the nail.

Namby-pamby Feeble; effeminate. Insipid. [Or. The seventeenth-century poet Ambrose (sneeringly nicknamed 'Namby' as a baby would pronounce it) Phillips.]

Nap **Catch napping** See under *Catch*.

Narrow **A narrow escape, majority,** *etc.* One which nearly did not occur.
I had a narrow escape from being run over by a bus this morning.
A narrow margin Very little (space, etc.).
John passed the examination by a narrow margin.
A narrow squeak [S] A success or escape only just attained.
We won the game, but it was a narrow squeak.

Nature **In the nature of things** Part of normal circumstances, routine, instinct, etc.
It's in the nature of things for children to behave in that way.

Near **Near by,** *or* **near at hand** Close; a short distance away.
Near the mark Nearly or approximately correct.

A near (*or* close) thing A success which was very nearly a failure.
I ran all the way and caught the train, but it was a near thing.

Necessity **Make a virtue of necessity** See under *Make.*

Necessity is the mother of invention New ways of doing things are usually contrived because of a pressing need.

Of necessity Unavoidably.

Under the necessity of Compelled; forced to. [Old f.]
I am under the necessity of selling my house.

Neck **Get it in the neck** [S] Be punished or reprimanded.

Neck and crop Entirely. [Or. The 'crop', or gorge, is the lower part of a bird's neck.]
The Cabinet was thrown out, neck and crop.

Neck and neck (*or* neck-to-neck) Side by side; level.
It was a neck and neck race.

Neck or nothing Desperate; risking everything. [Or. Racing. To win by the length of the horse's neck, or not at all.]

Negative **In the negative** No.

Neither **Neither here nor there** See under *Here.*

Nerves **Get on one's nerves** Irritate (usually by the repetition of some annoying action, usually slight).
George's continual sniffing gets on my nerves.

Have the nerve to Have the courage, or impertinence, to.

Nest **Feather one's nest** See under *Feather.*

Nest egg [LIT] An artificial egg left in the nest to encourage the hen to further laying. [MET] Money saved for one's old age or for some specific purpose in the future.

Never **Never mind** Do not trouble or concern yourself.

Never say die! Never give up hope of success.

Well I never! Expression of surprise.

New **New broom** A newcomer who intends to demonstrate his efficiency, ideas, etc. [Or. The proverb 'A new broom sweeps clean'.]

New-fangled A slightly contemptuous term applied to any new invention or method, usually of a minor type.

Next **Next door to** [LIT] In the adjoining house. [MET] Any form of nearness.
Her statements are next door to lying.

Next to nothing Practically nothing.

What(ever) next? Expression of surprise, literally suggesting 'What can occur subsequently which can possibly be more absurd, surprising, shocking, etc.?'

Nicety **To a nicety** Precisely; exactly.
The coat will fit you to a nicety.

Nick **In the nick of time** Just in time, at the right and vital moment. [Or.

The old custom of marking long sticks with 'nicks' or notches at intervals to indicate numbers.]

In the nick of time they were saved from drowning.

Nigger **The nigger in the woodpile** [S] The concealed object or aim; the hidden intention behind a statement or action. A person or circumstance creating trouble, difficulty, etc., in an otherwise favourable or happy situation.

Night **Have a good (*or* bad) night** Sleep well (or badly).

Overnight [LIT] The period between one day and the next. [MET] In a very brief time.

He became famous overnight.

Niminy-piminy Irritatingly affected and trivial.

Nine **Nine days' wonder** See under ***Wonder.***

Nines **Up to the nines** Magnificently; gorgeously. [Or. The Oriental regard for the number nine as indicative of the highest splendour and generostity, e.g. presenting a guest with nine camels, nine cases of jewels, etc.]

Here comes Pamela, dressed up to the nines.

Nip **Nip in the bud** End any project before it has a chance of maturing.

No **No one else** No other person.

No such thing An emphatic negative.

He said I had promised to go, but I told him I had done no such thing.

There's no accounting for taste Some people have very unexpected or odd likes and dislikes.

Nod **On the nod** Without objection.

The committee approved the whole plan on the nod.

Noise **Noise abroad** Cause to be widely known.

Nose **Cut off one's nose to spite one's face** Commit, through revenge or spite, some foolish action which injures oneself.

Follow one's nose Go straight forward.

Keep one's nose to the grindstone Make one work incessantly.

Lead by the nose See under ***Lead.***

Pay through the nose Pay far too much; pay extortionately.

You'll have to pay through the nose if you stay at that hotel.

Plain as the nose on one's face Very obvious.

Poke one's nose into Interfere with, pry or intrude into.

Put one's nose out of joint [S] Supersede; supplant in position, or affection.

I hope the new baby won't put young Peter's nose out of joint.

Turn up one's nose at Sneer at; scorn.

Jane turns up her nose at a seat in the gallery nowadays.

Under one's nose A near and obvious place.

The cat stole the fish from under my nose.

Not **Not in the least; not a bit** Not to any degree whatever.

I was not in the least afraid.

Not so No; a general negative.

Note **Take note (of)** Pay attention (to).

Nothing **Can make nothing of** Cannot understand.

Have nothing to do with Not be concerned with.

Nothing to choose between them; nothing in it Practically equal.

Both brothers are clever; there is nothing to choose between them.

Nothing for it No option; no other choice.

If I fail to get this job, there'll be nothing for it but to emigrate.

Nothing like as (so) good as In no way as good as.

Nothing more nor less; nothing short of Completely; absolutely.

The film was nothing more nor less than a disaster.

There's nothing to it It is easy.

Notice **At short notice** At the end of an unexpectedly short period.

We have to leave for America at short notice.

Now **Just now** Almost, but not quite at the present time.

George was here just now.

Now or never The unique opportunity.

Null **Null and void** Non-existent and consequently non-effective. [Or. Legal.]

Almost every new law makes some old one null and void.

Number **Number one** [S] Oneself.

He's too much concerned with number one to have much concern for other people.

Nut **A hard nut to crack** A difficult problem or person to deal with, or matter to decide.

Be nuts on [S] Passionately interested in.

Off one's nut [S] Crazy; mad.

Nutshell **In a nutshell** Stated very briefly.

This book will explain the whole problem in a nutshell.

O

Oar **Put in one's oar** Intervene; interfere.

I am settling the matter—you need not put your oar in.

Rest on one's oars Cease work for a time.

Oats **Sow one's wild oats** Commit the usual follies of youth.

Obligations **Discharge one's obligations** Repay what is due.

Under an obligation Compelled, either by law or by one's sense of duty.

Please don't feel under any obligation to come.

Oblivion **Sink into oblivion** Become completely forgotten.

Occasion **Have occasion** Have need, reason, justification.
If the occasion arises If there is reason, opportunity.
On occasion; as occasion arose Sometimes; when necessary.
Rise to the occasion Show the required qualities.
Take the occasion to Seize the opportunity to.

Occupy **Occupy one's time, energies, talents,** *etc.* 'Occupy' here used in the sense of 'employ', 'use'.

Occur **It occurs to me; it has just occurred to me** The idea has come to me; I have just realized.
It occurs to me that if we go to the concert tonight we won't get back in time.

Odds The **'odds'** represent the terms upon which one may bet upon a particular horse. **'Long odds'** mean that the chances of its winning are considered slight, and the phrase is used to indicate improbability.
It's long odds against Arthur coming home from Australia this year.
'The odds', on the other hand, may imply the reverse, a probable event.
The odds are that Jim will be able to come.
What's the odds! What does it matter!
Odds and ends Small, unclassified objects; what remains when more important things have been dealt with.

Odour **In bad odour** Unpopular; regarded unfavourably.
I'm in rather bad odour with my bank manager just now.

Off **Badly off** Poor.
Be off 1. An imperative order to depart.
2. Depart.
I must be off to catch my train.
3. Be unfit to eat or drink; stale. (Also **go off.**)
Don't eat that meat—it was bought last week, and must be (have gone) off by now.
4. Be unavailable; off the menu, all supplies being exhausted.
I'm afraid apple-pie is off.
Off colour Slightly unwell.
Off one's food Disinclined to eat; without an appetite.
Off one's guard In a state of relaxation and unawareness.
Off one's hands Disposed of.
I wish we could get that old wardrobe off our hands.
Off-hand 1. Without preparation; impromptu.
I can't give you the figures off-hand; I shall have to look them up.
2. Casual and irresponsible.
I dislike the young man's off-hand manner.
Off-putting [S] Discouraging; repelling.
The length of the drive is rather off-putting.

O

Offshoot A branching-off; a lesser concern or business which has developed from the original one.
Simpson's Cleaning Agency is an offshoot of Simpson's Stores Limited.
Off the beaten track In a remote place.
Off the map [S] Vanished. Not existing.
Off the point Irrelevant.
Well off 1. Rich.
2. In comfortable and satisfactory circumstances.
You shouldn't grumble about the house; you don't realize when you're well off.
On the off chance In the hope (usually faint).
I called on the off chance that Tom would be in.

Oil **Burn the midnight oil** Sit up late at night to work or study.
Oil and water Applied to two dissimilar or irreconcilable things, people, points of view, etc.
Pour oil on troubled waters Speak or act soothingly and tactfully in order to bring a quarrel to an end. [Or. It is stated that a young eighth-century priest was given by his bishop a bottle of oil to pour on the sea if it became rough, and actually calmed the waves by this means. It has been proved that oil sprayed upon the surface does help to calm a high sea.]

Ointment **Fly in the ointment** See under *Fly.*
Old **Of old** Belonging to the distant past.
An old hand Person very skilled or experienced at something.
Old hat Out of date. Well known.
These plans are very old hat.
Old head See *Head.*
Old as the hills Very old indeed. Frequently applied to an out-of-date object.
I can't wear that hat—it's as old as the hills.
Old maid An elderly spinster, or one with fixed habits. [Old f.]
Old stager Similar to **old hand.**
Olive **Olive-branch** A gesture of peace. [Or. The olive-branch was, in the past, a symbol of peace.]
After a long war, the exhausted enemy held out the olive-branch.
On **On and off** Intermittently; occasionally.
We visit them on and off.
Once **At once** Immediately.
Once and for all Finally.
She told him, once and for all, that she would not marry him.
Once bitten, twice shy Pain, loss, etc., teaches caution.
Once in a blue moon Very rarely. Similar to **a month of Sundays.**
Once in a way Occasionally, but not often.
Once in a way we visit the theatre.

Once-over [S] A brief examination.
I'll give the car the once-over before we start.
Once upon a time At some period in the past.

One **One and all** Everyone.
The entertainment was greatly enjoyed by one and all.
One-sided (agreement, treaty, *etc.*) Made from one point of view
and for the advantage of one party only. (Present-day official
equivalent, 'unilateral'.)
*We could not agree to such a one-sided arrangement with a European
power.*
Have one over the eight [S] Become intoxicated.

Open **Open and above-board** Entirely frank and candid.
He was entirely open and above-board in his statements.
Open (a discussion, proceedings) Begin.
Open the door to Lead to; encourage; result in.
*These innumerable minor regulations open the door to innumerable
minor crimes.*
Open secret A fact supposed to be secret, but known to everybody;
no secret at all.
Open sesame Any simple and miraculous method of solving a
problem. [Or. From the story of 'Ali Baba and the Forty Thieves',
in which a cave containing immense treasure could be entered only
by the utterance of those words.]
*The Chancellor thinks that taxing the rich is the open sesame to universal
prosperity.*
With open arms Enthusiastically. Heartily.
The hotel welcomed us with open arms.

Opinion **Be of the opinion** Believe; consider.
Golden opinions Very great admiration; general praise.
*The new President has already won golden opinions, even from his
political opponents.*
Matter of opinion Subject for dispute. Opposite of **matter of fact.**
Pass an opinion Express an opinion or view.
I don't know enough about paintings to pass an opinion.

Opportunity **Take (*or* seize) the opportunity** Make use of a particular moment.
*May I take this opportunity of expressing our gratitude for your
kindness.*

Opposition **Meet with opposition** Be opposed.
Any attempt to tax bachelors would meet with strong opposition.

Order **Order of the day** The current fashion.
Fifty years ago high, stiff collars were the order of the day for men.
In good order Fit for use.
In order 1. In succession; according to a pre-arranged plan.
The candidates will be interviewed in alphabetical order.

O

2. Tidy, neat.

Please see that this room is in order when the visitors arrive.

3. Officially correct.

You will be in order if you speak after the chairman.

On order Requested from the manufacturer but not yet supplied.

Our new cooker has now been on order for five weeks.

Out of order 1. The reverse of **in order** (2).

All these papers are out of order.

2. The reverse of **in order** (3).

You will be out of order if you interrupt the Chairman.

Take orders from Obey orders given by.

Take (holy) orders Become a clergyman.

Ordinary **Ordinary run of things** (*or* **course of events**) Events which may be expected to happen normally.

In the ordinary run of things I play tennis nearly every weekend.

Out of the ordinary Unusual; exceptional.

In our grandfathers' time it was quite out of the ordinary for a woman to go to college.

Other **On the other hand** On the contrary.

The other day Recently; not long ago.

The other day I met your brother.

Out **All out** Using all one's speed or effort.

Be out 1. Be mistaken in one's judgment.

We were out in thinking him unsociable.

2. Not at home.

I am sorry we were out when you called.

Flat out At full speed. Using all one's energies.

Have it out See *Have.*

Out and about Outside, in motion.

Out-and-out Thoroughly, completely.

The man is an out-and-out genius.

Out-at-elbows Shabby; wearing torn and ragged clothes.

Out for Engaged in seeking.

He's out for all the credit he can get.

Out of 1. From.

He did it out of kindness.

2. Without any (applied to something normally available).

The grocer was out of coffee.

See **out of stock.**

3. Having no share or part in.

He was feeling rather out of the fun.

Out of breath Breathless.

I reached the station completely out of breath.

Out of character Not typical.

His behaviour yesterday was very out of character.

Out of condition 1. As **out of sorts,** but applying particularly to animals. 2. Unfit for special exertion, because untrained.

Out of date Belonging to the past; unfashionable.

This guide-book is completely out of date.

Out of doors In the open air; exposed to the weather.

We'll go out of doors when the rain stops.

Out of joint Restless, uncomfortable, and generally unsatisfactory.

The political situation is out of joint.

Out of one's mind [LIT] Insane. [MET] Extremely foolish or rash.

Out of place See under *Place.*

Out of pocket See under *Pocket.*

Out of print Term applied to a book of which all copies are sold.

Out of sight Invisible.

Out of sorts See under *Sort.*

Out of the question See *Question.*

Out of stock Not available, owing to supplies being exhausted.

I am sorry, but that brand of cigarettes is out of stock.

Similar to out of (?)

Out of training Similar to **out of condition** (2).

Out of one's way 1. On a detour.

It's a little out of my way, but I'll drive you there.

2. To some trouble, inconvenience.

The neighbours went out of their way to be helpful when we first came to live here.

Out of the way 1. Unusual.

It was an out-of-the-way request.

2. Remote.

The house was in an out-of-the-way village.

3. In a position which causes no obstruction.

Please put the cushion out of your way.

Out of the wood Freed from one's trouble and difficulties.

He has worked hard to make up for lost time, and is now out of the wood.

Out of work Without employment.

Over **All over** See under *All.*

Over and above In addition to; extra to.

I've been given a week's holiday over and above my normal entitlement.

Over and over (again) Repeatedly; many times.

Over one's head Beyond one's comprehension.

Overshoot; overshoot the mark Go too far; exceed; exaggerate.

He overshot the mark when he said there were a thousand people present.

Owe **Owe it to oneself** Consider it necessary to one's self-respect or happiness.

I owe it to myself to explain how it all happened.
Owing to Because of.

Own **Get one's own back on** Revenge oneself on.

Hold one's own Maintain one's position.

He can hold his own in most sorts of argument.

On one's own [S] By oneself; without companionship or assistance.

I've been living on my own since February.

Off one's own bat On one's own initiative or responsibility.

Own up Make a confession.

P

Pace **Keep pace** Keep level; go at the same speed [LIT and MET].

I can't keep pace with your plans.

Put through one's paces Test a person in order to discover his knowledge or ability. [Or. Horsemanship. A purchaser of a horse 'puts it through' its various 'paces'—walking, trotting, etc.]

Pack **Packed like sardines** Crowded as closely together as sardines are in the tins in which they are sold.

We were packed like sardines in the train.

Pack of lies Many lies.

Pack up Finish. Go out of action.

Send packing Dismiss peremptorily.

Paddle **Paddle one's own canoe** [S] Manage one's own affairs without help or interference.

Pains **Be at (or take) pains to** Take trouble to.

I was at great pains to make the occasion a success.

Get for one's pains Receive for one's exertions or trouble.

All he got for his pains was ingratitude.

Paint **Not so black as is painted** Not as bad as represented.

Paint the town red Have a specially enjoyable night-out.

Palm **Palm off on** Substitute something of inferior value. (A conjurer 'palms', or conceals in the palm of his hand, a card or other small object he does not wish the audience to see.)

I asked for butter, but they palmed off margarine on me.

Palmy days Times of great prosperity.

In the palmy days of gold-mining, many rough and uneducated men became millionaires.

Pan **Pan out** [S] Succeed. Work out; finally result. [Or. Mining.]

Out investment didn't pan out satisfactorily.

Paper **Commit to paper** Write, with the special object of keeping a record.

On paper By report. Hypothetically. To judge from what is written down.
On paper, these policies seem very sound.

Par **Below par** Below the expected standard.
He's feeling a little below par this morning.
On a par with On the same terms as.
That remark is on a par with his normal behaviour.
Up to par At the expected level.

Parallel **Draw a parallel** Compare to indicate similarity.
We can draw a parallel between the fate of the Kaiser and that of Napoleon.

Parcel **Parcel out** Divide and distribute in portions.

Pare **Pare down** Reduce by degrees. ('Pare' is to peel or shave off the surface.)
We have pared down expenses to the limit.

Parlour **Parlour tricks** Minor social accomplishments—amateur singing, playing, etc. Now used ironically to mean minor roguery or incompetence.

Parrot-fashion As a parrot talks; from memory, with little or no regard to the real meaning.

Part **For my part** As far as I am concerned.
For the most part In most cases.
Part and parcel An essential and necessary part.
Take in good part Not be offended at.
Take the part of Support. Back up.

Parthian **A Parthian shot** A parting retort. (The Parthians used to fire arrows as they galloped away from their enemies.)

Partial **Be partial to** Like; enjoy.
I am rather partial to duck and green peas.

Pass **Make a pass** Make a threatening movement or gesture towards.
The dog, as he rushed away, made a pass at the man.
Pass *(at cards)* Refrain from playing at that particular moment of the game.
Pass away, over Formal and rather old-f. phrase for 'die'.
Pass by Go past.
I passed by your house yesterday.
Pass one's comprehension Be more than one can understand.
Pass judgment Express a final and definite opinion.
It is difficult to pass judgment on the affair when we know so little about what happened.
Pass muster Be regarded as up to the necessary standards; just good enough. [Or. Military. Soldiers are 'mustered' and examined for correctness of uniform, etc., before going on parade.]

Your clothes aren't smart, but they'll pass muster in a crowd.

Pass off 1. Ignore; treat as if it were unimportant.

She hated his familiarity, but passed it off as a joke.

2. Intentionally convey a false impression concerning some person or object.

The boy was only twelve, but liked to pass himself off as much older.

3. Disappear by degrees or stages.

There was a thick mist at first, but it soon began to pass off.

Pass out Faint.

Pass over 1. Ignore.

I shall pass over the first paragraph.

2 Forgive; excuse.

His father passed over the boy's foolishness.

A pretty pass (*or* mess)! A fine state of affairs! (Always used ironically.)

Things have come to a pretty pass!

Pass the time Spend or use up time.

Pass the time of day Spend a few moments in conversation.

Pass a remark Utter; make a remark.

George passed a remark about the weather, but his wife was not listening to him.

Passing **Passing rich, fair,** *etc.* More than. Surpassing. [Old. f.]

Past **Past-master** An expert; a highly experienced person. [Or. A past-master in any guild or Association is one who has in the past achieved the position of Chairman or Master.]

My husband is a past-master in the art of growing strawberries.

Patch **A good (*or* bad) patch** A period of good (or poor) luck, success, etc.

The school's football is going through a bad patch this season.

Not a patch on Not worthy to be compared with.

Patch up (a quarrel, *etc.***)** Repair. Set to rights (usually hastily or temporarily).

Patience **Out of patience; having lost patience** With no patience left; exasperated.

She became completely out of patience with the children.

Pave **Pave the way to** Lead to; result in.

This treaty will pave the way to peace.

Paved with good intentions Well-meaning. [Or. Old saying, 'The road to hell is paved . . .']

Pay **The devil to pay** [S] Tremendous trouble; a general upheaval; serious consequences.

If you don't post that letter tonight, there'll be the devil to pay.

Pay attention Listen and observe intently and carefully.

Pay attention to your teachers, and don't waste your time.

Pay back 1. Return what has been lent or given. 2. Punish, in return for some injury.

Pay off 1. Pay the whole of what is due.

The man's paid off his son's debts.

2. Naval. A ship is said to be 'paid off' when she returns to port and discharges her crew.

Pay out 1. [Nautical.] Slacken or loosen a rope. 2. Pay; disburse money.

We've paid out nearly £50 this month.

Pay the piper Pay whatever the cost, financial or otherwise, may be. Be in a position of power because one has the authority (especially financial) to demand obedience. [Or. Abbrev. of 'He who pays the piper should call the tune'.]

Pay one's way Pay expenses out of one's income.

I doubt if that shop will ever pay its way.

Pay up Pay what one owes.

Put paid to Finished. Settled.

A broken leg put paid to his walking holiday.

Peace **Hold one's peace** Remain silent.

Keep the peace Refrain from quarrelling, or causing any other disturbance.

Pipe of peace American Indians celebrated the end of warfare between two tribes or two individuals by smoking a pipe as a symbol of their being at peace with their recent enemies. See **bury the hatchet.**

Pearl **Cast pearls before swine** Present or introduce something of value or beauty to those who are entirely unable to appreciate it. [Or. Biblical.]

Pearls of wisdom Wise sayings, advice, etc.

Peg **Peg away** [S] Continue steadily; persevere.

If you peg away long enough, you'll be able to learn any language.

Peg down Confine to a certain level.

No government has yet succeeded in pegging down prices.

Peg out [S] Die.

Take someone down a peg (or two) Humble him.

Penalty **Pay the penalty** Suffer what is due and inevitable as the result of an action.

If you smoke when you're young, you'll pay the penalty in your old age.

Penny **In for a penny, in for a pound** (Frequently abbrev. to 'In for a penny'.) Being slightly involved, one may as well be involved still further.

Penny-dreadful An old-f. term for the cheap and sensational magazines of the last century.

A penny for your thoughts A facetious offer, made to arouse someone who has been silent and withdrawn.

Penny wise Careful in saving small sums, but wasteful in large matters. [Or. Abbrev. of the proverb 'Penny wise and pound foolish'.]

A pretty penny A large sum of money.

That house must have cost a pretty penny.

Take care of the pennies (and the pounds will take care of themselves) Care of small matters will reduce problems with large ones.

Turn (or earn) an honest penny Earn money (usually by extra work, or unusual methods).

Period **At no period** At no time; never in the past.

At no period have so many people been interested in politics.

Person **In person** Personally.

The Queen will open Parliament in person.

Perspective **In perspective** Viewed, or thought of as from a distance.

Viewed in perspective, the quarrel seemed to have been very trivial.

Pick **Pick and choose** Select carefully.

You haven't time to pick and choose.

Pick holes in Criticize. Show the faults in.

Pick-me-up A quick restorative, after weakness or fatigue.

Pick on Select from others, for special treatment.

It's a pity he had to pick on next weekend to go away.

Pick a quarrel Deliberately begin a quarrel.

That dog will pick a quarrel with any other one he meets.

Pick up Acquire by chance; obtain casually.

I picked up that old oak table in a Welsh village.

Pick one's way (or one's steps) Walk deliberately and carefully among difficulties and obstructions.

We had to pick our way through the mud.

Pick one's words Select carefully what one says.

Piece **All of a piece** All part of, or connected with.

His latest good deed is all of a piece with the rest of his character.

A piece of one's mind One's candid opinion. A rebuke.

Go to pieces Deteriorate completely. Opposite, **pick up the pieces**: correct a damaged situation.

Since his wife's death, he has gone to pieces.

Pull to pieces Analyse; examine closely with the object of finding fault. Similar to **pick holes in.**

Pig **Pig in a poke** Something acquired without knowing its value, and without previous examination or knowledge. Usually used with the verb 'buy'. (The word 'poke' here means a pocket or small sack.)

P

Pigs might fly Wonders might occur. (Used ironically.)

Pile **Make one's pile** [S] Make as much money as one needs. [Or. Gold-mining. A man's 'pile' was the amount of gold he accumulated.]

Pile it on Exaggerate.

Pile on the agony Increase or intensify distress or discomfort.
It's a good film, but it does rather pile on the agony.

Pill **A bitter pill** An unpleasant, humiliating or intensely disappointing fact.
The news of his failure was a bitter pill to swallow.

Gild (*or* sugar) the pill Do something to make an unpleasant task, statement, piece of news, etc., less so.

Pin **Pin down** 1. [LIT] Fix; fasten firmly.
2. [MET] Compel to deal with some particular fact or substantiate a statement.
The plumber promised to come, but it was difficult to pin him down to an exact time.

Pin one's faith on Believe in completely; trust absolutely.

Pin one's hopes on Attach one's hopes to; concentrate one's hopes on.
We are pinning our hopes on having a longer holiday next year.

Pin-money See *Money.*

Pins and needles The tingling sensation felt in a limb which has become stiff and numb.

Pinch **At a pinch** In an emergency; if absolutely necessary.
We've a good many guests, but at a pinch one or two can sleep in the lounge.

Where the shoe pinches Where the difficulty lies.

Pink **In the pink** In the best of health.

Pink of perfection Absolutely and completely perfect. [Old. f.]

Pipe **Pipe down** Talk less.

Pipe up Speak. Interrupt.

Put that in your pipe and smoke it [S] A facetious form of defiance, meaning 'Just you think about *that*!'

Piping **Piping hot** [LIT] Hot as water that is 'piping' or singing in a kettle just before reaching boiling-point.

Pit **Pit against** Place in competition against; compel to fight.

Pitch **Pitch into** [S] 1. Attack violently, either with one's fists or tongue.
2. Begin with energy one's work or a meal.
Here's your supper—pitch into it.

Pitch one's tent [LIT] To 'pitch' a tent is to erect it, usually for a limited period. [MET] To settle anywhere.

Pity **What a pity (*or* shame)!** A general expression of regret.
What a pity that you won't be able to come to the party.

Take pity on Feel sympathy for.

Place **In the first place** Firstly, at the beginning.
In the first place, I must explain that I can't speak English very well.
(Similarly second, third, etc., place.)
In place of Instead of.
Out of place Unsuitable; in the wrong surroundings.
Take place Happen; occur.
The wedding will take place next week.

Plain **Plain dealing** Honest and open business methods.
Plain as a pikestaff Obvious; unmistakable. [Or. The pikestaff or long stick carried by pilgrims and on which was fastened a statement of their devotion to Christ.]
Plain sailing A course of action without any difficulties.
Plain speaking Frank and honest speaking.

Play **Child's play** Extremely easy to perform or solve.
This crossword is mere child's play.
Play one's cards well (badly, *etc.*) Make good (bad) use of one's opportunities.
Play the devil (*or* deuce) [S] Ruin or seriously injure.
My indigestion plays the devil with my concentration.
Play down Reduce the importance of.
Play by ear 1. Perform on a musical instrument without having been taught or without using music.
2. [S] Follow a course of action without any advance planning.
Play false Betray; cheat.
That was the telephone ringing, unless my ears play me false.
See **double-cross** and **double-dealing**.
Play fast and loose Behave recklessly without consideration for others, and regardless of one's promises.
Play to the gallery Try to achieve popularity; degrade one's abilities in order to obtain popularity. [Or. Theatrical.]
Play the game [LIT] Observe the rules. [MET] Behave honourably.
Play into the hands of Behave so that one's actions are an advantage to someone else, usually an opponent or enemy.
By neglecting his work, he played into the hands of the manager, who had always wanted an excuse to dismiss him.
Play off Use two opponents, one against the other, to one's own advantage.
Play second fiddle Be in a subordinate position. (The first fiddle is the most important member of an orchestra.)
I refuse to play second fiddle to a man who knows less about this than I do.
Play truant Remain away from school.
Play up [S] 1. Support; follow the example set. [Old f.]
2. Cause trouble.

My car's playing me up again.
Play upon Take advantage of.
Play upon words A pun; a verbal joke.
Play with fire Act dangerously.
Played out Exhausted; finished; out of date.
That old sewing-machine is completely played out.

Plead **Plead the cause** Speak favourably for; help by supporting.
I am here to plead the cause of many unfortunate people who cannot plead for themselves.

Please **Please oneself** Do as one desires.
I am going home—you can please yourself.
Pleased as Punch [S] Extremely pleased.

Pledge **Pledge oneself** Make a solemn and formal promise.
Sign (take) the pledge Formally undertake never to drink intoxicants—wine, spirits, beer, etc.

Plentiful **Plentiful as blackberries** Extremely plentiful. (Blackberries grow in large numbers in the English hedges in autumn.)

Plight **Plight one's troth** Make a formal promise to marry. [Or. Troth = truth.] [Old f.]

Plot **The plot thickens** The affair becomes more complicated and exciting.

Plough **Plough back** Reinvest (e.g. profits in a business) in order to increase further.

Pluck **Pluck up courage** Acquire confidence and conquer fear.
She plucked up courage, and confronted the shop-keeper.

Plume **Plume oneself** Take pride in. [Old f.]

Pocket **In one's pocket** In one's control.
Out of pocket Poorer financially.
I am ten pounds out of pocket as a result of the arrangement.
Out-of-pocket expenses Expenses incurred and paid in transacting business.
I had to travel to Sheffield, and the out-of-pocket expenses came to over £5.
Pocket an insult Submit to an insult without protest; ignore it.
Pocket one's pride Become humble under compulsion or necessity.
I pocketed my pride and asked my uncle to lend me the fare home.

Point **Carry one's point** See *Carry*.
A case in point An example.
Many politicians owe much to their wives; Gladstone was a case in point.
Come to the point Arrive at the crux, or what is really important.
We talked for an hour before I had enough courage to come to the point and ask her to marry me.
Culminating point Climax.

The culminating point of the opera is the magnificent duet in the second act.

Make a point Contribute something to an argument.

I was able to make my point before the discussion ended.

Make a point of Take special care and trouble about.

She always made a point of warming her husband's slippers.

A moot point A point or detail which is unsettled and open to discussion or argument.

The precise centre of England is a moot point.

Not to put too fine a point on it To speak bluntly.

On the point of On the verge of.

The point The object.

The point of these discussions is that they enable the ministers concerned to get a clear idea of what is happening.

Point blank Direct; without any qualification. [Or. Gunnery. Fr. *point-blanc*—the white centre of the official target.]

He denied point-blank that he had ever entered the house.

Point a moral Emphasize some moral truth.

Napoleon's death points a moral to those who would sacrifice everything for power.

Point out Indicate; remind a person.

May I point out that you have not yet paid your bill.

Possession is nine points of the law If one possesses something, one is almost entitled to it. (Nine points = nine-tenths = virtually the whole.)

A sore point A subject upon which one is sensitive.

The fact that he is only five feet tall is a sore point with him.

Stretch a point Concede a certain amount.

The landlord will stretch a point, and let us stay another week.

Strong point Distinctive characteristic; special skill.

Golf is not my strong point.

To the point Directly relevant. Relevantly.

He spoke bluntly and to the point.

Point of view Personal opinion or aspect.

From the smokers' point of view the tobacco tax is too high.

A weak point A particular weakness.

Pole **Pole to pole** i.e. From the North to the South Pole. All over the world.

You can hear English spoken from pole to pole.

Poles apart A very great distance apart.

The management and the trade union are poles apart on the matter of working conditions.

Up the pole [S] In a difficulty.

Polish **Polish off** Finish quickly.

I can polish off the job in five minutes.
Polish up Improve. Smarten.

Possession **In possession of** Possessing; having.
The thief was in possession of a large quantity of stolen property.
See *Point.*

Post **At one's post** At one's appointed place, or official position.
The sentry was found sleeping at his post.
Left at the post Hopelessly beaten in competition. [Or. Racing, the 'post' being the starting-post, the point at which a race begins.]
Post-haste Very quickly.

Pot **Go to pot** [S] Become totally ruined. [Or. The 'pot' into which waste metal is put to be melted down.]
If you don't attend to your garden, it will go to pot.
Keep the pot boiling [S] Enable any kind of enterprise, etc., to remain in an active condition.
Pot-boiler Any literary or artistic work turned out merely to provide money for necessities.
The pot calling the kettle black One person accusing another of faults of which he is himself guilty.
A pot shot A shot fired deliberately at some stationary object.
Take pot luck See *Luck.*

Pound **Pound away** [LIT] Strike heavily and repeatedly. [MET] Work vigorously.
If you pound away at the job, you'll have finished before dark.
Pound of flesh Full and complete payment, regardless of circumstances. (Usually jocular.) [Or. Shakespeare's comedy *The Merchant of Venice*, in which Shylock, the moneylender, claims a pound of flesh rashly promised by a man who cannot pay his debts.]

Power **More (*or* all) power to your elbow!** Good luck to your efforts.
The powers that be Those in command; the authorities.
If you want to go to the races, you'll have to ask the powers that be.

Pray **Past praying for** Impossible to alter, to repair or to improve.
This old suit is past praying for.

Preparation **In course of preparation** Being prepared.
The visitors found a magnificent dinner in course of preparation.

Present **At present** At the present time; now.
At present we are living in Beckenham.

Press **Be pressed for** Have scarcely enough.
Press forward *or* on 1. [LIT] Push in a forward direction.
The crowd pressed forward to see his arrival.
2. [MET] Hasten.
I want you to press on with that work.

Go to press, i.e. the printing-press. Usually applied to a periodical, or to a book.

'The Weekly Gazette' goes to press on Thursday.

Pretty **Pretty good, active,** *etc.* 'Pretty' here is used in the sense of fairly, moderately, comparatively.

He is in pretty good health, considering his age.

Pretty well (or nearly) Almost.

Father will be coming soon—he has pretty well finished.

A pretty pass (or mess) See *Pass.*

Prevail **Prevail upon** Persuade.

Prey **A prey to** Suffering from.

She has been a prey to melancholy ever since her husband died.

Prick **Prick up one's ears** Become suddenly alert and attentive (as an animal raises its ears at hearing an unfamiliar sound).

Pride **Pride of place** Exalted position.

Put one's pride in one's pocket Same as **pocket one's pride.** See *Pocket.*

Take pride in Derive satisfaction from. Be proud or careful of.

Primrose **The primrose path** The pleasant, easy-going, unthinking way of living. [Or. Shakespeare's *Hamlet*, 'The primrose path of dalliance'.]

He has always followed the primrose path, and his family suffer for it.

Prison **Commit to prison** Formally order to be sent to prison.

Probability **In all probability (or likelihood)** Very probably; very likely.

Progress **In progress** Being done or undertaken.

Repairs to many of the houses were in progress.

Proof **Proof against** Able to resist.

This coat is proof against the severest weather.

Proof positive Definite proof.

The proof of the pudding is in the eating The value or wisdom of any action can only be discovered by actual experience. [Or. Proverb.]

Put (or bring) to the proof Test.

I think the plan will work, but let us put it to the proof.

Proportion **Out of all proportion** Far more than is deserved.

The cost is out of all proportion to the benefits we should get.

Prospect **In prospect** Being considered.

I have a much better job in prospect.

Pull **Pull a (long) face** Express disagreement, disgust, distaste.

Pull off [S] Succeed in completing.

I've managed to pull off a first-class bargain.

Pull one's leg Tease.

Pull strings Use private and personal influence.

Pull together Work together unitedly. [Or. The game of 'tug-of-war' in which each 'side', pulling at opposite ends of a rope, tries to drag the other side across the line between them.]

If we pull together, success is certain.

Pull one's punches [LIT] Fail to give the fullest force to one's blows (in boxing.) [MET] Speak (or act) gently. (Usually used in negative.)

Pull one's weight Use all one's efforts in support.

Pull oneself together Make an effort to regain one's normal mental state.

Pull through Survive.

Pull up 1. Noun. A stopping-place where drivers, etc., may stop for rest, food, etc. 2. Verb. Halt; stop.

The coach will pull up at Kingston.

Pull up short Stop abruptly, and before one intended.

Purpose **On purpose; purposely** Intentionally.

To the purpose Direct to the subject, practically and sensibly.

John never wastes time; he speaks plainly and to the purpose.

To no purpose Uselessly; without success. See *Serve.*

We begged him not to go out in the storm, but to no purpose.

To some (or little) purpose With some (or little) result.

Put **Put about** 1. Worried; anxious. [Old f.]

2. Nautical. Turn in the opposite direction.

The ship put about and returned to port.

3. Circulate; make publicly known.

It was put about that the Cabinet was in disagreement.

Put across [S] Successfully narrate, convince or influence.

He is a good teacher, who puts his subject across very well.

Put all one's eggs in one basket See *Basket.*

Put in an appearance Arrive and be present.

I am glad you were able to put in an appearance at the meeting.

Put it on Pretend. Feign or exaggerate an emotion, etc.

He says he's unwell, but I think he's putting it on.

Put one's back up [S] See under *Back.*

Put by Save, usually for a special purpose.

I've managed to put by £10 for the holiday.

Put to death Execute; kill.

Put down 1. Cease to hold.

Please put the shopping-bag down on the table.

2. Suppress.

The General put down the rebellion in six weeks.

3. Store for future use (wine, etc.)

We've put down two dozen bottles of port.

4. Write; record.

Please put down the following facts.

5. (Of animals.) Painlessly kill.

The dog was very old and we had him put down.

6. Ascribe. Attribute.

I put his irritability down to his ill-health.

Put to flight Compel to run away.

Put one's best foot (*or* leg) foremost See *Foot*.

Put one's foot down Act firmly, decisively.

Put one's foot in it Behave tactlessly.

Be put in (*or* into) force Same as **come into force**, under *Force*.

Put one's nose out of joint [S] See *Nose*.

Put off 1. Delay. Postpone. Evade.

Never put off till tomorrow what you can do today.

2. Repelled. Discouraged.

I meant to go, but was rather put off by the snow.

Put on airs; put on side Try to impress people by one's superiority.

Put on the screw (*or* screws) [S] Compel a person by pressure (as a screw increases pressure) to do what is desired.

Put on steam Make a special effort to progress.

Put out 1. Extinguish.

He put out the light.

2. Remove from a house or other building; eject.

He put out the cat.

3. Annoy; perturb. Inconvenience.

The old lady seemed put out.

4. Dislocate. Strain.

I put my back out by moving the piano.

Put over Communicate.

Put oneself out Take extra trouble.

We always put ourselves out to please grandfather.

Put a spoke in one's wheel Thwart one's intentions, plans, etc.

Put a stop (*or* an end) to Terminate; end.

The Government ought to put a stop to official waste.

Put to it; hard put to it Tested; confronted with difficulties. Pressed.

He was hard put to it to decide whether to stay in England or go abroad.

Put two and two together (and make four) Deduce from obvious facts.

Putting two and two together, he realized that the firm would soon be bankrupt.

Put up 1. Receive as a temporary guest; provide with a bed.

We can easily put you up for the night.

2. Provide for a definite purpose, usually an investment.

I'd like to acquire the business, if my uncle will put up the money.
Put up at Reside; live at temporarily.
We put up at my brother's when we go to Oxford.
Put up with Endure.
I can't put up with this toothache any longer.
A put-up affair A previously arranged affair; a plot.
The two men appeared to be quarrelling, but I soon realized that it was a put-up affair, and not genuine.
Put upon Impose upon.
Mary is so good-natured that her friends constantly put upon her.
Put the wind up [S] Frighten.
Put in a (good) word Speak in favour of; recommend.

Q

Qualms **Have qualms** Have doubts; feel uneasy.
I had qualms about letting the child go out so late.
Quarter **In every quarter; in all quarters** Everywhere; in every direction.
Queer **In Queer Street** In an uncertain position financially; in difficulties.
[Or. The custom of writing *Quere* (enquire) against a person's account when it was considered advisable to make enquiries before trusting him.]
They say the company is in Queer Street.
Queer card (*or* customer) An eccentric and unusual type of person.
The old man was civil, but obviously a queer card.
Queer one's pitch Spoil one's chances beforehand, usually by secret dealings.
I'd rather speak to him myself: if anyone else sees him first, it may queer my pitch.
Quest **In quest of** In search of; to search for.
Question **Begging the question** (Usually) Avoiding an argument or decision by bringing forward some immaterial point. But see *Beg*.
Beyond all question Without doubt; certain.
Burning question A matter requiring an immediate examination and prompt action.
The treatment of young criminals is a burning question.
Call in question Express doubt about; challenge.
I call in question the morality of abortion.
In question Mentioned; referred to.
The person in question has a very good reputation.
Open question Not certain; debatable.
The advantage of being a rich man's son is an open question.
Out of the question Utterly impossible.

To build a tunnel from England to America is out of the question.
Vexed question A problem or question very difficult to decide.
The best age for marriage is a vexed question.
Without question Without doubt.

Quick **To the quick** See **cut to the quick.**

Quits **Be quits (with)** Be equal (with). Be revenged (on).
See **cry quits.**

R

R **The three R's** Reading, (w)riting and (a)rithmetic—the first
elements of education.

Rack **On the rack** In a condition of acute mental tension; intensely
anxious. [Or. Rack = old instrument of torture.]
I was on the rack until I received the doctor's report.
Rack one's brains Similar to **cudgel one's brains**
(Go to) rack and ruin Complete decay; destruction.
His health has gone to rack and ruin.

Racket **Stand the racket** [S] Face the consequences; pay the cost.

Rage **All the rage** Immensely popular or fashionable.

Rag-tag **Rag-tag and bobtail** Disreputable people.

Rails **Off the rails** Disorganized. Confused. (Usually applied to
behaviour of people under strain.)

Rain **It never rains but it pours** Events, fortunate or unfortunate, rarely
occur singly.
Rain cats and dogs Rain violently.
(Come) rain or shine [LIT] Whatever the weather. [MET]
Whatever happens.
A rainy day Time of need, especially financial.

Raise **Raise Cain** [S] Create a tremendous noise or disturbance.
His wife will raise Cain when she discovers how much he has spent.
Raise one's eyebrows Express surprise.
Raise one's glass to Toast the health of.
Raise one's voice 1. Speak.
No one raised his voice in opposition.
2. Speak loudly, usually in anger.
Please don't raise your voice to me.

Rake **Rake-off** [S] Commission; an agent's share after a purchase has
been completed; profit.
Rake up Recall unnecessarily from the past.
Why rake up a scandal that happened so long ago?

Random **At random** By chance; without deliberate selection.
The explorer chose ten men at random to accompany him.

Range **Within range** Within an effective distance or area. Near enough to be heard, seen, controlled, etc.
The subject should be within range of his knowledge.

Rank **Rank and file** The ordinary working members of an organization. [Or. Military. Technically, soldiers under the rank of lance-sergeant comprise the rank and file.]
The payment offered to the rank and file is extremely poor.
Rise from the ranks See *Rise.*

Rap **Not worth a rap** Worthless. [Or. A 'rap' was a halfpenny issued in Ireland in 1721 and actually worth about half a farthing.]
Rap on the knuckles A sharp reproof.
The bank-clerk received a rap on the knuckles for his carelessness.
Rap out Speak sharply; snap.
The captain rapped out an order, and the men marched away.
Take the rap Accept responsibility.
If anything goes wrong, I'll take the rap.

Rate **At any rate** In any circumstances; whatever has happened or may happen.
The Government, at any rate, is not to blame.

Reach **Out of reach** Beyond the furthest distance to which one can stretch, or [MET] communicate.
We'd telephone Mary, but she's out of reach.
Reach-me-downs [S] Cheap, ready-made clothing.
Within reach Accessible.

Read **Read between the lines** Grasp the hidden significance of something spoken or written.
Reading between the lines, it's plain from her letter that she is unhappy.

Reality **In reality** Actually; in fact.
He thought her perfect; in reality she was selfish and vain.

Reap See *Sow.*

Rear **Bring up the rear; be in the rear** Travel behind; be at the back, as the last member of the party.

Reason **Hear (***or* **listen to) reason** Allow oneself to be persuaded.
Stand to reason Be obviously reasonable or logical.
If you go out in the rain, it stands to reason that you'll get wet.
Within reason Within the bounds of moderation.
I'll do anything within reason, but he's asking too much.

Reckon **Reckon among** Include among.
Reckoning That which is due, or owing, financially or otherwise.
Reckon on Rely upon. Similar to **count upon.**
Reckon up Count. Summarize.
Reckon with Include in one's plans (usually as a difficulty).

147

If you go swimming this morning, you'll have to reckon with a strong tide.

Reconcile **Reconcile oneself** Subdue one's dislike or objections.
You must reconcile yourself to getting up early.

Red **In the red** In debt. [Or. Banks' practice of registering overdrawn accounts in red ink on customers' statements.]

Like a red rag to a bull An exasperation; an intense annoyance. [Or. The belief (widespread but erroneous) that the sight of any red article infuriates a bull.]

Red-handed In the act of doing something wrong [Or. Probably reference to a murderer with his hands still stained with the blood of his victim.]
We caught the cat red-handed eating the butter.

Red herring An attempt to divert attention from the chief facts by introducing some detail of no importance. [Or. The old trick of drawing a red (dried) herring across the path by criminals when they are been followed by bloodhounds, to destroy the scent.]
The Prime Minister's speech was a mere red herring.

Red-letter day Day of rejoicing. [Or. The custom of indicating holidays and important saints' days in red lettering.]
Tuesday will be a red-letter day—my daughter is getting married.

Red tape Official and frequently trivial formalities. [Or. The old custom of Government officials and lawyers tying up their papers with red tape.]
We have given up trying to build a house—there is too much red tape involved.

To see red To become enraged.

To see the red light To have warning of difficulty or danger.

Reference **In (or with) reference to** Referring to; in connection with.
With reference to your letter of yesterday, we cannot accept the offer.

Without reference to Irrespective of. Without consulting or taking into account.
He acted without reference to his superior.

Reflection **Due reflection** Appropriate time for considering the matter.
After due reflection, we have decided to refuse.

On reflection After reconsideration.
On reflection, I think I was wrong.

Refresher **Refresher course** An additional course of studies, following an earlier one, taken to refresh one's memory.

Refusal **The first refusal** The first chance of buying an object before it is offered elsewhere.
I like the house, and the owner has given me first refusal.

Regular **Keep regular hours** Do the same thing at the same time every day.

Regular as clockwork Regular as the movements of a clock.
He comes home at six every night, regular as clockwork.

Rein **Give rein to** Allow to escape without restraint.
She is a child who likes to give rein to her imagination.

Relish **No relish for** No liking for.
I've no relish for long walks in wet weather.

Render **Render an account** Present a bill for payment.

Resolution **Form (*or* make) a resolution** Determine; definitely decide.
I've made a resolution never to go to bed later than eleven.

Respects **In all respects; in every respect** In every way.
The new washing-machine is better in all respects than the old one.
Pay (*or* send) one's respects Present (*or* convey) one's polite
greetings.

Rest **Rest assured** Be satisfied.
Rest on one's laurels Having earned distinction or honours, to
remain satisfied and do nothing further.
Rest on one's oars Remain passive, after making progress. [Or.
Rowing.]

Retreat **Beat a retreat** Depart defeated; go away ignominiously. [Or.
Military, from the signal to retreat being given by drum-
beats.]

Rhyme **Neither rhyme nor reason** Nonsense; rubbish. [Or. The author of
a worthless volume took it to Sir Thomas More, who told him to
turn it into verse. When this had been done, More said, 'That will
do. 'Tis rhyme now; before it was neither rhyme nor reason.']
No rhyme or reason No reason whatever.
There's no rhyme or reason why I shouldn't go.

Rid **Get rid of; rid oneself of** Dispose of; remove permanently.
I shall have to get rid of this worn-out carpet.

Ride **Ride one's hobby-horse** See *Horse.*
Ride roughshod Proceed without consideration or regard for other
people's views or feelings. [Or. A horse is 'roughshod' when it is
wearing specially roughened shoes, to prevent slipping.]
The Chairman rode roughshod over all objections to his plans.
Taken for a ride 1. Deceived. Tricked.
The car-salesman took him for a ride.
2. [LIT] Conveyed on a journey.
He took me for a ride on his motor-bike.

Riff-raff Worthless members of society. [Or. Riff = sweepings, raff = rags.
Both words are obsolete Anglo-Saxon.]

Right **By rights** Rightly; justly.
By rights, this house belongs to my father.
Serves you right See under *Serve.*
Right as rain (*or* a trivet) In satisfactory condition. [Or. A trivet

is a metal plate on three legs on which toast, etc., is stood to keep hot.]

Joan was feverish last night, but she's as right as a trivet this morning.

Come right See under *Come.*

Right and left (*or* **right, left and centre**) On all sides. In all ways.

The home team were beaten right, left and centre.

Right-hand man Chief assistant or supporter.

Arthur was my right-hand man when I built the garage.

Right of way Pathway, road, etc., established over private property by long-standing usage.

Ring **Ring a bell** Remind one of something, very vaguely.

Ring the changes Change the order of a limited number of items, so as to produce variety, e.g. mutton, beef, lamb, etc., for dinner. [Or. The variations produced by ringing Church bells in varying order.]

Ring off End a telephone call.

Run (make) rings round Do something very much better than.

He can run rings round me at tennis.

Ring up Contact by telephone.

Rise **Rise from the ranks** Be promoted from a private soldier to a commissioned officer. The phrase is also used in connection with anyone who has risen from a very inferior position to an important one in the same organization.

The Managing Director has risen from the ranks.

Rise in the world Become socially or financially more important.

Rise to Succeed in acting in a manner appropriate to.

The hotel rose to the occasion by producing a magnificent wedding-breakfast.

Rise with the lark Get up early—strictly speaking at sunrise, when the lark begins to sing.

Take a rise out of anyone Make a person look ridiculous, generally by deceiving him.

You'll find it difficult to take a rise out of a Scotsman.

Rob **Rob Peter to pay Paul** Take from one person (or thing) to pay another. (The origin of this phrase goes back to the twelfth century.)

Rock **(At) rock-bottom** (At the) lowest possible (point).

Public confidence in the Government is at rock-bottom.

On the rocks [S] [LIT] Shipwrecked. [MET] In financial or other difficulty. [Or. Naval.]

They were happy for a year or two, and then their marriage went on the rocks.

Rod **Make a rod for one's own back** Prepare trouble for oneself.

Rule with a rod of iron Govern or control with great severity.

Their father ruled the children with a rod of iron.

Roll   **Roll-call** The list of names of those who should be present at some assembly. (See **call the roll.**)

Rolling in money Very rich.

Roll up 1. [LIT]

Roll up the plans of the City.

2. [MET] [S] Assemble; appear.

I want all our friends to roll up on this occasion.

Rolling   **Rolling stone** One who never settles long in one place. [Or. Proverb: 'A rolling stone gathers no moss', i.e. a wanderer gathers no riches.]

Rome   **Do in Rome** Adapt yourself to the habits and customs of those among whom you are living. [Or. Proverb: 'Do in Rome as the Romans do.']

Room   **Not room to swing a cat in** Very little space.

Prefer a person's room to his company Prefer that he were absent, somewhere else.

Room for improvement Less than satisfactory state of affairs, and capable of being better.

There is room for improvement in her behaviour.

Room and to spare Plenty of space.

There's room and to spare in that box for my hat.

Root   **Root and branch** Every part; the whole organization.

The police are going to put an end to the vandalism, root and branch.

The root of the matter, trouble, *etc.* The base; the foundation of.

The root of the whole trouble is that teachers are underpaid.

Root out Remove completely; extract from its surroundings.

I am going to root out every wasps' nest in the garden.

Rope   **Give one enough rope** Allow one to continue in error until he brings the consequences upon himself. [Or. Proverb: 'Give a man rope enough, and he'll hang himself.']

(Know) the ropes (Be familiar with) the method and procedure.

Bill had better act as chairman, as he knows the ropes.

Rose   **Bed of roses** Pleasant and easy condition.

Life isn't always a bed of roses.

Through rose-coloured spectacles Cheerfully, optimistically.

He always sees life through rose-coloured spectacles.

Rotten   **Rotten to the core** Utterly bad.

Rough   **Rough and tumble** 1. Adjective. Disorderly. 2. Noun. Jostling behaviour.

Rough diamond An uneducated or unsophisticated but worthy person.

Rough-house Disturbance, row.

Rough it Live primitively.

If you go camping, you must be prepared to rough it.
Rough on [S] Severe on; a hardship for.
Jack's wife has run away with the man next door—which is rough on the man next door.
Roughly 1. In a rough manner.
The police handled the prisoners roughly.
2. Approximately.
There are roughly half a million people in the city.
Sleep rough Sleep out of doors, on park-benches, etc.
Take the rough with the smooth Be prepared to tolerate inconvenience, hardship, etc., as well as to accept the more agreeable aspects of life, etc.

Round **Going the rounds** A 'round' is a regular tour which a watchman makes to ensure that all is well, or a tradesman to deliver goods. [MET] Circulating; travelling around.
There's a curious rumour going the rounds.
Roundabout way, route, *etc.* A straggling, indirect way.
We came into Liverpool by a roundabout way.
Round numbers Strictly speaking, this idiom should refer to complete hundreds, thousands, etc. It is, however, constantly used in the sense of 'approximately'.
There are in round numbers 1,750 people in the village.
Round off Complete; add a final finish to.
He rounded off the performance with a song.
Round robin A letter or other document, usually of complaint, upon which all those concerned sign their names in a circle, so that everyone has the same responsibility and the leader remains anonymous. A petition passed from hand to hand for signature.
Round-table conference A meeting at which representatives of all parties to a dispute meet on equal terms to discuss matters.
There will be a round-table conference of employers and men tomorrow.
Round on Blame violently, and frequently undeservedly.
He lost his temper and rounded on the porter.
Round trip Journey which ends at its starting-point.
Round up Gather together.

Rub **Rub up** 1. Polish.
I want you to rub up the car.
2. Revive one's knowledge of a subject.
I must rub up my History for the examination.
Rub up the wrong way Irritate; annoy. [Or. From annoying a cat by rubbing its fur in the wrong direction.]
Her tactlessness always rubs people up the wrong way.

Rule **As a rule** Usually. More often than not.

Golden rule Basic, most important rule which ought never to be forgotten.
In golf, the golden rule is to keep one's eye on the ball.
Rule of the road The general rules governing traffic.
Rule the roost (*or* roast) Be in the position of one who issues orders, and is in command.
George's mother rules the roost in the household.
(*Note.*—Rule the roost.—Derived from the cock who is master of the farmyard 'roost', or hen house.
Rule the roast.—Derived from the cook whose duty it was to regulate the cooking of the meat on the kitchen fire.)
Rule of thumb [LIT] Measuring lengths by one's thumb. [MET] Measuring by guesswork based on experience.
Rule out Exclude.
Ruling passion The chief incentive in one's life.
Her ruling passion was to attract attention.
Work to rule Observe every rule and regulation in precise detail, thus making efficiency impossible. (Device used as alternative to open strike in industrial disputes, having the advantage of qualifying the employee for wages.)

Run 1. Verb. Manage.
He ran a grocery business.
2. Noun. An extended number of performances or issues.
The play had a run of 500 nights.
In the long run Eventually.
In the long run, crime does not pay.
On the run Being pursued from place to place.
Run across Meet casually and unexpectedly.
I don't often run across such an interesting pub.
Run after Seek; pursue.
He runs after every pretty girl he meets.
Run against Similar to **run across.**
Run amuck (*or* amok) Dash about wildly and senselessly.
The kitten has run amuck with my knitting-wool.
Run off (*or* away) with 1. Steal and depart with.
The assistant has run off with the week's takings.
2. Win easily.
We expect to run away with the Cup.
Run away with the idea Assume hastily and incorrectly.
I don't want you to run away with the idea that I'm dissatisfied.
Run close Be very near in race, competition, merit, etc.
St Helens is probably the ugliest place in England, but Runcorn runs it close.
Run counter to Be in opposition to.

Your suggestions run counter to what we arranged yesterday.

Run down 1. Collide with and injure or kill. Similar to **run over.**

If you drive so fast, you'll run down some unfortunate pedestrian.

2. Overtake, and frequently capture as well.

They ran down the escaped convict just outside the town.

3. Speak ill of.

She's always running down her neighbours.

4. Visit.

I'll run down and see you on Monday.

5. In poor health, through overwork, etc.

The poor woman is terribly run down.

Run dry Cease to flow.

Run to earth Find after a search. [Or. Fox-hunting, from following a fox to its den, or 'earth'.]

I ran the quotation to earth in Shakespeare's Othello.

Run for it Run for some especially urgent reason.

If you want to catch the bus, you'll have to run for it.

A run for one's money Time and opportunity in which to be free, or enjoy oneself.

The prisoner was recaptured, but he had had a month's run for his money.

Run the gauntlet See *Gauntlet.*

Run high Become heated; excited.

Feelings always run high during an election.

Runs in the family Is an inherited trait or characteristic.

Twins run in my family.

Run into See **run across,** also **run down** (1) and **run over** (2).

Run into debt Incur debt.

Run like mad See under *Mad.*

Run low Become scanty.

Our oil-supplies are running low.

Run mad Become fantastically exaggerated and unreal.

The plans for rebuilding the City show capitalism run mad.

Run on Hasten ahead.

Run on, and see if dinner's ready.

Run out 1. Come to an end.

My patience has completely run out.

We ran out of coal, and had to burn wood.

2. Cricket. A batsman is 'run out' when the ball is thrown against the wicket before he has had time to complete a run.

Run over 1. Flow over.

The water ran over the edge of the jug.

2. Drive over; collide with.

The train ran over the fellow as he was crossing the line.

3. Glance over; read through and check.

You'd better run (your eye) over these instructions before you go.

Run rings round See *Ring.*

Run riot Behave in a completely undisciplined way.

The children in that family run riot.

Run a risk Incur a risk or danger.

You'll run a risk of cutting your feet if you don't wear shoes.

Run to Reach; have sufficient money or ability for.

This novel runs to over four hundred pages.

I think I can run to another round of drinks.

Run to seed 1. [LIT] Grow rank and straggling. As a plant does after it has blossomed. 2. [MET] Deteriorate, with an effect of neglect and decay.

A house will soon run to seed if left unattended.

Run short of Be left without a sufficient supply.

I ran short of milk because the cat knocked over the jug.

Run through 1. Exhaust; squander.

I ran through my pocket money very quickly.

2. Read quickly.

I'll just run through these letters, and then we'll go out.

3. Pierce completely.

The needle ran through her finger.

Run up Stitch rapidly.

I'll soon run up this seam.

Run up a bill Incur debts, usually recklessly.

He ran up a bill for over £100.

Run wild Similar to **run riot.**

Runner-up The competitor immediately after the winner.

Jim won the swimming race, and Bill was the runner-up.

Running Consecutive.

We met several days running.

(*Note.*—This adjective invariably follows the noun.)

In the running With a chance of victory.

He's in the running for promotion.

Out of the running With no chance of winning.

Running fight A fight throughout which the defenders are running away and the attackers pursuing them.

Rush **Rush one's fences** [S] Be in too great a hurry for results. [Or. Hunting.]

Rush headlong Rush recklessly, with all one's energy.

Peter is always rushing headlong from one job to another.

S

Sack **Get (*or* be given) the sack; be sacked** [S] Be dismissed from one's work. [Or. Travelling workmen used to keep their tools in sacks or bags. When a man's work was finished he was given back the sack, in which he replaced his tools before going on to seek another job.]

Sackcloth **In sackcloth and ashes** Deeply penitent. [Or. Biblical. To dress oneself in sackcloth and put ashes on one's head was an indication of mourning and sorrow.]

Saddle **In the saddle** [LIT] Riding a horse. [MET] In office; in control of an enterprise.
Saddled with Burdened with.
He was saddled with the responsibility of educating three small children.

Said **No sooner said than done** Accomplished as soon as requested; finished very soon after being ordered, mentioned, etc.
I asked him for a report, and it was no sooner said than done.

Sail **Full sail** [LIT] With all sails spread. [MET] Without hindrance.
The cyclist went full sail over the handlebars.
Sail near (*or* close to) the wind Go very near to something which is improper, illegal, dangerous, etc. [Or. Nautical.]
The magistrate warned the defendant that he was sailing very near the wind.
Sail under false colours Pretend to be something that one is not. [Old f.] [Or. Nautical. Pirate ships used to hoist the flags of friendly nations to deceive other vessels.]
Set sail Start on a sea voyage.
The captain set sail for America early in May.

Sally **Sally forth** Go forth; come out (often in numbers, and suddenly or dramatically.)
Now that the rain has stopped we can sally forth.

Salt **Salt away** Save (money, etc.).
Salt of the earth Person(s) who are valuable members of society. [Or. Biblical: 'Ye are the salt of the earth'; St Matthew, ch. 5, v. 13.]
You'll enjoy meeting Harold: he's the salt of the earth.
Not worth one's salt (*or* keep) Worthless; not worth the cost of the salary one is paid. (*Note.*—The word 'salary' is derived from the Lat. *salarium*, salt. Originally 'salt money' was money paid to Roman soldiers in lieu of salt.)
Take with a grain of salt Accept a statement, but with some doubt as to its complete truth.

We take most of what he says with a grain of salt.

Salvation **Work out one's own salvation** Discover, by experience, the solution to one's problems.

Sand **Happy as a sandboy** Very happy. [Or. Sandboy = boy who hawked sand for sale.]

The sands are running out There is not much time left. [Or. The grains of sand running through the hour-glass, once a common substitute for the clock.]

You had better hurry—the sands are running out.

Satisfaction **Give satisfaction** Satisfy; be what is required.

I think these stockings will give satisfaction.

Sauce **Sauce for the goose** What is suitable for one person is equally suitable for another; the same rule applies to all people in similar circumstances. [Or. Proverb: 'What's sauce for the goose is sauce for the gander.']

Save **Save appearances (*or* one's face)** Prevent or minimize embarrassment; deal tactfully with any embarrassing situation.

The carpet was very old and shabby; my aunt, to save appearances, said that it was a family heirloom.

Save one's breath (to cool one's porridge) Say nothing; keep one's advice to oneself.

I warned her, but I might just as well have saved my breath.

Save the mark Expression used to emphasize a statement (usually one expressing surprise or irony) or to apologize for mentioning something unpleasant. [Or. Archery. When anyone shot especially well, the cry was 'God save the mark!', i.e. 'May God prevent the arrow being displaced by a later shot'.]

In our free country—save the mark!—council-house tenants can't even paint their own front doors.

Save the situation Find or provide a way out of difficulty.

I ran out of petrol, but a passing motorist saved the situation.

Say **Have one's say** Say all that one wishes to say in one's own words. (Opposite: **have no say**.)

We were all tired of speeches, but the woman was determined to have her say.

Go without saying Be too obvious to deserve mention.

I say An introductory phrase to a remark conveying surprise or special interest.

I say, look at the view from over here.

Say-so [S] [U.S.A.] 1. Opinion. 2. Decision.

Saying **As the saying is; as they say** A half-facetious, half-apologetic excuse for using a hackneyed phrase or cliché.

Well, hard work never hurt anyone, as the saying is.

Scales **Hold the scales** Be an impartial judge.

Scales of justice The scales traditionally held with each side exactly level by the blindfolded figure of Justice. (The figure is erected over the Central Criminal Court in London, as an emblem of the Law's fairness towards all who are tried there.)

Turn the scales 1. Weigh.

The boxer turned the scales at 14 stones.

2. Bring about a decisive change in fortunes.

Rain on the second day of the Test match turned the scales in Australia's favour.

Scatter **Scatter-brained** Careless; easily distracted; unable to concentrate on one thing.

Scarce **Make oneself scarce** Depart quickly, and efface oneself.

Scene **Behind the scenes** [LIT] Backstage in a theatre. [MET] Not in the public eye.

This Treaty would not have been possible without a lot of work behind the scenes.

Create (*or* make) a scene Cause any violent emotional disturbance.

Don't lose your temper and create a scene.

Scent **Scent (a mystery, scandal, *etc*)** Suspect.

Score **On that score** As far as that matter is concerned.

As far as travel is concerned, you need have no fears on that score.

Pay off (wipe off *or* settle) old scores Cancel an old injury or injustice by inflicting another adequate punishment. [Or. Score = Anglo-Saxon: a cut or scratch; debts used to be recorded by making such marks in long sticks. When such debts were paid, the 'score' was removed.]

Score off Triumph over; make one's opponent look foolish or embarrassed.

Scorn **Point the finger of scorn** [Old f.] Sneer at; speak about with contempt.

Scot **Scot free** See under *Free*.

Scrape **Get into a scrape** Get into trouble; commit some foolish action leading to trouble.

Scrape acquaintance with Take special trouble to become acquainted with; deliberately set out to become friends with.

Scrape through Succeed by a narrow margin (usually applied to examinations).

Scrape together Succeed, with difficulty, in accumulating something.

He scraped together just enough from his salary to take a week's holiday.

Scratch **Bring (*or* come up) to the scratch** Reach a definite decision; decide to take definite action. [Old f.] (See **up to scratch.**) [Or. Prize-fighting. The 'scratch' is the line marked in the prize-ring to which the boxers were led at the beginning of a fight.]

Scratch the surface Not penetrate deeply into.

The Minister's speech only scratched the surface of the problem.

Scratch team, crew, *etc.* A number of people collected casually, not regular members.

Although we'd only a scratch team, we won all three matches.

Up to scratch [S] Fit to deal with one's work; equal to what is required.

I've had influenza, and am still not up to scratch.

You scratch my back and I'll scratch yours If you help me, I will help you. [Vulgar.]

Screw **Have one's head screwed on** Have good sense.

George has got his head screwed on (the right way).

Put on the screw(s) See *Put.*

A screw loose [S] Something wrong or irregular.

I can't understand these accounts; there's a screw loose somewhere.

Have a screw loose [S] Be mentally deficient.

Scruple **Make no scruple; have no scruples** Have no hesitation.

[Frequently applied to some action which might involve some 'scruple' or sense of what is right and wrong.]

The soldiers made no scruple about robbing their prisoners.

Sea **At sea** Unaware; confused.

She stayed over an hour, but I am still completely at sea concerning her reason for coming to see me.

Get one's sea-legs Learn to walk successfully on the moving deck of a ship; accommodate oneself to the rise and fall of the waves.

Half seas over [S] Intoxicated.

Put to sea Leave the shore to start on a voyage.

Seal **One's lips are sealed** One is completely silent.

I can tell you nothing; my lips must be sealed.

Sealed book A subject completely unknown.

Fifteenth-century art was a sealed book to him.

Set the seal on Conclude. Formally end. Give distinction to.

His fourth goal set the seal on the match.

The presence of numerous international golfers set the seal on the tournament.

Season **For a season** For a short time.

The play will run for a short season at Stratford before transferring to London.

Close season Period during which certain sports are not played.

In season and out of season At all times, whether suitable or unsuitable.

He talked of his travels in season and out of season.

Out of season Unseasonable; at a wrong or inappropriate time.
Oysters are out of season in August.

A word in season Advice given at an appropriate time.

Second **(At) second hand** 1. Not new. 2. By hearsay.

Come off second-best Be overcome by a superior force.
The thieves attacked the postmistress, but found that they came off second-best.

Second childhood Childish behaviour at an age when it is not expected.

(Play) second fiddle (Be of) secondary importance (usually to another person).

Second to none Better than all others.

Second nature Instinctive; an action which has already taken place so many times that it has become automatic.
It had become second nature to light the fire and prepare breakfast for her husband.

Second thoughts Later, more mature consideration.
On second thoughts, I won't go to the theatre tonight.

Second wind In exercise, easy breathing after initial breathlessness. Also applied to other circumstances in which continued practice, experience, etc., makes them easier, more pleasant, etc.
After a year in this job, I'm just finding my second wind.

Secret **Make no secret of** State openly, without concealment.
Napoleon made no secret of his hatred for England.

Security **Hold as security** Retain, in case of loss or failure to repay.
The bank are holding the documents as security against the loan.

See **I'll see** I'll consider the matter before deciding.

See with half an eye See immediately, with no effort at all.
One could see with half an eye that she was very ill.
Similar to **see at a glance.**

See fair play Make sure that the rules are obeyed, that there is no cheating.

See fit Choose; decide.
He didn't see fit to take her into his confidence.

See how the land lies Discover the state or condition of affairs.

See off Accompany to the starting-place.
We saw him off at the station.

See one's way Manage. Contrive.
Can you see your way to repairing it immediately?

See red Become infuriated.

See through 1. [LIT] Perceive through something transparent.
I saw him through the window.
2. [MET] Perceive the truth, in spite of attempts to deceive.

Any idiot can see through most television advertising.
3. Ensure that a job is completed.
We are going to see the work through.
(Note alteration in order of words.)
See to Give one's attention to.
The plumber said he would see to it tomorrow.
Not see the wood for the trees Be unable to see the general picture, the full overall effect, because of impeding detail.

Seed **Run to seed** See under **Run.**

Send **Send down** Suspend or expel from membership of university.
Send packing Dismiss peremptorily. Also **send someone about his business.**
Send up 1. Write, usually requesting information. (Also **send off.**)
I'll send up for the firm's catalogue.
2. Satirize. Parody. (Also noun **send-up.**)
The play sends up the advertising industry.
Send word Dispatch a message.
I'll send word that we'll be arriving late.

Sensation **Create a sensation** Produce a startling effect.
The murder created a tremendous sensation.

Sense **Sense of humour,** *etc.* Ability to appreciate what is humorous, etc.
Come to one's senses 1. Recover consciousness.
She came to her senses in hospital.
2. Recover one's sense of proportion and of what is intelligent and just.
Take leave of one's senses Appear to have lost one's normal balance or sane state of mind.
He's behaving like a man who's taken leave of his senses.

Sensible **Sensible of** Aware; conscious of.
I am sensible of your great kindness.

Separate **Separate the sheep from the goats** Separate worthy people, or (more loosely) those suited to a particular purpose, from those who are the reverse.
Separate the wheat from the chaff Separate what is worth keeping from what is rubbish.

Sepulchre **Whited (or painted) sepulchre** One whose virtuous appearance and manner conceals inward vice; a hypocrite. [Or. Biblical.]

Serve **Serve someone right** Punish justly and appropriately.
He fell through the ice; it served him right, for he had been told it was dangerous.
Serve its turn Prove useful for a limited time.
I used a stick to support me; it served its turn until I could procure a crutch.
Serve its purpose Be suitable for what it is required to do.

Opposite: **serve no purpose.**

The greenhouse is dilapidated, but it serves its purpose.

Service **Render** (*or* **do, perform) a service** Be useful to; assist.

If you'll deliver this parcel, you will render me a great service.

Service flat One in which domestic help, meals, etc., are provided by the management.

Set **Set about** 1. Begin; commence.

I'll set about preparing supper.

2. Attack violently. Also **set on.**

The three thugs set about the barman.

Set one's affections on Concentrate one's liking upon; desire intensely.

Mary has set her heart on the big doll in the toyshop.

Set against 1. Opposed to.

His parents are very much set against the marriage.

2. Balanced against.

The £5 you've paid now will be set against the £20 you borrowed last year.

Set aside Disregard; place on one side.

Set-back A reversal or arrest of progress. A relapse.

The injury to the full-back was a great set-back to the team's chances.

Set back 1. Impede or reverse the progress of.

The drought will set the country's progress back several years.

2. [S] Cost.

The evening-out set me back a fiver.

Set down 1. Write; place on record. 2. Deposit passengers.

Set by the ears Exasperate; cause to quarrel.

Set eyes on Emphatic form of 'see'.

I haven't set eyes on him for many years.

Set an example Exhibit oneself as an example or model to be followed.

Big boys should set an example to small boys.

Set one's face against Oppose firmly.

I've always set my face against organized religion, and I always shall.

Set foot in Enter.

I will never set foot in that shop again.

Set on foot Start; initiate.

An enquiry will be set on foot to find out the cause of the accident.

Set forth, off, out Start; depart.

Set free, at liberty Release.

Set one's hand to Undertake.

Whatever he sets his hand to, he always does it well.

Set one's heart on Strongly desire to obtain.

S

Set one's house in order Arrange one's own affairs properly; correct one's own faults.

Set in Begin (applied to something which will continue for some time).

Winter has set in early this year.

Set off 1. Start on a journey.

He set off to Sheffield early next day.

2. Make more effective; embellish.

The roses set off the dark beauty of her hair.

Set on See **set about** (2).

Set phrase Formal phrase.

He thanked me in a number of set phrases for my help.

Set purpose Determined purpose; one already decided upon.

It was his set purpose to discover his father's old home.

Set at rest Cause to subside; eliminate.

What he told me set at rest all my fears.

Set right Make correct.

Set sail See under **Sail**.

Set the seal on Complete, make final. (A legal document is not completed until the principals have signed their names against a seal.)

That evening set the seal on our friendship.

Set store by See under **Store**.

Set (or lay) the table Prepare it for a meal.

Set one's teeth on edge See under **Teeth**.

Set the Thames on fire Achieve sensational success.

He'll never set the Thames on fire.

Set-to Contest; fight.

There was a set-to when the police asked the demonstrators to disperse.

Set to Become active; busy.

If we set to, we shall soon have the room tidy.

Set up 1. Formally establish; cause to exist.

The Prime Minister will set up a committee to investigate the matter.

2. Assume the right.

I don't set myself up as an authority on rare books.

Settle **Settle down** Become established; adopt regular habits; live a settled and normal life.

They have settled down very happily in their new home.

Settle someone's hash [S] Spoil or end someone's plans. Similar to **cook his goose**; **put paid to**.

Seven **In one's (or the) seventh heaven** In a state of intense delight or ecstasy. [Or. The outmost of the Seven Heavens or 'layers' with which it used to be believed that the earth was surrounded.]

S

Shade **Put in the shade** Appear more prominent than. Outshine. Overshadow.
Their record of slum-clearance puts other towns in the shade.

Shake **Shake the dust from one's feet** Depart from, usually in contempt or anger.
Shake in one's shoes Tremble with fear and apprehension.
Shake off Get rid of.
I wish I could shake off this cold.
Shake out Remove dust, etc., from garment, etc., by shaking.
Shake-out [S] A reform by removing inefficient or surplus elements.
A Cabinet shake-out is imminent.
Shake up 1. Mix by agitating. 2. Rouse.
Shake-up Similar to **shake-out.**

Shakes **No great shakes** [S] Unimportant; generally inferior.
I've seen her paintings, but they're no great shakes.

Shame **A burning shame** A great and terrible shame; one to make the cheeks burn with anger.
It is a burning shame that children should have to beg in the street.
Put to shame Cause to feel ashamed, or inferior.
The boy's playing would have put many a professional to shame.

Shank **Shanks' pony** One's own legs.
We missed the last train and used shanks' pony.

Share **Share and share alike** Divide everything equally.
The three partners in the business agreed to share and share alike.

Sharp **Sharp practice** Behaviour which, while still technically legal, practically amounts to swindling.
Sharp's the word; look sharp; be sharp Hurry up.

Sheep **Black sheep** A person with a bad record or reputation. [Or. A theory that, as among every flock of sheep there is always one which is black, so in every respectable family there is always one discreditable member.]
As well be hanged for a sheep as a lamb If one is in mild trouble, one might as well **go the whole hog** and incur serious trouble.
Cast sheep's eyes Gaze in a foolish and amorous way at a person.
See **Separate, Wolf.**

Sheer **Sheer off** [S] Break off (usually applied to metal bolts, etc., coming apart under strain).

Sheet **Sheet anchor** Chief support. [Or. Nautical. The sheet anchor is the largest and strongest of a ship's anchors.]
I earn my living in several ways, but fruit-growing is my sheet anchor.
Three sheets in the wind Intoxicated.

Shelf **On the shelf** No longer required to do active work; replaced by someone more effective. No longer capable of work. Also applied to a woman who is thought to be too old or unattractive to marry.

Shell **Come out of one's shell** Throw off one's reserve and become communicative.

Shell out [S] Pay.

Shift **Makeshift** See *Makeshift.*

Shift for oneself Take care of oneself.

Thanks for your help; I can shift for myself now.

Shift one's ground Adopt a new point of view or position in an argument, discussion, etc.

Shilly-shally Waste time trying to reach a decision. [Or. Probably a corruption of 'Will I, shall I?')

Shine **Take the shine out of** Make appear inferior and unimportant.

Cinderella's dress took the shine out of her sisters'.

Ship **Shipshape (and Bristol fashion)** Tidy and in good order. [Or. The reputation of Bristol as a port.]

When one's ship comes home (*or* in) When one becomes rich.

I'll buy you a fur coat when my ship comes in.

Shoe **Another pair of shoes** [S] An entirely different matter.

I'll lend you a pound, but £10 is another pair of shoes.

In a person's shoes In a similar position to him.

I shouldn't like to be in his shoes when his wife sees his condition.

On a shoe-string [S] [U.S.A.] With very limited resources (e.g. of money).

Where the shoe pinches The real trouble or worry; the chief cause of financial anxiety. [Or. The saying 'Only he who wears the shoe knows where it pinches'.]

See *Shake, Dead.*

Shoot **Shoot ahead** Make extremely rapid progress.

The magazine was started only six months ago, but it has shot ahead rapidly.

Shoot one's bolt Make a final effort, having nothing left in reserve. [Or. Bolt = short, heavy arrow of crossbow.]

The team shot their bolt too early and were easily defeated.

Shop **All over the shop** Everywhere.

I've looked for my slippers all over the shop.

Closed shop Factory, or part of one, in which employees have to be members of a trade union.

Talk shop Discuss one's profession, business, etc. (usually on informal or social occasions).

Jack is coming round this evening to talk shop.

Shorn **Shorn of** Stripped of.

Short **Short of** Without sufficient.

I can't offer you tea, as we're short of milk.

Short-circuit Deal informally and quickly with (an official document, etc.), omitting the usual procedure.

Is there no way of short-circuiting these formalities?

Short cut A short way from one point to another, as distinct from the usual one.

The distance by the road is three miles, but there is a short cut through the park.

Short-handed *or* **short-staffed** With an insufficient number of helpers; short of staff.

I'm sorry to keep you waiting, but we are short-handed this week through illness.

In short Summarized; stated briefly.

The rumour, in short, is not to be trusted.

Short-lived Not of long duration.

Short shrift Very little time for explanation before inflicting punishment, or administering reproof, correction etc. [Or. Shrift = confession to priest, prior to doing penance and receiving absolution.]

He tried to explain the mistake, but got very short shrift.

In short supply Available in insufficient quantities to meet the demand.

Short weight Less than was ordered or paid for.

The butcher has given us short weight again.

(Make) short work of Dispose of quickly.

The children made short work of the chocolates.

Shot **A good shot** An accurate or near accurate attempt. Opposite: **a bad shot.**

He made a good shot at repairing the toy.

Like a shot With extreme speed.

The frightened cat dashed away like a shot.

A long (*or* random) shot A casual suggestion; a mere guess.

Shoulder **Give the cold shoulder to** Treat coldly and formally; snub.

Have broad shoulders Be able to bear much responsibility.

Have on one's shoulders Support; bear.

It is a terrible responsibility to have on one's shoulders.

Head and shoulders See *Head.*

Old head on young shoulders See *Head.*

Put one's shoulder to the wheel Work hard and steadily. [Or. The fable of the lazy man who had his cart stuck in the mud. He appealed to Jove for help; Jove retorted that the man should himself put his shoulder to the wheel and try to move it before appealing to the gods.]

Rub shoulders with Come into intimate contact with; become acquainted.

Shoulder to shoulder United in effort.
Straight from the shoulder Directly and forcibly. [Or. Boxing.]
He's not the sort of man who normally speaks straight from the shoulder.

Show **Show cause** Give good reason.
Show-down A frank exposure; an open challenge.
Show off Display one's cleverness with the intention of attracting attention and obtaining praise.
Most small children show off in front of visitors.
Show of reason Apparent justice and logic.
The chef said, with a show of reason, that it was impossible to make an omelette without eggs.
Show up 1. Expose (usually to disadvantage).
The behaviour of those children shows up their parents.
2. Escort someone upstairs.
The visitors have arrived; show them up.
3. Be conspicuous, clearly visible (often to advantage).
The painting shows up well against that wall.

Shuffle **Shuffle off** Avoid. Abdicate. Hand over to someone else.
He tried to shuffle off responsibility upon the other driver.

Shut **Shut down** Close. (Usually applied to business.)
Shut one's eyes to Pretend not to notice.
Shut out Exclude.
Shut up [S] Shut up one's mouth; stop talking.
His father became tired of the boy's excuses, and told him to shut up.
Shut up shop [S] Give up business; end one's occupation, either for the day, or permanently.
He managed a circus, but when the war came he had to shut up shop.

Side **On every side; on all sides** From every direction, every source.
On every side we have heard approval of the Government's new housing plans.
On the side; as a side line In addition to one's normal work.
The garage mechanic earns quite a lot on the side.
Side by side Standing close together.
Side with Ally oneself with; openly sympathize with.
I know you will side with me in my dispute with the manager over wages.
Split one's sides Laugh very heartily.

Sight **At first sight** At the first (superficial) glance; immediately.
At first sight I don't much like the town.
In sight of Near enough to see.
We shall soon be in sight of Southampton.
In the sight of In the view of; as seen by.
In the sight of the world, they were a happily married couple.

S

Know by sight Be familiar with the appearance only.
I've never met him, but I know him by sight.
Lose sight of [LIT] Fail to see. Opposite: **catch sight of.**
At this distance you lose sight of the village.
[MET] Fail to realize, or to remember.
You've lost sight of the fact that you are no longer young.
Lose one's sight Become blind.
Out of sight Beyond one's vision.
The car dashed away, and was soon out of sight.
Sight for sore eyes [S] A very welcome, cheering thing to see.
Out of sight, out of mind One forgets that which is not present.

Sign **Sign of the times** Indication of present-day thought and feeling.
It is a sign of the times that children are taken to listen to debates in Parliament.

Signal **Give the signal (*or* sign)** Indicate by sign or speech when some event should happen.
The captain gave the signal for the men to attack.

Silence **Keep silent; keep *or* maintain silence** Continue to remain silent.
You will have to keep silent throughout the ceremony.
Silence is golden, but speech is silver To remain silent is better than to talk.

Silk **Make a silk purse out of a sow's ear** Change the real character of a person; make a gentleman of one who is not one; create something good out of poor materials.
Take silk See under *Take.*

Sing **Sing-song** 1. Noun. An impromptu concert, usually held by a community—soldiers, campers, etc.
We had a sing-song round the camp fire after supper.
2. Adjective. Monotonous; flat and lifeless.
The sentry repeated his instructions in a sing-song voice.
Sing the praises of Praise highly and in general terms.
Jack spent half the morning singing the praises of his fiancée.

Single **Singleness of aim, purpose, heart** Concentration; a single object in view.
With complete singleness of aim, Joan of Arc began the task of freeing France from its enemies.

Sink **Sink or swim** Rely on one's own efforts; succeed or fail.

Sit **Sit on** 1. [LIT]
Do you mind sitting on the floor?
2. [S] Repress. Rebuke. Snub.
If that child isn't sat on she'll be unbearable in a few years.
Sit tight [S] Remain firmly in one's place.
Sit up [S] Be startled.
That dress of yours will make the neighbours sit up.

Sit up for Wait after the usual bedtime for somebody's return.
We shall probably be late coming home, so don't sit up for us.

Six **At sixes and sevens** Muddled; in a state of confusion.
We have only just moved into the house, and everything is at sixes and sevens.

Six of one and half-a-dozen of the other An affair in which both sides deserve equal blame or merit.
The magistrates listened to the story of the quarrel between the two women, and decided that it was six of one and half-a-dozen of the other.

Skeleton **Skeleton in the cupboard** A disgrace which the family, community, etc., does its best to conceal.

Skin **By the skin of one's teeth** Very narrowly. Only just.
We caught the bus by the skin of our teeth.

Skin-deep Superficial; not lasting.
Beauty is only skin-deep.

Thick-skinned Insensitive (to criticism, other people, etc.).

Slap **Slap in the face** A rebuff; an insult.
Slap-up [S] First-class; splendid.
We went to the hotel and had a slap-up dinner.

Sleep **Let sleeping dogs lie** Refrain from stirring up trouble.
Sleep on a matter Allow a time to pass before finally deciding.
I'll sleep on the matter, and write to you tomorrow.

Sleep like a top Sleep peacefully and deeply. [Or. When a top is spinning at its greatest speed, it appears motionless and is almost soundless.]

Sleeping partner One who is a partner (e.g. in a business) but plays no active part.

Sleight **Sleight-of-hand** Extreme manual dexterity and quickness. (The phrase is generally used in connection with conjuring and in performing an illusion.)
By sleight-of-hand he made an entire pack of cards disappear.

Slide **Let things slide (*or* drift)** Do nothing; take no active steps; be negligent.

Slink **Slink away** Retreat silently, secretly, guiltily, unobtrusively.

Slip **Give the slip** Escape, and remain uncaptured.
Make a slip (*or* slip up) Make a slight (but frequently vital) error.
You've made a slip somewhere in these accounts.

Many a slip Many things may happen to prevent a desired or expected result. [Or. Proverb: 'There's many a slip 'twixt cup and lip'.]
He seems sure that he will pass the examinations, but there's many a slip.

Slip away, out, off, across, *etc.* Move unobserved or quietly or quickly.

Slip through one's fingers Escape; be lost.

I had the chance, but let it slip through my fingers.

Slip of the pen An error in writing.

Slip of the tongue A verbal error.

Slope **Slope off** Depart, usually furtively.

Slot **Slot in** Fit in (between two others). Accommodate.

The dentist slotted me in at short notice.

Slouch **Slouch** [S] Incompetent or slovenly worker, performer, etc.

He's certainly no slouch as a gardener.

Sly **On the sly** Secretly and artfully.

Small **Small beer** Trivial; unimportant.

The news is all very small beer.

Small talk See *Talk.*

Smoke **End (*or* go up) in smoke** Have no result; end in nothing.

The committee discussed various improvements, but it has all ended in smoke.

No smoke without fire All rumour has some truth in it, or some justification.

Snake **Snake in one's bosom** Person ungrateful for kindness shown.

Snake in the grass A hidden or hypocritical enemy.

Snap **Snap at** 1. Try to bite (usually applied to animals).

2. Speak irritably to. 3. Accept eagerly.

Snap one's fingers at Disregard; treat with contempt.

He was one of those who snap their fingers at all conventions.

Snap out of [S] Throw off. Get rid of.

I wish he would snap out of his present mood.

Snap up Seize hastily.

It's a bargain I snapped up in the market.

Sneak **Sneak off (*or* away)** Depart furtively.

Sneeze **Not to be sneezed at** Not to be treated as unimportant or insignificant. (Always used in the negative.)

The firm is offering a salary which isn't to be sneezed at.

So **Just so; quite so** I agree; it is as you have stated.

And so forth Similar objects; in a similar way, etc.

He dealt in chairs, tables, and so forth.

Similar to **and so on; et cetera.**

So-long [S] Good-bye.

So-so In inferior health; not too badly; moderately well.

His results in the exam were only so-so.

So-and-so 1. Such and such a person. Used as a general substitute for the specific name of a person or thing.

Choose something that you like; never mind what Mrs So-and-so is wearing.

2. A mild term of abuse.

I think the vicar is an old so-and-so.

So to speak; in a manner of speaking Speaking generally, without being literally exact; speaking with a certain amount of metaphorical exaggeration.
I agree with you in a manner of speaking.

Sober **Sober as a judge** Not at all drunk.

Sober down (*or* up) 1. Become more serious-minded and reliable.
The boy will sober down as he grows older.
2. Recover from a temporary attack of hysteria or drunkenness.
We put him on the bed to sober up.

Soft **A soft answer** A well-mannered answer.

Soft in the head Foolish.

Soft-hearted Sympathetic and understanding (sometimes too much so).

Soft job Very easy job (in view of the salary).

Soft option [LIT] An easy choice. [MET] Same as **soft job**.

Soft soap 1. Flattery; ingratiating behaviour.
You won't persuade me by using soft soap.
2. Verb. Behave ingratiatingly.

Soft-spoken Gently and politely speaking.
She's a pleasant, soft-spoken girl.

Sold **Sold a pup** [S] Swindled; cheated.

Soldier **Come the old soldier (over)** Claim greater experience (than), and consequently superior wisdom.
He becomes rather irritating when he tries to come the old soldier.

Old soldier [LIT] A former soldier. [MET] Person of experience.

Soldier on Continue, despite the difficulties.

Soldier of fortune Originally a professional soldier who hired himself as such to any country. A wanderer who lives by his wits.

Some **Somebody (someone, some person, somehow, for some reason, something) or other** 'Other' is here used as a vague alternative to an unspecified individual or thing, i.e. somebody or other = 'any person'.
Somebody or other has left the gate open.

Song **For a song; a mere song** Extremely cheap; at a merely nominal price. Similar to **cheap as dirt**.
The painting was going for a song, so I bought it.

Make a song about Create a fuss, disturbance, quarrel about (usually for trivial reasons).
The repair-bill is not worth making a song about.

Soon **Sooner or later** Eventually; in the end.
If you drive like that, sooner or later you'll have an accident.
Similar to **before long**.

Sort **A good sort** A good fellow; a helpful person.

Of a sort; of sorts Not fully deserving the name.
He's a billiards-player of sorts.
Out of sorts Not in good health; depressed and irritable. Similar to **off colour.**

Soul **Be unable to call one's soul one's own** Be dominated by a person.
He is so intimidated by his wife that he daren't call his soul his own.
Not a soul Absolutely no one.
When I reached the station, there was not a soul on the platform.
Soul of discretion The essence of prudence.
You can confide in my deputy: he's the soul of discretion.

Soup **In the soup** [S] In difficulty.

Sour **Sour grapes** Something referred to disparagingly, but only because it is out of reach. [Or. Æsop's fable of the fox who, after vainly trying to reach some grapes he wanted, consoled himself by saying that they were sour.]
When he couldn't get a ticket, he said he had never really wanted to go anyway, but it was sour grapes.

Sow **Reap what one sows** Be faced with the results of one's own actions.
Sow the seeds of Originate; begin.
The referee's strictness sowed the first seeds of dissension.
Sow the wind and reap the whirlwind Perform ill-advised action and produce even worse consequences.

Spade **Call a spade a spade** Speak quite plainly or bluntly.

Spanner **Throw a spanner in the works** Interfere with, and check another person's plans. [Or. A spanner is a small tool used for turning metal nuts.] Similar to **put a spoke in one's wheel.**

Speak **In a manner of speaking** See **so to speak,** under *So.*
On speaking terms Just acquainted. Opposite: **not on speaking terms,** which also means 'having quarrelled'.
Plain speaking Uttering one's real and unflattering opinion. Also **speak one's mind.**
There was a good deal of plain speaking, and they parted in anger.
Speaks for itself Demonstrates without words; requires no explanation.
His record speaks for itself.
Speaking likeness A vivid and realistic likeness.
Speak up 1. Speak more loudly. 2. Speak one's opinion (e.g. **for** or **against** something). Also **speak out.**
Speak volumes Convey much, while actually saying little or nothing.
The glance she gave him spoke volumes.
Speak well of Praise. Be to the credit of.
It speaks well of a teacher's authority if he never has to shout.

S

Strictly speaking Speaking exactly, or according to a rule or promise.
Strictly speaking, I ought not to tell you this.

Spell **Spell out** Explain very clearly.
The solicitor spelled out the consequences of taking legal action in the matter.

Spick **Spick and span** Extremely neat and tidy. [Or. Nautical. A 'spick' is a spike or nail, a 'span' a chip of wood; a spick-and-span ship is one in which all wood and metal is new.]

Spike **Spike a person's guns** Take some (sudden) action which ends opposition. [Or. Military. Old-fashioned cannon were fired by applying a light to the 'touch-hole', one bored into the near end of the barrel. The object of an attacking enemy was always to hammer a spike or iron into this hole, making the cannon useless.]

Spin **In a flat spin** In a state of panic.
Spin out Draw out; prolong. Endure.
I don't think this gin will spin out for much longer.
Spin a yarn Tell a story. [Or. Nautical.]
The old man could spin many yarns of his youth.

Spirit **In high spirits** Cheerful. Opposite: **in low spirits.**
The spirit of the law The real meaning or intention of the law, as opposed to **the letter of the law,** the strict interpretation of its words.

Spite **In spite of** Despite; notwithstanding.
We're going to get married, in spite of the opposition of her family.
Out of (or from or in) spite With malicious intention.

Splash **Make a splash** [S] Cause a sensation, excitement.
We're going to make a splash by giving a big party on John's birthday.
Splash out (on) Spend liberally (on).

Splice **Splice the mainbrace** [S] Take a stimulating drink to keep one's spirits up. [Or. Nautical. The 'mainbrace' is the rope which fixes the main (or chief) mast in position.]

Spoil **Spoiling for a fight** Anxious and eager to quarrel or fight.
I realized that he was spoiling for a fight.
Spoil-sport One who impedes (by his words or behaviour) the enjoyment of others.

Sponge **Sponge on** Systematically and constantly obtain money from one's friends.
He's done no work for years, and lives by sponging on his relations.
Throw up the sponge Submit. Admit defeat. [Or. Boxing, where sponge was formerly thrown into ring by a man's seconds to signify his withdrawal from the contest.]

Spoon **Born with a silver spoon in one's mouth** Born of rich parents; born lucky.

S

Spot **A spot of** A small quantity of.
I'd like a spot of that cake, please.
Spot [S] Discover.
We soon spotted George in the crowd.
Spot cash Immediate payment in cash.
I've sold my bicycle for £5, spot cash.
Spot the winner Bet successfully.
I was lucky enough to spot the winner in the two o'clock race.
On the spot 1. At that particular place; there.
The police were on the spot within ten minutes.
2. Immediately; without delay.
I'll attend to it on the spot.
Similar to **there and then.**
Put on the spot Place in a difficult position.
If it gets into the newspapers he'll be put on the spot.

Spout **Up the spout** [S] In the pawnshop; pawned. [Or. The spout is the channel up which goods upon which money has been lent are sent to the storeroom to remain until claimed.] Also, in difficulty.

Sprat **Throw (*or* set) a sprat to catch a mackerel** Risk a little to gain much. Make a small gift or concession in the hope of obtaining a large one.

Spur **On the spur of the moment** Suddenly, without previous consideration.

Square **All square** Level; equal.
If I buy the next round, we shall be all square.
Back to square one Back to the beginning.
On the square [S] Honest; genuine.
I don't think he's on the square.
Square a man Bribe him.
Square peg in a round hole Person not fitted for his position.
His personality makes him something of a square peg at the factory.

Stable **Lock the stable door** Take precautions when the accident they are to prevent has already happened. [Or. Proverb: 'It is useless to lock the stable door when the steed is stolen.']

Staff **Over-staffed** With more employees than are needed.
Under-staffed The reverse. Similar to **short-handed.**

Stake **At stake** Dependent upon what is about to happen.
The future of the whole country is at stake.
Have a stake in Be involved in (the welfare of).
All ratepayers have a stake in the matter.

Stand **It stands to reason** It is logically clear and certain.
It stands to reason that two people cannot live as cheaply as one.
Stand aghast Be shocked, appalled.
I stand aghast when I see what the motor-car is doing to London.

Stand aloof Remain detached; refuse to share or co-operate with.
Stand aside 1. [LIT] Stand where the progress of others will not be impeded. Also **stand back.**
If you'll stand aside, these people can pass.
2. [MET] Give someone else an opportunity.
Stand by 1. Wait in a state of readiness.
The troops have been ordered to stand by.
2. Support by word or deed.
He stood by his friend through all his troubles.
3. Be an observer.
I will not stand by and do nothing.
Stand on ceremony Behave stiffly and ceremoniously. (Usually used in the negative.)
Don't stand on ceremony—make yourself at home.
Stand a chance Have any possibility.
I don't think your horse stands a chance of winning.
Stand corrected Admit to being wrong.
I am sorry for the mistake—I stand corrected.
Stand down Retire.
Stand on one's dignity Show—often absurdly—a sense of one's importance.
Stand fast (*or* firm) Remain immovable.
Stand one's ground Refuse to change one's statements or opinions.
The police tried to make her admit that she had made a mistake, but the girl stood her ground.
Similar to **stand (*or* stick) to one's guns.**
Stand on one's own (two) feet (*or* legs) Accept full responsibility for one's own actions; accept no assistance.
My uncle offered to help me, but I told him I would rather stand on my own legs.
Stand in a person's light Prevent his advancement; spoil his career. (Usually used in the negative.)
Stand-offish Haughty; consciously superior; curt.
Stand out 1. Remain in opposition; refuse to co-operate.
The conspirators did their best to persuade all the men to join them, but three stood out.
2. Be conspicuous.
The statue stands out against the trees.
Stand out for Insist upon.
The workmen are standing out for higher wages.
Stand over 1. Stand near, usually to enforce an order.
She stood over the boy while he washed his face.
2. Put aside for a time.
The accounts can stand over till next week.

Stand on one's rights Insist upon one's legal rights.
If he stands on his rights, he can claim all his wife's savings.
Stand in good stead Prove useful to.
This old coat will stand me in good stead if the weather turns cold.
Stand to Similar to **stand by** (1).
Stand to win (*or* **lose)** Be in a position where one is capable of
winning (or losing).
If this horse wins, I stand to lose £10.
Stand up for Support openly, by speech or action.
He stood up for his brother.
Stand up to 1. Confront boldly; oppose.
If the lawyer tries to bully you, stand up to him.
2. Be capable of. Bear. Tolerate. Carry the weight of. Endure.
This roof won't stand up to the winter weather.

Standard **Standard of living** Degree of material comfort achieved by a
person, society, etc.

Standstill **At a standstill** No longer moving or functioning.
During the strike, all work in the factories was at a standstill.

Star **Star turn** A 'turn' or act by a famous performer. Frequently
applied to any conspicuous or successful incident.
The star turn of the party was Uncle George's limerick.

Stare **Stare one in the face** Confront; be evident and obvious.
The troops saw defeat staring them in the face.

Stark **Stark staring mad** Extremely mad.

Start **A fresh start** A new beginning.

Stave **Stave in** Smash inwards. Crush out of shape.
If the fire takes hold the walls will stave in.
Stave off Avert. Ward off.
A late goal staved off defeat.

Steal **Steal a march on** Gain an advantage for which one's adversary
was not prepared.
Steal one's thunder Forestall him. [Or. Playwright's remark when
stage-effect of thunder he had intended for his own play was used
first in another.]
Steal upon Creep softly upon.

Steam **Get up steam** Summon energy for a special effort.
Let off steam Get rid of surplus energy.
Steamed up [S] Angry.

Steer **Steer clear of** Avoid; evade.
If you want to steer clear of trouble, don't get married.
Steer a middle course Avoid extremes; act moderately;
compromise.

Step **Retrace one's steps** Return in the direction one had come.
He retraced his steps, looking for the purse.

Step by step Slowly and methodically.
Step by step she taught the dog to obey her.
Step in Intervene.
Step on it [S] Hurry.
Stepping-stone (*or* stones) [LIT] Stones in a stream used to enable one to cross with dry feet. [MET] Anything which may act as a means to an end (usually to an improvement).
He regards his present job purely as a stepping-stone.

Stew **Stew in one's own juice** Suffer the consequences of one's own (misguided) actions.

Stick **In a cleft stick** In such a position that it is very difficult to make a decision.
Stick it; stick at it; stick it out [S] Endure; persevere under difficulties.
This road is terrible, but if we can stick it we shall save over a mile.
Stick-in-the-mud An unenterprising, unambitious person.
Stick at nothing Stop at nothing; be restrained by no scruple or impediment.
She is one of those women who will stick at nothing to get what she wants.
Stick out Same as **stand out** (2).
Stick out a mile [S] Be very prominent.
It stuck out a mile that he wasn't interested.
Stick out for Same as **stand out for**.
Stick in one's throat (*or* [S] gizzard) [LIT] Choke one. [MET] Cause disgust or aversion.
It sticks in my throat to have to admit defeat.
Stick to one's guns Not to be budged from one's position.
Stick up to Offer resistance to.
Stick up for Same as **stand up for**.

Stiff **Stiff as a poker (a ramrod, buckram)** Rigid; formal.
The old lady sat upright, stiff as a poker, and glared at me.
Stiff upper lip Firmness of character.
It is not now regarded as fashionable to keep a stiff upper lip.

Still **Still life** A phrase applied by artists to compositions in which there are only inanimate objects—flowers, fruit, furniture, etc.
Still waters run deep Streams which flow silently are usually deep. Quiet, undemonstrative people are frequently those who have depths of emotion, etc., even though they are successfully concealed.

Stock **Lay in a stock of** Acquire supplies of.
On the stocks Being made, but not finished. [Or. Shipping.]
I have two novels on the stocks.
Stock still Absolutely motionless.

The boy stood stock still, too terrified to breathe.

Stock-in-trade [LIT] A tradesman's stock, or supply of goods for sale. [MET] Any possession, tangible or otherwise, which one employs in one's business or profession.

Her stock-in-trade consisted of plenty of confidence, a knowledge of French, and a charming smile.

Take stock of Consider the value or possibilities of.

He took stock of his present position.

Stone **Leave no stone unturned** Use every possible effort to find out; investigate thoroughly.

The police will leave no stone unturned to discover the murderer.

Stone blind (*or* deaf) Totally blind or deaf. Also, with the same effect, **stone cold** and **stone dead.** (But not, for some reason, stone dumb.)

Stone's-throw A short distance (theoretically, as far as one can throw a stone).

The house was within a stone's-throw of the sea.

Stony-broke Entirely without money.

Stoop **Stoop to conquer** Humiliate oneself to achieve success in the end. [Or. Goldsmith's comedy, *She Stoops to Conquer.*]

Stop **Come to a full stop** Cease completely.

A dead stop A complete and sudden halt.

The car came to a dead stop in the middle of the road.

Stop-gap Temporary solution.

Stop-gap measures will not solve this crisis.

Stop at nothing Ignore all impediments.

Stop by [S] [U.S.A.] Call in on a casual visit.

Store **In store** About to come.

I think you've a surprise in store.

Set store by Value; attach importance to.

I've kept all your mother's letters, as I know you set great store by them.

Storm **Bow before the storm** Yield to public indignation.

The Town Council wanted to close the gardens on Sunday, but they bowed before the storm.

Storm in a teacup Much excitement and trouble over a trivial matter.

Story **The story goes** It is said.

Straight **Keep a straight face** See under *Face.*

Straight away; straight off Immediately.

The doctor will see you straight away.

Straightforward 1. Without complications. 2. Honest.

Straight from the shoulder See under *Shoulder.*

Straight off Without hesitation.

Straight tip [S] A definite hint; also private and accurate information. [Or. Betting.]
Take a straight tip from me, and stay away from that shop.

Strain **Strain at a gnat and swallow a camel** Object to some trivial matter while condoning or permitting a far greater offence.
Strain one's eyes 1. Make an extra effort to see.
If you strain your eyes, you can just see the church.
2. Tire one's eyes.
Don't strain your eyes by reading such small print.

Straw **Clutch (*or* grasp) at a straw** Grasp at anything, however trivial, to escape disaster; gain hope from the slightest sign that may appear favourable. [Or. The saying that a drowning man will clutch at even a straw to save himself.]
The last straw Any final unendurable event; a culminating injury. [Or. Proverb: 'It is the last straw that breaks the camel's back.']
Make bricks without straw See under *Brick.*
A man of straw See under *Man.*
Not care a straw (*or* two straws) Care nothing at all.
A straw will show which way the wind blows A trivial thing will indicate what is likely to happen. (Hence, **a straw (*or* straws) in the wind.** Hints which indicate **which way the wind is blowing,** i.e. what is likely to happen.)
The President has not made any firm promises, but his latest speech is taken as a straw in the wind.

Stream **Go (*or* drift) with the stream** Follow the example of the majority.

Stretch **At a stretch** 1. With an effort; only by straining one's resources.
We can manage to entertain ten people at dinner at a stretch.
2. Continuously.
Some lorry-drivers are working ten hours at a stretch.
Stretch one's legs Take exercise by walking.
Stretch a point Make an exception to a rule. Extend an arrangement, rule, law, etc., beyond its legitimate extent.
The bus conductor stretched a point and allowed fifteen standing passengers.

Strides **Make rapid strides** Progress quickly.

Strike **On strike** Refusing to work until some grievance is corrected.
Strike a bargain Reach an agreement.
Strike a blow for Do something on behalf of.
The revolt struck a blow for freedom.
Strike at Aim a blow at.
Strike at the root of Threaten destruction to.
Aircraft noise strikes at the root of civilized living.
Strike back Return a blow.

S

The Opposition struck back very successfully.
Strike the happy medium Arrive at the best possible compromise.
Strike home Strike a vital blow; strike directly at the heart or emotions.
It was only a short speech, but it certainly struck home.
Strike while the iron is hot Take advantage of a suitable opportunity.
Strike off 1. Remove from an official list or record.
His name was struck off the register of doctors.
2. Print (illustrations, etc.)
Two hundred copies of the etching were struck off.
Strike on Luckily encounter.
I've struck on a plan for solving the problem.
Strike out 1. Make violent movements with one's arms or legs.
The swimmer struck out for the shore.
2. Similar to **strike off** (1).
Strike terror, fear, *etc.* Create terror; terrify.
Within striking distance (of) Near enough (to).
If we leave early we should be within striking distance of Stafford by lunch-time.

String **String together** [LIT] Link, as by a string or cord. [MET] Arrange in sequence.
I've strung together a few ideas for discussion.

Stroke **A stroke (of work)** Any work. (Usually used in negative.)
I haven't done a stroke all weekend.
A stroke of luck Unexpected good fortune.
On the stroke (of) Punctually (at).

Strong **Strong box** A metal box designed to protect valuable papers from fire or thieves.

Struck **Struck all of a heap** [S] [MET] Stunned; utterly astonished. [Old f.]
Stuck **Stuck up** [S] Vain; arrogant.
Study **In a brown study** See under *Brown.*
Make a study of Pursue knowledge in.

Stumble **Stumble upon** Discover by chance.
I stumbled upon some interesting old letters.
Stumbling-block Obstacle.
The biggest stumbling-block is the size of the kitchen.

Stump **Stumped for** At a loss for.
He never seems to be stumped for ideas.

Stung **Stung (or wounded or cut) to the quick** See under *Cut.*
Subject **Change the subject** Talk of something else.
A sore subject A subject about which one is particularly sensitive.
We didn't discuss his son's absence, as we knew it was a sore subject.
A subject for A matter for. A cause of.

His success is a subject for congratulation.

Such **Such-and-such a person** See **so-and-so.**

Such being the case Considering the present state of affairs.

Such being the case, we were very lucky to find a house.

Suchlike Things, people, etc., of that kind.

I don't much care for night-clubs and suchlike.

Sum **Sum up** Give a final résumé and analysis of what has occurred.

One may sum up the situation by saying they are living in a condition of uneasy peace.

Summer **Summer time** The official alteration of Greenwich time, in order to allow more hours of daylight in summer to be used.

Sun **A place in the sun** Favourable situation.

Under the sún In the whole world.

There's nothing new under the sun.

Sure **Make sure; make certain** Render absolutely certain.

I will make sure that the letter is posted tonight.

Sure enough In accordance with something anticipated.

I said you'd come, and sure enough here you are.

Sure as Fate Beyond a doubt, with absolute certainty.

As sure as Fate, I shall get a letter tomorrow telling me to go home.

Surprise **Taken by surprise** Suddenly surprised; astonished.

She was so taken by surprise that she burst into tears.

To my surprise Contrary to what I expected.

Suspense **In suspense** In a condition of uncertainty.

We shall be kept in suspense until we receive further news.

Swallow **Swallow an insult** Submit to an insult without protest.

Swallow up Engulf; cause to disappear.

An earthquake can swallow up an entire town.

His wife's debts swallowed up all his savings.

Swear **Swear by** Have great belief in. Recommend. Resort to frequently.

My wife swears by these indigestion-tablets.

Swear like a trooper Use particularly bad language. [Or. A trooper is a soldier, a member of a troop of horse.]

Sweat **In a (cold) sweat** [LIT] Perspiring. [MET] 1. In a state of anxiety. 2. In a hurry.

Sweat on [S] Count on. Rely on.

I'm sweating on the car's being repaired by tonight.

Sweated labour Men employed for long hours for low wages.

Sweep **Make a clean sweep (of)** Get rid or dispose (of).

The new manager is going to make a clean sweep of the whole establishment.

Swell **Swell the ranks of** Add to an already large number of people or things.

George has lost his job, and now swells the ranks of the unemployed.
Swelled (swollen) head Conceit.

Swim **Go swimmingly** Proceed smoothly and well; become a complete success.
I am sure your party tomorrow will go swimmingly.
In the swim Fully involved in what is going on.
We're new to the district, and not yet in the swim.

Swing **In full swing** Making full progress.
The fête was in full swing when the storm came.
Go with a swing Proceed in a lively and enjoyable manner.
The whole event went with a swing.

Swoop **At one fell swoop** In one complete and sudden disaster.
She lost her husband, her son and her home at one fell swoop.

Sword **Cross swords with** Quarrel with. Engage in rivalry or controversy with.
He's not a man I'd like to cross swords with.
Sword of Damocles A disaster liable to occur at any moment; a threat to one's peace and happiness. [Or. The story of Damocles who, being invited by Dionysius to a splendid feast, looked up from his seat to see a sword suspended above his head by a single hair.]
Put to the sword Executed.

T

T **Cross the T's** Be very accurate. Correct or finish something in detail.
To a T Exactly. [Or. The T-shaped piece of wood used by carpenters to make sure that joists are exactly at right angles.]
This measurement is correct to a T.

Tackle Undertake (usually with a little difficulty).
I'll tackle the job as soon as I have time.

Tag See **rag tag and bobtail**

Tail **Tail between his legs** Cowed and humiliated, like a frightened dog.
Tail off Become weaker.
Turn tail Turn one's back and run away.
With one's tail up In good spirits.

Take **Taken aback** Disconcerted; surprised.
The man was utterly taken aback when they recognized him.
Take account of See **take into account**.
Take after Resemble, physically or otherwise.
Mary takes after her father, and is very musical.
Take a running jump Term of contempt or disagreement.

If you think I'm going out in this weather, you can take a running jump.
Take back Withdraw.
I take back everything I said.
Take a back seat [S] Become less important and prominent; be supplanted.
Now that the President has arrived, the Vice-President will have to take a back seat.
Take the bit between one's teeth See *Bit.*
Take the bull by the horns Confront a difficulty boldly and without any evasion.
Take the cake (*or* the biscuit) [S] See *Biscuit.*
Take care Be careful.
Take care that you don't slip on the frosty road.
Take a cue Understand a hint. Follow someone's example. [Or. The 'cue' is the word which indicates when an actor is to appear.]
Take down 1. [LIT]
*Take down that book (*or take that book down*) from the shelf.*
2. [MET] Record; write.
Take down this letter, please.
Take down a peg [S] See *Peg.*
Take effect Come into operation. Make an impact.
The new regulations will take effect from next year.
Take one's fancy Charm; attract; interest.
I saw nothing in the shop to take my fancy.
Take flight; take to flight Depart quickly.
The thieves, hearing footsteps, took to flight.
Taken for a ride Deceived.
Take for granted Assume as a fact.
Take in good (bad) part Accept good-naturedly (or angrily).
I hope you'll take my advice in good part.
Take in hand Undertake. Control.
The workmen will take the repairs in hand next week.
Take to heart Be seriously affected.
He has taken your words to heart, and will try to be more careful in future.
Take heed of (*or* to) Attend; be warned by.
Take heed of what I've told you.
Take a hint Pay attention to, and act on, a gentle suggestion, without needing explicit guidance.
Take hold of Seize; grasp.
The boy took hold of the ladder, and began to climb.
Take in 1. Mislead; deceive.
We were completely taken in by his story.
2. Buy regularly. (More usually, simply **Take.**)

I take (in) the 'Gardeners' Magazine'.
3. Receive, as a means of livelihood.
Miss Brown takes in lodgers.
4. Escort to a dining-room, etc. [Old f.]
Our host took in the principal guest.
Take into account Include in one's calculations, plans, ideas, etc.
I didn't take into account the possibility of such a long delay.
Take it from me [S] Accept what I say as true. Also **take my word for it.**
Take a liking, dislike, fancy, *etc.,* **to** The same as 'like', etc., except that the effect is rather more emphatic and spontaneous.
Take off 1. Mimic.
He took off the headmaster perfectly.
2. Rise from the ground.
The aeroplane will take off at three o'clock.
Take-off Piece of mimicry or caricature.
Take oneself off Depart, generally abruptly or indignantly.
They took themselves off without saying good-bye.
Take offence (*or* **umbrage)** Be annoyed; angry.
He always takes offence at any kind of criticism.
Take on Accept responsibility for.
I've taken on the organization of our Hospital Fête.
See **take upon oneself.**
Take out 1. Obtain the issue of (in a legal sense).
I am taking out a patent for the invention.
2. Extract.
The dentist took out five of Mary's teeth.
3. Accompany (for a walk, etc.); in charge of.
Father isn't at home; he's taken out the dog.
Take it out of one 1. Exhaust; weaken.
So much hill-climbing takes it out of me.
2. Have revenge. (More usually, **take it out on.**)
Just because you're in a bad temper, don't take it out on the dog.
Take over Take the place of someone else.
You stay with the children until ten o'clock, and then I'll take over.
Take-over bid Attempt by a company to purchase another.
Take pains (*or* **trouble)** Make a considerable effort.
I took pains to explain the facts clearly.
Take part in Share; co-operate; act with others.
Her sister takes part in all local events.
Take a person's part Support; identify oneself with.
The boy's mother will naturally take his part.
Take place Happen; occur.
The race will take place tomorrow.

T

Take the rough with the smooth Accept philosophically both
pleasant and unpleasant things.
*If one becomes a teacher, one must be ready to take the rough with the
smooth.*
Take the shine off (*or* out of) [S] Cause to appear inferior;
supersede.
Take sides Support one adversary against another.
A judge should remain impartial, and not take sides.
Take silk Become a Queen's Counsel, an honour which entitles a
barrister to wear a silk gown in Court, instead of the cloth one
previously worn.
Take one's stand Decide upon a mental attitude; base one's
argument.
I take my stand on the fact that all men are born free.
Take stock of Examine thoroughly and in detail.
He decided to take stock of the present condition of affairs.
Take by storm Capture by a violent attack. [Or. Military.]
Captivate sensationally.
The film has taken everywhere by storm.
Take to Form a liking for.
The baby took to the kitten at once.
Similar to **take a liking to**.
Take to one's bed Go to bed, usually for some time, as the result of
illness, etc.
My husband feels so ill that he has taken to his bed.
Take to task Blame; reprove.
His wife took him to task for his forgetfulness.
Take too much Become intoxicated.
Though Bill enjoys a drink he never takes too much.
Take in tow [LIT] Attach a cable, etc., to a vehicle, ship, etc., to
pull it along. [Or. Nautical.] [MET] Take charge of; be responsible
for.
Bill seems to have taken most of his wife's family in tow.
Take on trust Believe without evidence or proof.
We are prepared to take on trust the facts you have told us.
Take up 1. Absorb; occupy.
Attending to a husband and six children takes up most of her time.
2. Lift.
We will take up the carpet and send it to be cleaned tomorrow.
Take up the threads Resume after an interruption.
She came home from a long holiday to take up the threads of her old life.
Take up with Become friendly or intimate with.
Take upon oneself Assume or accept responsibility without being
asked.

T

I've taken it upon myself to ask the Bishop to dinner.
Take the will for the deed Accept the desire to be kind and helpful, even if nothing practical results.

Tale **Old wives' tale** Superstitious tradition, often foolish but believed to be true by some people at the moment and many in the past. Also, an unconvincing story.
His cure for rheumatism is a real old wives' tale.
Tale-bearer One who spreads rumours, and who tells malicious stories of other people.
Tell its own tale Need no explanation.
The canary's feathers in the cat's mouth tell their own tale.
Tell tales out of school Reveal another person's private affairs; discuss them with inappropriate people, or at inappropriate times.
Thereby hangs a tale There is an interesting story or explanation concerned with that event. [Or. Quotation from Shakespeare's *The Taming of the Shrew.*]

Talk **Idle talk** Foolish, useless talk; gossip.
Small talk Talk concerning trivialities; formal and polite conversation.
The Duke of Wellington once said that he had no small talk when conversing with Queen Victoria.
Table-talk Conversation of the friendly and entertaining type which takes place among intimates at a meal. Applied especially to the talk of famous people.
Talk the back (*or* hind) legs off a donkey (*or* horse) Be very talkative.
Talk over 1. Discuss.
We talked over his plans for the future.
2. Convince; bring to one's own way of thinking. Similarly, **talk round**.
He wouldn't come at first, but we talked him over.
Talking of As we are discussing.
Talking of money, have you paid the gas bill yet?
Talk through one's hat Talk nonsense.

Tall **A tall order** [S] An order or request difficult to carry out.
Tall story One difficult to believe; an exaggerated and improbable story.

Tape **Get (*or* have) somebody (*or* something) taped** [S] Have person or thing summed up, understood, solved, etc.
The electrician seems to have got the job all taped.

Tar **Tarred with the same brush** Having the same defects.
She is rather conceited, and her son is tarred with the same brush.

Taste **There's no accounting for taste** Everyone has different tastes, some of them difficult to understand.

They get on together very well: there's no accounting for taste.
A taste for A natural appreciation of, or liking for.
I have no taste whatever for Japanese art.
Tear   **Tear to tatters, ribbons,** *etc.* [LIT] Tear roughly into small pieces.
[MET] Destroy (e.g. someone's argument).
Tear oneself away Make oneself leave (usually used in negative).
*It was such a good exhibition that I could hardly tear myself
away.*
Tear one's hair Be angry, very anxious, perplexed.
I was tearing my hair with impatience at the delay.
Tears   **Bathed, drowned** *or* **dissolved in tears** Weeping excessively.
Crocodile tears Hypocritical grief; tears shed by one who is not, in
fact, grieving at all. [Or. The legend, based on the sucking and
oozing sounds made by the movement of crocodiles in the
swampy ground in which they live, that the animals deliberately
weep noisily, so that travellers go to rescue what they imagine to
be a lost child.]
Reduce to tears Compel to weep by pity or distress (or,
occasionally, by excessive laughter).
Teens   **In one's teens; teenage** At any age from thirteen to nineteen
inclusive.
Teeth   **In the teeth of** In spite of; without regard to.
They married in the teeth of her parents' opposition.
Lie in one's teeth Tell serious and blatant untruths. (Emphatic
form of 'lie'.)
Make someone's teeth chatter Cause one to tremble or shiver so
much that the upper and lower teeth click together.
The bitter north wind made their teeth chatter.
Set one's teeth on edge [LIT] Cause a grating or tingling sensation
around one's teeth, through their contact with acid, etc. [MET]
Cause a general discomfort at some particularly harsh sound, or by
embarrassing action or speech.
For heaven's sake oil that wheel—it sets my teeth on edge.
Skin of one's teeth See under **Skin**.
Tell   **Tell one's beads** Say a series of prayers as one passes one's fingers
over the beads of a rosary; say the Rosary. ('Tell' in this sense means
'count'.)
Tell off 1. Select a number of persons by name for a special
purpose.
The captain told off six men to act as escort to the prisoners.
2. [S] Reprove. Express one's views frankly and unfavourably.
I told him off for keeping me waiting.
Tell that to the Marines (or, more correctly, **the Horse Marines**,
such a corps being non-existent, as Marines are a sea-going force)

T

Tell that story to someone who doesn't exist, since no one who does exist is likely to believe it.

You're telling me! [S] I am quite aware of that.

Temper **Lose one's temper; be out of temper** Exchange one's good temper for a bad temper; be angry, irritable, in an unpleasant mood. Opposite: **keep one's temper.**

Temper the wind to the shorn lamb Arrange matters to suit the weakest element.

Ten **Ten to one** It is ten chances to one that it will happen; very probably. (Similarly other numbers.)

Tell him you've broken the vase; ten to one he won't be angry.

Tenterhooks **On tenterhooks** In a state of acute anxiety or suspense. [Or. Tenterhooks are hooks on which cloth is stretched after being woven.]

The students were on tenterhooks to hear the result of the examination.

Terms **Come to terms** Reach a formal and businesslike arrangement.

If you're willing to sell your house, we can soon come to terms.

Couched in terms Expressed in words.

What he said was couched in terms of deep affection.

On good (*or* bad) terms with Having a friendly (or unfriendly) relationship with (normally applied to relationships between people). Similarly **on speaking terms** = in a relationship which is such that both parties speak to one another.

We have always been on bad terms (we are not on speaking terms) with our neighbours.

On one's terms With the conditions (e.g. price, rules) laid down by one.

We shall have to accept the goods on their terms.

Thank **Thank goodness, heaven,** *etc.* A general ejaculation of gratitude.

Thank goodness it hasn't rained today!

Thank one's (lucky) stars Be grateful. [Or. The stars are supposed to protect a person and bring good fortune—and the reverse.]

You may thank your lucky stars that you weren't in the house when the party was on.

Thanks to Owing to; because of.

No thanks to No credit or gratitude is due to.

It's no thanks to you that the house wasn't burnt down.

That **At that** Thereupon. Then.

At that, the meeting broke up.

In that Since. In so far as.

I could understand his point of view, in that I'd been in a similar position myself.

That's that [S] A concluding emphasis to a statement.

I refuse, and that's that.

That is to say To express differently, or more fully.

He's a cutler—that is to say, a man who sells knives and sharp tools.

Thick **(As) thick as thieves** [S] Very intimate.

A bit thick [S] Unreasonable.

It's a bit thick to be asked to wait longer.

In the thick of In the densest, most congested part [LIT and MET].

We were in the thick of the crowd.

Don't disturb me—I'm in the thick of a job.

Thick-skinned Not sensitive to reproach, criticism, etc.

He's too thick-skinned to see the impression he makes.

Through thick and thin Through every trouble or difficulty, good fortune or bad fortune.

His wife said she loved him, and would follow him through thick and thin.

Thing **Have a thing about** Be obsessed by.

Just the thing; the very thing Exactly what is needed or appropriate.

This carpet is just the thing for the bedroom.

Know a thing or two Be experienced, shrewd.

Of all things From among all the things which might have happened.

And now we're told—of all things!—that we shall have to leave the house.

On to a good thing Engaged in a profitable or beneficial activity.

As the only vet in the town, he's on to a good thing.

Taking one thing with another Weighing the advantages against the disadvantages; considering all the circumstances.

Taking one thing with another, we are better off in England.

The thing (to do) *or* **the done thing** The correct procedure. The custom. The fashion.

Think **I don't think!** [S] Used as a term of ironic dissent.

Electricity pylons certainly improve this landscape—I don't think!

Think better of it Abandon an unwise decision.

He was going to argue with the shop-assistant, but thought better of it.

Think fit (*or* proper) Decide; consider suitable or appropriate. (The phrase is frequently used ironically.)

The young man, having no job and no money, thought fit to get married.

Think highly (*or* much) of Admire.

Think little (*or* nothing) of Treat casually; regard as normal.

In Australia, one thinks nothing of riding fifty miles to a dance.

Think no end of Have a very high opinion of.

We think no end of our new shopping-centre.

T

Think no more of Forget.
Think out Meditate upon; consider.
We must think out some other way of repairing it.
Think over Consider at some length.
I'll need a few days to think it over.
Way of thinking Point of view; personal aspect.
According to my way of thinking, all wars do more harm than good.

This **This, that and the other** Various unspecified things.

Thorn **A thorn in the flesh (*or* in one's side)** An infliction; an annoyance which one has to endure. [Or. The custom of the ancient Pharisees of putting thorns in their garments to prick their legs when walking.]
That aunt who lives with the Wilkinsons is a permanent thorn in the flesh.

Thought **A penny for your thoughts** What are you thinking about?
Quick as thought Instantly.
Second thoughts Further consideration.
On second thoughts, I'll go by train.
Take no thought for Do not worry or concern yourself about.
Take thought Consider thoroughly.
Take thought before you do it.

Thread **Lose the thread** (of an argument, etc.) Stop understanding.
Pick up the thread(s) Resume after an interruption.
It's difficult to pick up the thread of this book after a week.
Thread (*or* edge) one's way Move to one's destination through narrow or crowded streets.
We threaded our way through the crowds at the station.

Threshold **On the threshold** [LIT] The 'sill' (horizontal piece of wood or stone) that forms the bottom of the door-frame at the entrance of a building. [MET] The beginning of anything.
The scientist felt he was on the threshold of solving a tremendous mystery.

Through By means of.
He obtained the information through his own efforts.
Through with [S] Finished with.
I'll be through with the job in half-an-hour.

Throw **Throw away** Lose by neglect or recklessness.
He threw away his chances of winning.
Throw dust in the eyes of Obscure the facts; mislead.
The Prime Minister was accused of throwing dust in the public's eye.
Throw a fit [S] [LIT] Have a fit. [MET] Become highly agitated or excited.
Father will throw a fit when he hears that the car's broken down again.
Throw in Give in addition.

190

The herrings were ten for 50p, and the fishmonger threw in an extra one.
Throw light upon Make plainer.
This information may throw light upon the mystery.
Throw off Discard. Get rid of.
He appears to have thrown off his cold.
Throw off the scent Distract from what is of true importance, from the true facts. [Or. Hunting.]
The police were completely thrown off the scent, and arrested the wrong man.
Throw open Make accessible.
They intend to throw open the house to the public.
Throw out Reject. Distract.
Throw out a suggestion Make a suggestion, usually tentatively.
Throw over Abandon; discard; have no further association with.
He was engaged to Jane, but she threw him over.
Throw up the sponge Surrender; abandon abruptly; admit complete defeat. [Or. Boxing. The sponge used to bathe the boxers' faces was thrown into the air when the loser admits his defeat.]
You've still a chance of finishing it; don't throw up the sponge.

Thumb **Thumbs up!** Exclamation expressing satisfaction.
Under one's thumb Under one's control or influence.
She has her husband completely under her thumb.

Thunder **Like a thunderclap (*or* thunderbolt)** Causing great astonishment.
The news of his resignation was like a thunderclap.
Thunders of applause Applause so noisy and continuous that it suggests thunder.
There were thunders of applause when the curtain fell.
Thunderstruck Overcome with astonishment.

Tick **Half a tick** [S] A very short space of time.
On tick [S] On credit, hire-purchase; without immediate payment.
Tick off 1. Check (by placing a small mark, e.g. against items in a list).
Please tick the names off as I call them out.
2. Reprimand gently.
The doctor ticked me off for over-eating.

Tickle **Tickled to death** [S] Extremely amused.

Tide **Tide over** Continue until changed and usually improved conditions take place.
I need £1 to tide me over till I can get to the bank.

Tie **Black tie** A black tie worn with a dinner-jacket. (The idiom is used as indicating the whole outfit.)
White tie Similarly, a white tie worn with white waistcoat, coat with 'tails', and black trousers—the more formal evening dress.

Time **Against time** With all speed.

Ahead of time Before the expected time.

All the time Continuously.

At this point in time At the present state of affairs; at this moment.
At this point in time it is difficult to say how long the strike will last.

At one time Formerly.

At times; from time to time At intervals; occasionally.
He seems at times to know more than he says.
Similar to **now and then; now and again.**

Beat time The action of a conductor indicating the 'beats' in the music with his baton.

Before one's time Before one was born.
Compare **born before one's time.**

Bide one's time Wait patiently. [Or. 'Bide' is an abbrev. of 'abide' = stay, remain.]
If we bide our time it will all come right.

For the time being Temporarily; during the time that is immediately coming.
We are going to Rome as soon as we can, but are staying in London for the time being.

From time to time Occasionally.
I only go to the cinema from time to time.

A good time 1. A highly pleasurable time.
Jane and Joan are at Brighton, having a thoroughly good time.
2. A considerable period.
I am going into the town, and shall not be back for a good time.

Hard times Times of poverty, suffering, or discomfort.
He went through hard times when he was young.

High time Fully time.
It is high time that we went home.

High old time [S] A gay time.

In (the) course of time Eventually; after some time had passed.

In time 1. Before it is too late.
The doctor came in time to save her life.
2. After some considerable time had passed.
In time he forgot all about her.

In good time Early; with time to spare.
Be at the station in good time.

In the nick of time Just in time; almost, but not quite, too late.
The door of the tiger's cage was shut in the nick of time.

In no (or less than no) time Very soon; almost immediately.
We shall be ready in less than no time.
Similar to **in half a tick; two-twos; half a jiffy.**

Many a time Repeatedly; frequently.

Many a time we walk by the river.

Once upon a time Some time ago; in the past. (The traditional beginning to children's stories.)

Once upon a time there lived a king with three sons.

Overtime Extra time; additional hours of work for which payment is made.

Part-time Time which does not occupy all the usual working day.

Marjory has a part-time job taking care of young children.

Pass the time of day (with) Exchange greeting (with a person).

Pressed for time Short of time; very busy.

I can't stay more than ten minutes, as I am pressed for time.

Stand the test of time Remain valid, unaltered, strong, etc., despite the passage or effect of time.

Unlike some laws, this one has stood the test of time very well.

Stated time A time already fixed.

At the stated time the ship will leave the harbour.

Take time by the forelock Act promptly and without delay. [Or. Time is always represented as an old man, bald except for a 'forelock' or tuft of hair over his forehead.] Similar to **strike while the iron is hot.**

Time after time Repeatedly.

The fence has had to be rebuilt time after time.

Time and again Frequently.

The children have been warned about the danger time and again.

Time's up [S] The stated time has come to an end, is finished.

Time's up—you must say good-bye.

Time of day The time, the hour.

What's the time of day?

Time of life Age.

At my time of life I can't be expected to dance.

Time of one's life A most enjoyable period.

I had the time of my life at the party.

Time on one's hands Time to waste, to spare; superfluous time.

As I had a good deal of time on my hands, I decided to explore the City.

Time out of mind; from time immemorial Longer than can be remembered. [Old f.]

Farmers have fed their sheep here time out of mind.

Times out of (or without) number Many times; times beyond counting.

You've been told times without number to wash your hands when you come to dinner.

Times, days, years, *etc.,* **to come** In the future.

T

In times to come none of us will have to work.

Work against time Use special efforts to finish a piece of work within a stated time.
We are working aginst time to complete the house by Christmas.

Tip **A straight tip** [S] Definite and accurate information; also (frequently) a plain warning. Also **the tip-off**. A hint.
He got the straight tip—work harder, or you'll fail the exam.
Tip the wink [S] Warn; give a signal.
I'm going to sleep; tip me the wink when tea's ready.

Tiptoe **On tiptoe** [LIT] Standing on the tips of one's toes. [MET] a state of excitement and tension.
The children were on tiptoe when the day of the party arrived.

Tip-top [S] Excellent; the best of its kind.
We had a tip-top breakfast at the hotel.

Tit for tat An equivalent; something, frequently unpleasant, given in return for something else.
The little girl tore her brother's book, and tit-for-tat he hid her doll.

Tittle-tattle Idle, chattering gossip.

To **To and fro** (= To and from.) From one spot to another and back again.
The sentry paced to and fro.

Toe **Toe the line** Conform, usually under pressure, to rules, etc.
The Party expects M.P.s to toe the line.
Tread on one's toes Offend one's feelings, prejudices, etc.

Together **Together with** With; also.
I am selling the house, together with the furniture.

Token **By the same token** Further; moreover.

Tom **(Any) Tom, Dick or (and) Harry** Persons taken at random. Any unspecified people.
It's not the sort of club that admits any Tom, Dick or Harry.
Tom Tiddler's ground Imaginary place where great wealth may be obtained without effort.

Ton **Like a ton of bricks** Very heavily or severely.

Tongue **Give tongue** Repeat. [Or. Hunting. Hounds are said to give tongue, or utter their peculiar cry, when the fox is seen.]
I wouldn't give tongue to such gossip.
Hold one's tongue Become silent; cease to speak.
Lose one's tongue Be too bashful to speak. Opposite: **find one's tongue.**
On the tip of one's tongue On the verge of being spoken; almost but not quite uttered.
It was on the tip of my tongue to tell him, but I was too frightened.
Tongue-tied Silent through embarrassment or fear.

Wag one's tongue Talk indiscreetly, or too much.
Too many tongues have been wagging for the matter to remain confidential any longer.
With one's tongue in one's cheek Without meaning what one says; insincerely.
He said he was terribly sorry, but I knew he spoke with his tongue in his cheek.

Tooth **A sweet tooth** A liking for sweet things—jam, sugar, etc.
Long in the tooth Old. [Or. Horses, where age can be estimated from length of teeth because the gums recede.]
Tooth and nail With extreme fierceness.

Top **From top to toe** [LIT] From one's head to one's feet. [MET] From beginning to end.
She was impeccably dressed from top to toe.
Top dog [S] Victor. Master.
Top gear The highest gear of a car engine.
Top speed; full speed As fast as possible.
The car drove through the town at top speed.
Top of the tree (or ladder) The highest point in one's business or profession.
He has reached the top of the tree as a surgeon.
Top up Fill up something partly empty. Finish; conclude.
Please top up the oil and water.
See **Sleep.**

Topsy-turvy In a state of confusion or disarray. Inverted, the normal position reversed.
After the party, the whole room was topsy-turvy.
Similar to **upside down.**

Toss **Toss up** Decide by spinning a coin. See **heads or tails.** Hence **win the toss, lose the toss.**
A toss-up A complete uncertainty; as likely as unlikely.
It's a toss-up whether I will be able to come.

Touch **In touch with** In communication, or contact, with.
I haven't been in touch with him for some years.
Lose touch Cease to have any communication with. Opposite: **keep in touch (with).**
I used to see him fairly often, but I've lost touch with him lately.
Touch and go Extremely doubtful or precarious.
It was touch and go whether we should arrive in time.
Touch up Restore or improve by a number of small details (especially with a brush or pen).
Touch upon Refer to briefly.
The preacher touched upon the restlessness of the present time.
Touch wood Expression meaning 'I hope my luck continues'.

T

Wouldn't touch (it) with a bargepole [S] Wouldn't have anything to do with (it), because of (its) unpleasantness, etc.

Tower **Ivory tower** Pleasant shelter from harsh reality.
We are living in an ivory tower if we think we can ignore the growth of world population.
Tower of strength A great support and help.
In a towering passion (*or* rage) Dominated by tremendous danger.

Track **Beaten track** [LIT] A pathway which has been beaten or flattened by many feet. [MET] A regular routine; customary procedure.
They live on Dartmoor, well off the beaten track.
Make tracks [S] Hurry away.
I'd better make tracks for the post office.
Track down Find.
See *Keep.*

Trade **Of a trade** Following the same occupation.
Are both of you stamp-collectors, too? Then we're three of a trade.

Trail **Trail one's coat** Attempt to start a quarrel or argument. [Or. To trail or drag one's coat behind one was an accepted method of issuing a general challenge; any person stepping on the coat was considered to have insulted its owner.]
Trail off Become weaker and feebler.
He began by shouting, but his voice trailed off into a mere whisper.

Train **In the train of** Among those in an inferior position accompanying a great personage.

Tread **Tread on one's corns (*or* toes)** [S] Accidentally say or do something to cause embarrassment.
Tread on the heels of Follow immediately after.

Treasure **Treasure (up)** Retain, as something precious and valuable.
We should treasure every moment of such a day as this.

Trial **Give a trial** Test. Similar to **try out.**
We've decided to give the new soap a trial.

Tribute **Pay tribute** [LIT] To pay a fixed amount to a ruler or other governor. [MET] Admit one's indebtedness to some helper or benefactor.
I am delighted to pay tribute to all that he has done for the Association.

Trice **In a trice** [Oldf.] [LIT] A period of time equal to one-third of a second. [MET] Very quickly.
Don't go—I'm coming in a trice.

Trivet **Right as a trivet** In sound health or condition. [Or. Trivet = tripod for holding cooking pots. Right = steady, therefore good.]

Trivial **The trivial round** The routine of everyday life; the succession of small regular duties. [Or. Abbrev. of lines from Keble's hymn, 'The trivial round, the common task, will furnish all we need to ask'.]

Trot **Trot out** [S] Quote, often glibly or predictably; exhibit; produce in support.
He trotted out the old proverb that there's no time like the present.

Trouble **Ask for trouble** [S] Be rash; incur vexation.
If he buys that car he'll be asking for trouble.

Trouble brewing Trouble is likely to occur.
I'm afraid there's trouble brewing over that speech you made at the meeting yesterday.

Trouble in store Trouble likely to occur at some later time.

True **(Run) true to form** (Happen) predictably, in accordance with expectation or past experience.

Trump **Trump-card** Piece of valuable information, knowledge, etc., or an unexpected idea, produced surprisingly to outwit or defeat an opponent. [Or. Card-playing. 'Trump' is an abbrev. for French *triomphe*, a game of cards = triumph, and a trump-card is a 'triumph' or winning card.]
The Prime Minister played his trump-card by saying that negotiations had in fact already begun.

Trump up Falsely state; tell maliciously and untruthfully.
He came to me with a trumped-up story about my brother.

Turn up trumps See ***Turn.***

Trumpet **Blow one's own trumpet** Boast of one's own work or actions.
He spends most of the time blowing his own trumpet.

Trumpet-call [LIT] Tune played by a trumpet or trumpets alone, usually in manner of a summons. [MET] An urgent summons to action.
His speech was a trumpet-call for public protest.

Truth **Home truths** Unpalatable facts about oneself.
Unless his conduct improves, he'll have to be told a few home truths.

The naked (plain, simple, sober, *or* stark) truth The truth, and nothing but the truth.

Arrive at the truth Discover what really occurred.

Truth is stranger than fiction Things which actually happen are sometimes more unexpected that the things which are invented in literature.

Try **Try conclusions** Start a struggle that must have a definite ending.
The Government is certain to try conclusions with the House of Lords.

Try one's hand at Attempt.
I'm going to try my hand at cooking while Jane is away.

Try on Put on a garment to see if it fits.
You'd better try on the coat before you buy it.

Try-on [S] An impudent attempt.
He asked me to lend him some money, but it was merely a try-on.

Try out Put to the test.

T

Tuck **Tuck in** [S] Have a good meal.

Tuck up Wrap closely in bedclothes, etc.

Tug **Tug-of-war** See **pull together**.

Tune **Change one's tune** Assume a different style of manner or language. Similar to **sing a different tune**.

In tune In agreement. In harmony. Opposite: **out of tune**.

To the tune of At a cost of.

The town is building a new hall to the tune of seventy thousand pounds.

Turn **As it turned out** As it resulted; happened; as the sequel.

Everyone thought farmers would be ruined, but as it turned out they were more prosperous than before.

Do a good (or bad) turn Help (or the reverse).

I thought I would do Mary a good turn by minding the baby.

Done to a turn Cooked perfectly.

Not turn a hair Remain calm, in control, unperturbed.

She sang the very difficult solo without turning a hair.

Take a turn Pass from one state of health to another.

The injured man took a turn for the worse on Monday.

Take turns; take it in turns Act in rotation or regular order.

We took turns in mowing the lawn.

To a turn Exactly.

Turn to (good) account Use; make use of successfully.

I can turn all this timber to good account.

Turn adrift Cast out to wander. [Or. Nautical. A vessel is adrift if it is floating without control wherever the winds and current may take it.]

Turn against Change from like to dislike; regard with aversion.

He became so irritable that many of his old friends turned against him.

Turn aside Alter the direction in which one is going. Temporarily leave one occupation for another.

The Professor would turn aside from his studies to play with his little grandson.

Turn one's back on Deliberately ignore.

Turn the corner Pass a crisis successfully.

The patient has turned the corner, and will recover.

Turn a deaf ear to Refuse to listen to.

Turn down 1. [LIT] Fold over and flatten down.

He turned down the collar of his coat.

2. [MET] Refuse or decline definitely.

He turned down every offer of help.

Turn of events Change in the course of events, or happenings.

A year later, owing to a strange turn of events, I found myself in Paris again.

Turn of phrase Manner of speech.

Turn one's hand to Undertake a variety of work, or work that is not one's normal occupation.

I'm a carpenter by trade, but I can turn my hand to bricklaying or painting.

See *Head.*

Turn an honest penny See under *Penny.*

Turn in Go to bed.

The travellers were so fatigued that they all turned in early.

Turn inside out [LIT] Turn so that the inner is outside, and vice versa. [MET] Examine or explore with extreme thoroughness.

I've turned my desk inside out, but cannot find the missing paper.

Turn off (*or* on) Stop (or start) something by turning (a tap, knob, switch, etc.).

Please turn off the light.

Turn-out Display.

The Lord Mayor's show was a magnificent turn-out.

Turn out 1. Manufacture.

We can turn out twenty gross of cups a week.

2. Compel to leave, evict.

The family were turned out of their cottage because they could not pay their rent.

3. Empty (usually to tidy).

He turned out his desk.

4. Transpire. Be the final outcome.

It turned out that he was George's father.

5. Similar to **turn off.**

Turn over 1. Cause to fall over. 2. **Hand over.**

Turn-over Amount of money taken in a business, shop, etc.

Turn over a new leaf Change for the better.

Turn out well Succeed in life.

He's a sensible and clever boy, and ought to turn out well.

Turn (*or* tilt) the scales [LIT] Make the scale fall, and so register something slightly heavier than the weight on the opposite side.

He turned the scale at eleven stone.

[MET] Finally decide some matter which is in doubt.

The evidence given by his friend turned the scale, and the boy was set free.

Turn of speed Capacity for speed.

This car has a fine turn of speed.

Turn the tables Reverse the position.

The sudden arrival of the police turned the tables.

Turn tail Turn and run away.

Turn of the tide [LIT] The point at which the sea ceases to flow out and begins to flow back, or vice versa. [MET] The point at which success is followed by failure, or vice versa.

For Napoleon the turn of the tide came soon after he divorced Josephine.

Turn and turn about First one, then the other, for equal periods.
George and I kept watch, turn and turn about, for an hour at a time.
Turn turtle Turn upside down in the sea.
The great ship turned turtle and sank.
Turn up 1. Arrive; appear. 2. Find.
Our guests did not turn up until nearly midnight.
Turn up one's nose Sneer.
Now she has become well known she turns up her nose at plain food.
Turn up trumps Prove of great and vital service. [Or. See **trump-card**.]
Turn upon Blame or attack.

Twiddle **Twiddle one's thumbs** Waste one's time. Similar to **kick one's heels.**

Twinkle **Twinkling of an eye** Very quickly. [Or. 'Twinkling' means a rapid twist or turn, and is of the same origin as 'wriggle'.]

Twist **Twist one's arm** [LIT] Hurt one's arm by twisting it. [MET] Bring pressure to bear to persuade someone. [Or. Method of torture.]
I think he'll come if you twist his arm.

Twister [S] One who 'twists', or systematically cheats.

Two **In two-twos** [S] In a moment; almost instantly.

U

Under **Come under** Be classified with.
Cups and saucers come under crockery.
Fall under [MET] Similar to **come under.**
Under a cloud In disgrace.
My son's been under a cloud since he crashed the car.
Underdog Person in an inferior position.
The English are reputed to have a special sympathy for the underdog.
Under one's wing Under one's protection, guidance.
Under way See *Way.*

Understanding **Come to an understanding** Agree and co-operate, after discussions and explanations.
The two men held opposing views, but eventually came to an understanding.
On (*or* with) the understanding According to an agreement, instruction, etc.
You may go to the dance, on the distinct (clear) (precise) understanding that you are back before midnight.

Up **All up** See *All.*

On the up and up Improving.
Up against it In difficulties.
If it rains, we shall really be up against it.
Up and about Well enough to leave one's bed after an illness.
Up in arms Indignant; resentful.
She was up in arms at the idea.
Up to date See *Date.*
Up and doing Active; busy.
We must be up and doing if we are going to catch the train.
Ups and downs Good times and bad times.
We all have our ups and downs.
Up-end Place so that the small or narrow end is uppermost.
We shall have to up-end it to get it out of the room.
Up to the eyes Submerged.
I am up to the eyes in work.
Up to the hilt To the limit, the greatest possible extent. [Or. The hilt is the handle of a sword, at which the blade ends.]
The property is mortgaged up to the hilt.
Up to the mark [S] In one's normal state of health; capable of doing something.
John does not seem up to the mark this morning.
Up the pole See *Pole.*
Come up to the scratch See *Scratch.*
Up to a thing or two [S] Alert; shrewd.
Mrs Jenkins may be old, but she's up to a thing or two.
Up to something Privately planning; plotting some scheme.
I guess by the look on her face that she is up to something.
Up stage [S] [LIT] The front of the stage, the position of most prominence. [Or. Theatre.] [MET] Haughty, conceited behaviour.
She has become terribly up stage.
Up to it Capable of doing anything.
The hill is steep: are you up to it?
(Not) up to much (Not) good.
I didn't think the party was up to much.
Up to you [S] The responsibility is yours.
It's up to you to win this fight.
Up the spout See *Spout.*
Up a tree [S] In a state of desperation.
I've lost my wallet, and am completely up a tree.
Upon **Upon which** When this occurred.
The boy admitted that he stole, upon which his father thrashed him.
Uppers **On one's uppers** Very poor; completely destitute. [Or. When the sole of a shoe is completely worn out, the wearer is walking on the 'uppers' or upper layers of leather.]

Sam lost his job six months ago, and he's now on his uppers.

Upside **Upside-down** Inverted.

Use **Make use of** Utilize, employ.

We can make use of these bricks to build a wall.

Use up Finish. Consume the remainder of.

You can use up the milk.

V

Vain **In vain** Ineffectively; without any result.

He shouted in vain for help.

Take in vain Treat lightly.

Valour **The better part of valour** Discretion. Carefulness. [Or. Proverb: 'Discretion is the better part of valour.']

The general decided on the better part of valour, and surrendered.

Value **Set a value on** Estimate the value of.

I asked him to set a value on the pictures.

Van **In the van** In the front. [Or. Nautical, from the French *avant*. Abbrev. for 'vanguard'; the foremost or leading position.]

That firm is always in the van with improvements.

Variance **At variance** In a state of quarrelling or disagreement.

The two brothers are always at variance (with one another).

Veer **Veer round** Change one's opinions, language, behaviour, mood, etc.

At first Simon agreed with me; then he veered round and agreed with Brian.

Veil **Draw a veil over** Remain silent about; conceal.

They prefer to draw a veil over the whole incident.

Take the veil Become a fully initiated nun.

Velvet **With velvet gloves** Gently.

Vengeance **With a vengeance** To an excessive degree.

There will be trouble with a vengeance when the boss hears what happened.

Vent **Give vent to** Give expression to; allow (one's emotions) to escape.

The old man gave vent to his anger when he heard the news.

Ventilate **Ventilate a grievance** See *Air*.

Venture **Nothing venture (nothing win *or* gain)** One must be bold (if one wishes to win something).

Venture on Take the risk of making.

I think I shall venture on a mild protest.

Verdict **Bring in (*or* return) a verdict** The legal phrase for a jury recording a decision.

The jury brought in a verdict of guilty.

Very **The very thing** See **just the thing**, under **Thing**.

Very well See under **Well**.

Vested **Vested interest** [LIT] Permanent rights. [MET] Personal involvement; keen commitment.

The old man has a vested interest in the farm.

Vet. Abbrev. for 'veterinary surgeon', one who examines and cures sick animals. Now frequently used as a verb in the sense of examining and, where necessary, correcting any form of work.

I shall be glad if you'll vet what I've written.

View **Bird's-eye view** A comprehensive view from above, such as a bird would obtain.

You get a bird's-eye view of Paris from the Eiffel Tower.

Bring into view Reveal to one's sight.

The telescope can bring into view objects a mile distant.

Extreme views Opinions which do not find favour with the majority.

In full view (of) Plainly visible (to).

To have in view To be contemplating, planning.

We have in view a new hospital for seamen.

In view of After consideration of.

In view of what you tell me, I shall not go.

In my view In my opinion.

In my view, war is a game in which both sides lose.

Meet (or fall in with) a person's views Do as he desires.

We will do everything we can to meet your views.

One-sided view A prejudiced and limited outlook.

On view Available for inspection. See **Point**.

Taking a long view Planning over a long period.

Taking a long view, they are buying land to build a factory ten years hence.

With a view to With the purpose of. In the hope of.

Virtue **By (or in) virtue of** As a result or consequence of.

By virtue of his position, the Lord Mayor is the chief magistrate of the city.

Make a virtue of necessity Gain an advantage, or pretend to be acting virtuously (e.g. out of a sense of duty or goodwill, etc.), when one is in fact under compulsion.

Have the virtue of Have the good quality of.

This sofa has the virtue of being convertible into a bed.

Visit **Visit the sins on** Punish a person for the sins someone else has committed. [Or. Bible: 'I will visit the sins of the fathers upon the children.']

Voice **Give voice to** Express; state publicly.

The newspapers gave voice to what most people were thinking.

Raise the voice Speak more loudly.

Please raise your voice when addressing an audience.
Opposite: **lower the voice.** Speak more softly.
At the top of one's voice As loudly as possible.
A voice in the matter A share in the control; a right to express one's views.
With one voice Unanimously.

W

Wait **Wait (up)on** 1. Pay a formal visit. (Now almost obsolete.) 2. Attend to the wants (of).
The dinner was good, but there weren't enough people waiting on the guests.

Wake **In the wake** In the footsteps or path of. [Or. Nautical. The 'wake' is the track left by a vessel as it passes through the water.]
Refugees follow in the wake of war.

Walk **Walk away with something** Win something very easily.
Walk of life Occupation; profession.
Walk-out Departure, usually as demonstration of protest.
The orchestra staged a walk-out when the conductor prolonged the rehearsal.
Walk out on Leave, unexpectedly and usually in pique (so that difficulties are caused).
You can't really blame his wife for walking out on him.
A walk-over An extremely easy victory.
The next race ought to be a walk-over for the Frenchman.

Wall **With one's back to the wall** Desperately, as a final defence.
We're fighting with our backs to the wall to win the election.

Wane **On the wane** Diminishing; decreasing in power. [Or. Astronomy. A star 'wanes' when its light decreases.]
Her influence was on the wane.

Want **For want of** Because of lack of.
It is rotting for want of paint.
In want of In need of.
The organization is in want of £200 immediately.

War **Be in the wars** Show signs of physical damage.
Cold war Unfriendly relations between nations shown by propaganda, lack of diplomatic or economic co-operation, etc., but not by fighting.
Wage war Conduct war.
War to the knife (*or* the death) A bitter and ruthless struggle.
War of nerves Unfriendly relationships between nations, when

W

attempts are made to undermine confidence, morale, etc., or to make threats, but not to fight.

Wash **Not wash** [S] Not stand up (to). See **stand up to** (2). Not bear examination. Work satisfactorily.
Those arguments simply won't wash.
Wash one's dirty linen in public Discuss or reveal one's own shortcomings, scandals, etc., publicly.
Wash one's hands of Refuse any responsibility for.
Do as you like; I wash my hands of the whole business.
Wash-out [S] Complete failure.
I tried to make my living as an artist, but it was a wash-out.
Wash out [LIT] Remove by washing.
I've washed out the stain on your coat.
[MET] Obliterate.
He tried to wash out the memories of the past.
Washed-out Tired, incapable of effort, as result of energetic activity (or over-indulgence).

Waste **Waste one's breath** Talk in vain.
You'll simply be wasting your breath if you talk to him.

Watch **On the watch** In a state of watchfulness. Similar to **on the alert**.
Set a watch Arrange for systematic watching.
A watched pot never boils Time seems long when one is waiting for something to happen. [Or. Proverb.]

Water **Hold water** 1. [LIT] Contain without leaking.
That bucket won't hold enough water.
2. [MET] Be true, and capable of being tested.
His account of the robbery won't hold water.
In hot water In trouble.
Of the first water Of the finest possible quality; to the greatest degree.
His action was a blunder of the first water.
Make one's mouth water Be intensely attractive, delightful to eat or see.
The prospect of a week's holiday at Christmas makes my mouth water.
Still waters run deep A reserved disposition or manner may conceal strong emotions or unexpected characteristics.
Throw cold water on Depreciate; discourage.
We want to start a fish shop, but Father is inclined to throw cold water on the idea.

Way **Across the way (street, road,** *etc.***)** On the opposite side of it.
All manner (*or* **sorts** *or* **kinds) of ways** A large variety of ways.
The new lodger will be useful in all manner of ways.

By the way Incidentally. (The phrase is used when a speaker wishes to pass abruptly from one subject to another which has little or no connection with it.)
By the way, I am leaving early tonight.
By way of 1. By passing through.
We came by way of Banbury.
2. As substitute for. With the intention of making.
He sent her flowers by way of an apology.
Get in (or out of) the way Obstruct (or the reverse).
Please get out of my way.
Is this ladder getting in the way?
Get into the way of Acquire the habit of doing.
You'll soon get into the way of using it.
Give way 1. [LIT] Break.
The railings gave way, and three people fell in the river.
2. [MET] Yield.
He begged his mother to come, and at last she gave way.
Go one's own way Follow one's personal desires, without accepting guidance or advice.
It is a waste of time warning him—he is determined to go his own way.
Similar to **have one's own way; follow one's own devices.**
Go the way of all flesh. Die.
Have one's own way Do as one wishes.
I want to do it, and I mean to have my own way.
In a small way In modest circumstances.
He's a builder, but only in a small way.
In a way In certain respects; to a certain extent.
He considers himself clever, and in a way he's justified.
In the way Obstructing; forming an obstruction.
I can't empty the bottle—there's a piece of cork in the way.
In the way of In a position to obtain.
She put me in the way of several good bargains.
Lead the way 1. Act as leader. 2. Show by example what ought to be done.
A long way off Very distant.
Those hills are a long way off.
Make one's way 1. Progress; travel on one's journey. 2. Succeed in one's profession.
That young man will make his way in the world.
Make way [LIT] Step aside. [MET] Retire from office.
He ought to make way for a younger man.
On the way Coming.
Once in a way Occasionally.
Out of the way See under *Out.*

Over the way Same as **across the way.**
Parting of the ways Time for important decision.
Pave the way for Take steps to prepare for some change or future development.
The withdrawal of the troops paves the way for the granting of independence to the country.
Under way Beginning; moving; starting. [Or. Nautical.]
We have several plans under way.
Ways and means Methods of overcoming difficulties.
I hope we can find ways and means of getting to the seaside.
Wing one's way Travel swiftly, as a bird flies.

Weak **The weakest goes (*or* go) to the wall** Those least able to help themselves are pushed aside or ignored. [Or. Said to be the benches lining the wall of the Chapel of the House of Commons, specially put there for the old or sick, at time when no other seating existed. Originally, therefore, the expression was one of concern.]

Wear **Fair wear and tear** The normal lessening in value due to constant use.
Apart from fair wear and tear, the bicycle is in excellent condition.
Wear away Cause to disappear by friction.
The leather on the writing-case was completely worn away.
Wear down Exhaust. Tire.
The children's incessant requests finally wore him down, and he promised to take them for a game.
Wear one's heart on one's sleeve See *Heart.*
Wear off Diminish and finally disappear.
The effects of the shock will soon wear off.
Wear on Pass or diminish slowly.
The hours wore on; night came.
Wear out 1. [LIT] Render useless by wear.
My boots are worn out.
2. [MET] Exhaust.
The woman had not slept all night and was completely worn out.
Wear well (*or* badly) Last a long (or short) time. Remain in working order, or presentable, for a long (short) time. (Also, jocularly, of people: retain (or lose) one's strength of youthfulness.)
My climbing boots have worn extraordinarily well.

Weather **Make heavy weather of** [S] Treat as though it were a very serious matter. Find difficult.
Under the weather [S] Unwell, or depressed, or both.
John seems rather under the weather tonight.
Weather the storm Survive. ('Storm' is frequently used for financial and other troubles.)

W

Wedge **The thin end of the wedge** A small or trivial beginning which is likely to develop into something of much greater importance.

Weigh **Weigh down** Overburden.

Weigh in 1. Enter a race or contest, having been weighed. 2. Enter forcefully.

Weigh one's words Choose what one says very carefully.

Weigh up Estimate. Come to a judgment about.

He's a very difficult person to weigh up.

Well **As well** Also.

Come early, and bring your sister as well.

As well as In addition to.

Let well alone Do not interfere.

Very well A general expression of agreement and assent.

(All) well and good Unemotional or neutral acceptance of decision, etc.

If you decide not to believe me, well and good.

Well built, *or* **well set-up** Physically well constructed; fit.

He was a well set-up man of forty.

Well disposed (to) Inclined to favour.

The Council is well disposed to the idea.

Well done! Exclamation of approval.

Well founded Justifiable.

It turned out that his fears were well founded.

Well, I never! Abbrev. of 'Well, I never heard anything so extraordinary!' A common expression of astonishment.

Well-lined purse Plenty of money.

One needs a well-lined purse to stay at that hotel.

Well off See under *Off.*

Well out of something [S] Fortunate not to be involved in something any longer.

I never enjoyed the job and am well out of it.

Well-rounded (*or* -turned) phrases, sentences, *etc.* Elegant and graceful speech.

Well-to-do Fairly rich.

West **Go west** [S] Die; or become destroyed, or useless. [Or. 1914–18 War slang for 'die'.]

My old raincoat has finally gone west.

What **I tell you what** I make this suggestion.

I tell you what—let's go to a cinema.

Know what's what Be able to discriminate between what is of value and use, and what is not.

You won't deceive Henry; he knows what's what.

What have you [S] Anything else similar.

Put the cases and what have you in the boot.

What's-his-name; what do you call him? A substitution for a name one has forgotten.
This morning I met that tall man with red hair—old what's-his-name.
Similar to **so-and-so.**

Wheel **Put a spoke in one's wheel** Interfere with one's plans.
Similar to **throw a spanner in the works.**
Wheels within wheels Small, often unknown motives and influences, which contribute to the general result. Secret procedures.

Wherewithal **The wherewithal** That which is necessary to accomplish something. Money.

Whether **Whether or no** Whether or not.

While **A little while** A short time. (Opposite: **a long while.**)
I'll telephone you in a little while.
Once in a while At long intervals. Occasionally. Similar to **from time to time.**
See **Worth.**

Whip **Have the whip hand** Be in a position to control.

Whistle **Wet one's whistle** [S] Indulge in a drink.
Whistle for 1. Summon by whistling. 2. Give up any hope of obtaining.
If you want a house in this village, you'll have to whistle for it.

Whit **Not a whit** Not at all. [Or. Whit = a speck, the smallest visible particle of matter.]

White **White (*or* pure) as driven snow** Absolutely white. [Or. Driven snow is snow that has been 'driven', or blown, by the wind.]
White as a sheet Extremely pale; colourless.
When she heard the news, she turned as white as a sheet.
White at the lips Extremely angry. Very afraid.

Whole **Go the whole hog** [S] Insist on having everything, or the best obtainable.
On the whole Having considered all sides of the matter.
I think, on the whole, we had better stay at home.
Whole-hearted Enthusiastic. Without doubts.

Why **The why and wherefore** The reasons for any action or the existence of any condition. The explanation.

Wide **Broke to the wide** [S] Completely without money.
Wide awake 1. [LIT] Entirely awake. 2. [MET] Alert, aware.
He is very wide awake where making money is concerned.
Give a wide berth to Avoid.
It is advisable to give a wide berth to that particular shop.
Wide of the mark Inaccurate. [Or. Shooting.]
You're very wide of the mark if you think I want to work here all my life.
Widespread Found in many places.

Wild   **Wild goose chase** A practically hopeless search or other enterprise.
Wild guess Utterly haphazard guess.
Wild horses wouldn't (get me there, *etc. etc.*) Not even the strongest persuasion would (prevail on me to go there, etc.).

Wildfire   **Like wildfire** With extreme rapidity. [Or. An inflammable mixture very difficult to extinguish. It was used in fighting at sea.]
The news spread like wildfire.

Wile   **Wile away (the time, *etc.*)** Pass, occupy (the time).

Will   **Against my will** Contrary to my wishes.
At (one's own sweet) will Exactly as one pleases.
One is allowed to wander about the grounds at one's own sweet will.
Free will Right, or power, to decide one's own course of action.
Hence **of my own free will**: without any compulsion being exercised on me.
Where there's a will there's a way If there is determination to do something, a means of doing it will be found.
A will of one's own Spirit, determination, of one's own.
Our baby is only a month old, but he's already shown that he has a will of his own.
Willy-nilly Just as one pleases. Whether one likes it or not. [Or. Abbrev. of the old 'will-he, nil-he'.]
We just can't park the car here willy-nilly.
With a will Energetically.

Win   **Win hands down** Succeed very easily.
Win over Convert to one's own point of view; persuade to become one's ally.

Wind   **Get wind of** Obtain early information about something that is likely to happen.
Wellington got wind of Napoleon's plans, and altered his own.
Get the wind up Become scared; frightened. [Or. Royal Flying Corps slang, 1914–18.]
It's an ill wind that blows nobody good It is a very unfortunate event which is of no benefit: someone is almost sure to profit from a loss. [Or. Proverb.]
In the wind Likely to happen.
Our train is stopping just before the frontier; I wonder what's in the wind.
Like the wind Extremely quickly.
Put the wind up Frighten.
Sail near the wind Verge on the indecent, or the dishonest.
Straw in the wind See *Straw.*
Take the wind out of one's sails Disconcert, usually by gaining an advantage over one, e.g. by anticipating one's arguments or suddenly revealing a secret.
Which way the wind blows What developments are likely to

happen. What opinions are being held. What the position is, or is likely to become.

Wind up Conclude; bring to an end.
The party finally wound up in the small hours.

Wing **Clip the wings** See under *Clip.*
Take under one's wing Protect (as a hen takes her chickens under her wing).
Please take the new typist under your wing until she settles in.
Take wing Start flying.

Wink **Forty winks** A short sleep.
Wink at Tactfully ignore.

Wise **Get wise to** [S] Become aware of.
Put someone wise (to) Inform someone (of).
Wise after the event Knowledgeable when it is too late. Failing to foresee.

Wish **Wish to goodness** Wish intensely, emphatically. (Polite version of 'Wish to God'. 'Goodness' is similarly used in 'Hope to goodness' and 'Trust to goodness'.)
I wish to goodness you'd come down to breakfast punctually.
Wish a person joy Wish him, or her, luck; congratulate.
Wish a person joy of Hope he may find some pleasure or satisfaction in.
Wishful thinking Thinking, or belief, based on wishes rather than facts.

Wishy-washy Feeble. Unsystematic.

Wit **Addle one's wits** Make one's mind hopelessly confused. [Or. 'Addled' is applied to an egg upon which the bird has been sitting for some time, and then has deserted.]
The problems involved are enough to addle any man's wits.
At one's wits' end See under *End.*
Have (*or* keep) one's wits about one Be alert, observant and intelligent.
You'll need to have your wits about you at the interview.

Withers **Wring one's withers** [Old f.] Cause acute distress. [Or. The 'withers' of a horse are the muscles joining the back and shoulders, and these are often made painful ('wrung' in Shakespeare's *Henry IV*) by a badly fitting saddle.]

Within **Within an ace of** Close to.
I was within an ace of being run down by the van.
Within call (*or* hail) Near enough to hear the sound of a voice.
Within (easy) reach Accessible; capable of being reached, physically or by communication.
There are shops within easy reach of the house.
Within oneself Not using one's whole energies.

He ran well within himself, but still won the race easily.

Wolf **Cry wolf** See under **Cry.**

Keep the wolf from the door Live without suffering acute poverty.
He earns scarcely enough to keep the wolf from the door.

Wolf in sheep's clothing A plausible deceiver; one whose
apparent harmlessness conceals his true character. [Or. Biblical:
also Æsop's fable, in which a wolf covered himself with the
sheep's skin and succeeded in deceiving a herd of sheep—but not the
shepherd.]

Wonder **Do wonders** Have remarkable success.

Nine days' wonder An event which causes great excitement for a
short time and is then forgotten.

No wonder Not surprising. (The phrase is often used on its own,
meaning 'I am not in the least surprised'.)
It is no wonder that she is always tired.

Wool **Be wool-gathering** Allow one's thoughts to wander.
Finish your work—you've been wool-gathering.
Similar to **day-dreaming.**

Word **As good as one's word** Faithful in keeping a promise.
*She said she would marry him when he came out of prison, and was
as good as her word.*

Break one's word Fail to keep one's promise.

Fine words butter no parsnips Words are less adequate than
deeds.

Give one's word Make a promise.

Hard words Harsh and unpleasant statements, not necessarily true.

Have the last word Make the final (and supposedly decisive)
contribution in a discussion, altercation, quarrel, etc.

Have a word with Talk briefly to.

Have words Quarrel.

In a word In brief. To sum up.

In so many words Verbally and explicitly.
He told me, in so many words, that he did not trust him.

Keep one's word Do as one promised.

The last word The latest, or best, of its type.
The train is the last word in speed and comfort.
See also **have the last word.**

Leave word Leave a message.
Leave word at the office about your holiday plans.

A man of his word One who can be trusted to keep a promise.

Say a good word for; put in a good word for Speak in favour of.
He offered to say a good word for me with the prison Governor.

Send word Transmit a message.

Take at one's word Accept a statement literally, and as the truth.

When the hotel manager promised us a first-class dinner, we foolishly took him at his word.

Upon my word! Exclamation, expressing astonishment. [Old f.]

Waste words Talk in vain. Talk with no result.

Word for word Exactly as spoken or written; verbatim.

This is, word for word, the message he gave me.

Word of honour Solemn promise.

A word in the ear A private statement, or hint.

Word in edgeways Any entry into a conversation.

She talks so much that one can't get a word in edgeways.

(By) word of mouth Verbally; spoken, as contrasted with written, speech.

The General informed them by word of mouth that peace would shortly be arranged.

Word in season Well-timed advice.

Word-perfect Exact, absolutely accurate.

Work **At work on** Engaged or employed on.

Donkey-work Rough or hard work, necessary for the completion of a task. [Or. A 'donkey-engine' is a small engine which supplies power for minor work on board ship.]

You have only to arrange the furniture in your room—the cleaners have done all the donkey-work.

Make short work of Finish quickly.

The new machine makes short work of the washing.

Work one's passage Earn a privilege or advantage by doing work in return. [Or. Nautical. A passenger who has no money to pay his fare and works as a seaman instead, is said to work his passage.]

Work out 1. Solve.

Have you worked out the sum yet?

2. Be calculated.

The cost works out at £4 a square metre.

3. Plan.

I'll work out the details of our holiday over the weekend.

Work up 1. Create by degrees.

From one small shop, he worked up to a very fine business.

2. Rouse or excite.

It was a thrilling game, and the spectators became very worked up.

Work upon Exert influence upon.

That politician can work upon his hearers' emotions until they are prepared to vote for anything he suggests.

Work wonders Succeed remarkably.

The new headmaster has worked wonders at that school.

World **All the world and his wife** Everyone; all the people there are.

All the world and his wife seem to be present.

For all the world 1. Precisely.

She looks for all the world like her sister.

2. Under any circumstances.

I wouldn't like his job for all the world.

Make the best of both worlds Satisfy two opposing demands; compromise.

A man (*or* woman) of the world An experienced person; one familiar with the customs and habits of society.

The way of the world The customary behaviour of mankind, especially civilized, sophisticated mankind. (The phrase is generally used ironically.)

What in the world Whatever. (Used for special emphasis.)

I can't understand what in the world she's bought it for.

Worm **Even a worm will turn** Even the weakest person may be goaded into defiance or rebellion. [Or. Proverb.]

Worm (one's way) in Insinuate.

Worm out Discover by persistent questioning.

Worn **Worn out,** *etc.* See *Wear.*

Worse **The worse for wear** [LIT] Damaged by use. [MET] Not at one's best; tired out; unwell.

Worst **At the worst** In the worst possible circumstances; even if the worst happens.

Let's start in spite of the rain; at the worst we can only get wet.

If the worst comes to the worst If matters become as bad as they can possibly be.

Worth **Worth one's salt; worth one's keep** See *Salt.*

Worth its (*or* one's) weight in gold Very valuable or useful.

Worth while; worth one's while; worth it Worth spending time or trouble over.

I would try to sell the business, but it isn't worth while.

Wrap **Wrapped up in** Entirely devoted to; absorbed in.

He is wrapped up in his family.

Write **Nothing to write home about** Trivial. Unexciting.

The scenery in Belgium is nothing to write home about.

Write off Treat as no longer of any value.

The goods are unsaleable; we had better write them off.

Writing **The writing on the wall** Clear warning of disaster. [Or. Biblical. The writing on the wall was the warning given to Belshazzar as a plain indication that unless he altered his conduct, the end would be disaster.]

Wrong **Get hold of the wrong end of the stick** [S] Be completely mistaken.

Go wrong Make an error.

Wrong-headed Perverse and obstinate.
Wrought **Wrought up** Worked up. Tense and excited.

Y

Year **All the year round** Throughout the year.
Years of discretion An age at which one is supposed to have acquired a certain amount of wisdom and discretion.
Yellow **Yellow-livered** Cowardly. [Or. A tradition that the liver of a coward has a streak of yellow in it.]
Yellow press Sensational newspapers, usually with chauvinistic tendencies.
Yeoman **Yeoman service** Sound and excellent work.
Yet **As yet** Until now.
As yet, I have seen no signs of deterioration.
Yours **Yours truly** [S] I; me.
Yours truly will do his (i.e. my) best.
Yourself **Pull yourself together** Take control of your feelings.

A Concise Dictionary of English Idioms

Other Books of Interest

A Concise Dictionary of English Slang
William Freeman

The English Language: An Introduction
W. Nelson Francis

Language Made Plain
Anthony Burgess